TECHNICAL REPORT

Reforming Teacher Education

A First Year Progress Report on Teachers for a New Era

Sheila Nataraj Kirby, Jennifer Sloan McCombs,
Scott Naftel, Heather Barney, Hilary Darilek,
Frederick Doolittle, Joseph Cordes

TR-149-EDU

June 2004

Prepared for the Rockefeller Foundation

RAND EDUCATION

The research described in this report was conducted for the Rockefeller Foundation by RAND Education.

Library of Congress Cataloging-in-Publication Data

Reforming teacher education : a first year progress report on Teachers for a New Era / Sheila Kirby ... [et al.].
      p. cm.
   "TR-149."
   Includes bibliographical references.
   ISBN 0-8330-3647-5 (pbk.)
   1. Teachers—Training of—United States. 2. Educational change—United States. I. Kirby, Sheila Nataraj, 1946– II. Teachers for a New Era. III. Title.

LB1715.R354 2004
370'.71'1—dc22
                                                                          2004012731

The RAND Corporation is a nonprofit research organization providing objective analysis and effective solutions that address the challenges facing the public and private sectors around the world. RAND's publications do not necessarily reflect the opinions of its research clients and sponsors.

RAND® is a registered trademark.

Published 2004 by the RAND Corporation
1700 Main Street, P.O. Box 2138, Santa Monica, CA 90407-2138
1200 South Hayes Street, Arlington, VA 22202-5050
201 North Craig Street, Suite 202, Pittsburgh, PA 15213-1516
RAND URL: http://www.rand.org/
To order RAND documents or to obtain additional information, contact
Distribution Services: Telephone: (310) 451-7002;
Fax: (310) 451-6915; Email: order@rand.org

Preface

Teacher education is often regarded as a "black hole" by funders interested in K–12 education, and many of them—having given up hope of reforming the way teachers are prepared—are choosing to work directly with K–12 schools and districts instead. Yet persuasive evidence exists that teacher quality matters; that teachers have discernible, differential effects on student achievement; and that these teacher effects appear to persist across years. The Carnegie Corporation of New York decided to meet the challenge of reforming teacher education head-on and launched an ambitious reform initiative, *Teachers for a New Era* (TNE), in the summer of 2001. The aim of this initiative is to stimulate construction of excellent teacher education programs that are guided by a respect for evidence, are based on close collaboration between education and arts and sciences faculty, and integrate classroom experinces fully into the curriculum. Four institutions—Bank Street College of Education; California State University, Northridge; Michigan State University; and the University of Virginia—were selected in the summer of 2002 as the first TNE sites; they are to receive $1million for each of five years and substantial technical assistance to reform their teacher education programs to align with the TNE design principles.[1]

The Carnegie Corporation involved a number of other foundations in its selection process, and representatives from these foundations participated in the deliberations. Two—the Annenberg Foundation and the Ford Foundation—decided to join the initiative and provide funds to allow a larger number of institutions to be selected to participate in TNE. The Rockefeller Foundation, which had also participated in the process, decided to fund a national evaluation of the initiative to document how the initiative unfolds and assess whether the reform has an impact in changing the way teachers are prepared and on the effectiveness of teacher graduates. The Rockefeller Foundation asked the RAND Corporation and the Manpower Demonstration Research Corporation (MDRC) to undertake such a national evaluation and provided funding for eighteen months (December 2002–May 2004). This technical report documents our work during this first phase and describes the first year of the TNE reform as it played out in the four sites. The main body of the report provides an overview of the progress the sites made in the first year and some early lessons learned from a cross-site analysis. Appendixes A–D provide details on each institution, including a profile of the four institutions at baseline (prior to the start of the initiative), a summary of the design proposals developed by each of the institutions to carry out the reform, and detailed notes on

---

[1] In summer 2003, Carnegie selected seven additional sites for TNE funding: Boston College; Florida A&M University; Stanford University; the University of Connecticut; the University of Texas, El Paso; the University of Washington; and the University of Wisconsin, Milwaukee.

implementation progress. In addition, Appendix E describes the state policy contexts against which the reform is being carried out at each of the sites.

This report should be of interest primarily to educational researchers, funders interested broadly in K–12 education, and education policymakers at the national, state, and local levels who are struggling with issues of teacher quality and improving learning for all students.

This research was conducted within RAND Education, a division of the RAND Corporation, and reflects RAND Education's mission to bring accurate data and careful, objective analysis to the national debate on education policy.

The RAND Corporation Quality Assurance Process

Peer review is an integral part of all RAND research projects. Prior to publication, this document, as with all documents in the RAND technical report series, was subject to a quality assurance process to ensure that the research meets several standards, including the following: The problem is well formulated; the research approach is well designed and well executed; the data and assumptions are sound; the findings are useful and advance knowledge; the implications and recommendations follow logically from the findings and are explained thoroughly; the documentation is accurate, understandable, cogent, and temperate in tone; the research demonstrates understanding of related previous studies; and the research is relevant, objective, independent, and balanced. Peer review is conducted by research professionals who were not members of the project team.

RAND routinely reviews and refines its quality assurance process and also conducts periodic external and internal reviews of the quality of its body of work. For additional details regarding the RAND quality assurance process, visit http://www.rand.org/standards/.

Contents

APPENDIX

Figures

Tables

Summary

In a bold attempt to reform the way teachers are prepared in the United States, the Carnegie Corporation of New York, with the Annenberg Foundation and the Ford Foundation, launched Teachers for a New Era (TNE) in the summer of 2001. The goal of this initiative is to fundamentally reform teacher education in a selected number of teacher preparation programs by providing these sites with funding ($5 million over a period of five years) and technical assistance through the Academy for Educational Development (AED). Four institutions were selected for the TNE grant in FY2002: Bank Street College of Education; California State University, Northridge (CSUN); Michigan State University (MSU); and the University of Virginia (UVa).[2]

Bank Street College of Education is an independent institution devoted entirely to improving the education of children and their teachers. The college comprises three divisions: Children's Programs, which runs the School for Children; the Division of Continuing Education; and the Graduate School of Education devoted entirely to teacher education. The Graduate School offers master's degrees in education through a number of different programs that can be completed in as little as 12–15 months, although two years to completion is most typical. Generally, Bank Street graduates about 250 teachers per year from programs leading to initial certification.

CSUN offers multiple pathways for obtaining elementary and secondary teaching credentials, including undergraduate programs offered jointly by the College of Education and arts and sciences colleges. In addition, it offers several versions of the postbaccalaureate program (fifth-year program). In 2000–01, CSUN issued a total of 1,554 initial credentials. Overall, a little less than half of the graduates were minorities.

MSU's teacher education program is a five-year route to a bachelor's degree and a Michigan teaching certificate. The Department of Teacher Education also offers an 18-month certification program for postbaccalaureate applicants. MSU prepares approximately 550–600 teachers a year.

At UVa, the Curry School of Education and the College of Arts and Sciences offer a five-year integrated Teacher Education Program, the culmination of which leads to both the baccalaureate and the Master of Teaching degrees. In addition, the Curry School of Education offers a two-year postbaccalaureate program in which students with a completed BA degree in a noneducational field earn a Master of Teaching degree. There were 124 students

---

[2] In summer 2003, Carnegie selected seven additional sites for TNE funding: Boston College; Florida A&M University; Stanford University; the University of Connecticut; the University of Texas, El Paso; the University of Washington; and the University of Wisconsin, Milwaukee.

in the graduating class of 2002. Enrollment in the Curry School teacher education programs has been growing in recent years.

TNE Design Principles

The TNE prospectus outlined several design principles that Carnegie believes characterize excellent teacher education programs. The three major principles are:

- **A teacher education program should be guided by a respect for evidence.** A culture of research, inquiry, and data analysis should permeate the program. Attention needs to be paid to pupil learning gains accomplished under the tutelage of teachers who are graduates of the program.
- **Faculty in the disciplines of the arts and sciences must be fully engaged in the education of prospective teachers,** especially in the areas of subject-matter understanding and general and liberal education.
- **Education should be understood as an academically taught clinical practice profession.** This requires: close cooperation between colleges of education and actual practicing schools; appointment of master teachers as clinical faculty in the college of education; and a two-year residency induction period for graduates of a teacher education program, during which graduates will be followed and provided mentoring and support. (http://www.carnegie.org/sub/program/teachers_prospectus.html)

Each institution was required to develop a design proposal that detailed how it proposed to reform its teacher education program to align with these design principles and also addressed a number of other issues detailed in the TNE prospectus (such as recruiting from underrepresented groups in teaching; providing pathways for late deciders; and ensuring that teachers had a deep understanding of subject matter as well as pedagogical content knowledge that would allow them to teach imaginatively and productively, etc.). These design proposals were then translated into work plans with specific activities, milestones, and time lines. The sites received their first-year funding in November 2002–January 2003 and were required to report progress in the first year in October 2003.

The First Phase of the National Evaluation and Purpose of Report

RAND and MDRC are jointly conducting a national evaluation for the Rockefeller Foundation of the TNE initiative as it is implemented by these first four grantees. The first phase of this evaluation began in December 2002. The objectives of this first phase were to lay the foundation for the larger, longer-term evaluation, collect baseline data to describe where the institutions were at the start of the initiative, analyze the design proposals to understand how the institutions proposed to align their programs with the TNE design principles, collect early implementation data on the programs and the institutions, and analyze the environments in which these four institutions are operating with respect to state and district policies. This report uses data collected during extensive site visits at the beginning and end of the first year.

This report describes the results of the first phase of the study. Because the sites had only been implementing TNE for about nine months at the time of our site visit, the report is largely descriptive.

Cross-Site Observations Regarding Implementation in Year 1

The sites have made progress over the past year in implementing their work plans, especially given that their "year" really consisted of between eight and ten months. Several cross-site themes emerged in the first year.

Recognition by Top-Level University Administrators and Strong Project Leadership Enhanced the Credibility of TNE. The insistence of the funders that the leadership for TNE should rest in the provost or president's office helped the projects gain visibility and prestige. The open and vocal support of university leaders attracted arts and sciences faculty into the TNE fold. Appointing senior and well-respected faculty from both arts and sciences and education to head the projects helped facilitate dialogue across the campus departments and fostered implementation.

The Sites Structured and Supported Their Teams in Very Different Ways. Some sites provided release time and overt recognition for their leadership teams; others did not. Some provided release time or stipends for all faculty working on TNE; others did not. Often the release time or the stipend was reportedly insufficient to cover the time required by the TNE work. In recognition of the heavy demands on faculty of teaching, research, and service duties, the sites had or were attempting to hire new faculty or staff to help with the TNE work. The sites were hiring many of these new faculty under criteria that seemed somewhat different from those used for the typical academic hire. For example, the advertised positions at CSUN stressed direct experience in K–12 schools and/or demonstrated interest in pedagogy along with the more usual academic credentials and research.

Junior Faculty and Those Close to Promotion Points Were Concerned About the Effect of TNE on Their Advancement. Some junior faculty—while excited about the work—worried about refusing to participate, given the high visibility of the project, and felt they paid a heavy price for taking on this work. Some arts and sciences deans openly spoke of their concern about the publications records of junior faculty engaged in TNE, while some faculty members who were close to tenure points expressed fears about whether they had done sufficient work on their tenure review packages. Despite these issues, most faculty were excited about their TNE work.

Sites Adopted Different Strategies Tailored to Their Institutional Culture but Recognized That Changing Culture Is Challenging. The sites displayed perspicacity in choosing their overall approaches. Because CSUN and MSU already had a fair degree of overt and explicit collaboration between arts and sciences and education faculty, they chose to establish teams to work on the design principles with leaders from both colleges. UVa, playing to the research interests of its faculty, offered funding to arts and sciences and education faculty to conduct research focused on assessment issues and the opportunity to teach new, integrated courses. UVa also attempted to reach out to local school districts and to be sensitive to "turf" issues. Bank Street, realizing that it had the farthest to go in terms of educating its faculty regarding assessment and collaboration with arts and sciences, chose to establish small teams with some limited arts and sciences involvement that focused on developing a research base to help inform program improvement.

Overall, across the sites, most faculty reported that these collaborations were a rewarding experience, in that they learned to see through different lenses. But all the sites understand that changing institutional culture and making the project a cross-university endeavor is uphill work and will require time and patience.

Involving K–12 Faculty in Meaningful Ways Proved Harder Than Expected. Although increasing the involvement of K–12 faculty in the teacher education program is one of the central principles of TNE, this has proven to be harder for some sites than expected. Some of this difficulty is due to scheduling problems (for example, the different teaching times for university and K–12 faculty); some of the difficulty, however, is due to the sites having not yet determined how best to involve teachers.

Site Communication Both Within and Outside TNE Needs Improvement. TNE is large and complex, involving large numbers of participants. Communication is an issue both within TNE and between TNE and other non-TNE faculty, and the sites frequently mentioned the importance of clear and frequent communication of the vision, the process, and progress to get buy-in from both internal and external audiences.

There Was Some Redundancy in the Work Being Done by the Sites. Assessment is front and center in the TNE prospectus, but the work requires sophisticated technical expertise and access to high-quality data, both of which may be harder to come by in some institutions and some states than others. All the sites seemed to be going over the same ground—learning about value-added modeling and examining different ways of measuring the learning of both their teacher candidates and the pupils taught by their graduates. Induction is another area where current efforts have been marked by a great deal of redundancy with nearly all the sites conducting literature reviews of induction programs in an attempt to identify best practices. The sites expressed a desire for greater collaboration, believing that this would be particularly beneficial in such a challenging area as assessment.

Technical Assistance Played an Important Role in Facilitating Implementation. The role of the technical assistance provider is to manage the project, act as a spokesperson for the funders, arrange workshops on relevant topics, facilitate cross-site communication, and provide tools and techniques to help the sites manage the project. For example, the TNE grant required each site to produce a work plan detailing specific activities, milestones, and time lines. While this was somewhat alien to the academic culture, the sites ended up appreciating the discipline imposed by the work plans and saw them as a roadmap and an important referent. The workshops were seen as generally useful in helping the sites to think through different issues.

State Policy Environments Have Important Implications for TNE Implementation. State policies, in terms of teacher licensure and induction requirements, are already affecting all four institutions. In particular, all four sites are attempting to align the design of their TNE induction programs with those administered by districts and/or mandated by states. The TNE work would also be facilitated by access to longitudinal data that would allow the sites to track their teacher graduates over time and student-level test score data linked to teachers. Such data collection would be most efficiently done at the state level.

Despite reductions in state funding, the three public institutions have tried to protect their teacher education program from budget cuts. However, in some cases, faculty have been stretched thin because of universitywide cost-cutting measures (for example, a hiring freeze at UVa at the time TNE was launched). If there are further cuts, it is uncertain whether the institutions can continue to shield their teacher education programs. Reductions in faculty and/or support are likely to affect TNE implementation.

Recommendations

These observations translate into recommendations that might help improve implementation in future years. We should make clear that the sites are aware of many of these issues and are working on them in the second year.

- Providing tangible support and clear recognition of TNE leaders and participants would alleviate some of the time burdens and send a clear signal regarding the importance of the TNE work.
- Explicitly recognizing TNE work in promotion and tenure decisions, and wide dissemination of these changes, would encourage the participation and ongoing involvement of junior faculty in the work.
- Ensuring that new TNE faculty receive contracts that detail explicitly the criteria on which they will be judged for promotion and tenure is important.
- Paying greater attention to ways in which K–12 faculty can be integrated into the TNE work and/or providing substantive roles for teachers-in-residence would be helpful in achieving greater buy-in from these faculty.
- Working collaboratively on such issues as assessment and induction would be helpful. The technical provider could play an increased role in facilitating such collaboration.

This first year was a learning year for the sites. This report documents their successes and their challenges in the first year of the reform and sets the stage for the future. The lessons derived from the first year of implementation should prove useful to the four sites studied here, new TNE sites just beginning their first year of implementation, and the funders as they move ahead with the reform initiative.

Acknowledgments

The authors would like to thank the Rockefeller Foundation for funding this research and the Carnegie Corporation for supporting and encouraging RAND and MDRC to undertake a national evaluation of the TNE initiative. We particularly thank Fred Frelow, our project sponsor at Rockefeller, and Daniel Fallon, Chair of the Education Division at Carnegie, for their interest, time, and patience, and Karin Egan and Barbara Gombach, Program Officers, Education Division, for attending the meetings of the Technical Work Group, which is overseeing the project, and for participating in interviews. The Academy for Educational Development, the technical assistance provider funded by Carnegie, was very helpful in providing an overview of its role in the reform and sharing such materials as the design proposals, budgets, and workshop materials with us.

The work could not have been undertaken without the cooperation of the TNE sites. We are deeply grateful to the project directors, the leadership teams, and the TNE faculty at the four sites for their willingness to provide data and to share their thoughts and their opinions with us during phone calls and site visits. They were candid and honest about their progress and the challenges they faced. We also thank the TNE assistants for setting up the site visits and for shepherding us around.

We are grateful to our reviewers, Catherine Augustine and Susan Bodilly of RAND, for their critical and insightful reviews. Their recommended changes greatly improved the organization and clarity of the report. Both Dominic Brewer and Susan Bodilly also provided overall guidance for the project as directors of the program under which this report was produced. Our Technical Work Group (TWG) is providing guidance and advice during the course of the study, and we thank them for their constructive criticism and feedback. The members are: Daniel Goldhaber, University of Washington; Susan Moore Johnson, Harvard Graduate School of Education; Henry Levin, Teachers College, Columbia University; Judith Warren Little, University of California, Berkeley; Lee Shulman, The Carnegie Foundation for the Advancement of Teaching; and Warren Simmons, Annenberg Institute for School Reform. Henry Levin also provided some very helpful comments on how to conceptualize the potential benefits of the program.

We are also grateful to our editors, Paul Arends and Phyllis M. Gilmore, for their patient and careful editing.

CHAPTER ONE

Introduction

In the summer of 2001, the Carnegie Corporation of New York announced an ambitious reform initiative, *Teachers for a New Era* (TNE), to stimulate construction of excellent teacher education programs at selected colleges and universities. In its prospectus, Carnegie made clear that it was seeking "a catalytic revision of teacher education led by colleges and universities committed to a new future for teaching and learning in the nation's schools" (Carnegie, 2001). Carnegie also outlined some specific design principles that it expected to be used in reforming the teacher education programs, principally that the teacher education program should be guided by a respect for evidence; that faculty from the arts and sciences should be fully engaged in the preparation of prospective teachers; and that teaching should be regarded as a clinical practice profession. To assist institutions in this endeavor, Carnegie planned to make awards in the amount of $5 million over a period of five years to each of six institutions. Institutions were to be selected over three years, beginning with two institutions in FY2002. Carnegie involved a number of other foundations in its selection process, and representatives from these foundations participated in the deliberations. Two—the Annenberg Foundation and the Ford Foundation—decided to join the initiative and provide funds to allow a larger number of institutions to be selected to participate in TNE. As a result, four institutions were selected for the TNE grant in FY2002: Bank Street College of Education; California State University, Northridge (CSUN); Michigan State University (MSU); and the University of Virginia (UVa).[1] The awards were announced in April 2002. In addition to the funding, institutions are receiving substantial technical assistance by the Academy for Educational Development (AED), under a contract with Carnegie.

The Rockefeller Foundation, which had also participated in the selection process, decided to fund a national evaluation of the initiative to document how the initiative unfolds and assess whether the reform has an effect in changing the way teachers are prepared and on the effectiveness of teacher graduates. The Rockefeller Foundation asked RAND and the Manpower Demonstration Research Corporation (MDRC) to undertake such a national evaluation and provided funding for the first phase of the evaluation (December 2002–May 2004). This technical report documents our work during this first phase and describes the first year of the TNE reform as it played out in the four sites.

---

[1] Although the original prospectus called for funding two institutions per year, in FY2003, Carnegie pooled its FY2003 and FY2004 funds and added extra funds to enable it to fund six new institutions. Annenberg again joined Carnegie in providing funds for one new institution. As a result, seven new institutions were selected for funding in FY2003: Boston College, Florida A&M University, Stanford University, the University of Connecticut, the University of Texas at El Paso, the University of Washington, and the University of Wisconsin–Milwaukee. The awards were announced in July 2003. This study focuses only on the first four grantees.

Objectives of the National Evaluation

The long-term objectives of the RAND and MDRC evaluation are to provide evidence of whether the initiative has been "successful" from both the individual institution's point of view and that of the funders; to identify factors that foster or hinder the implementation of reform of teacher education programs at the program, institution, district, and state levels; and to promote an understanding of the many factors and actors that need to be aligned to successfully reform teacher education and improve student learning.

A set of research questions guides the evaluation:

1. To what extent did the grantees implement Carnegie's design principles (including the induction program) and other principles laid out in the prospectus? What did the grantees attempt to do with the Carnegie funds?
2. What factors fostered or hindered implementation?
3. What has been the impact on the ability of the institutions to produce well-trained, competent, and qualified teachers? How has this changed over time?
4. What has been the impact on teacher retention?
5. What has been the impact on student learning and achievement?
6. Are the grantees regarded as "exemplars"?
7. What has been the overall contribution of the Carnegie initiative to teacher education reform in the country, states, and districts? What are the lessons learned from this attempt at reform? To what extent was Carnegie's theory of change validated in terms of producing high-quality teachers with measurable impact on student learning?
8. What are the net social benefits of Carnegie's investment in teacher education?

Some of these questions can only be answered in the long term, after several cohorts of students have graduated from the newly designed programs and have been in the labor force for some time. Some, perhaps, will never be fully answered. Nonetheless, these are appropriate research questions and are the focus of the longer-term evaluation.

In the short term, we are limited to answering questions (1) and (2). However, answering these questions is crucially important for the evaluation. If implementation is weak or fails to occur, then examining questions (3)–(8) becomes moot to a large extent. More specifically, an assessment of program implementation is needed for four important purposes:

1. To monitor current activities to identify problems in program implementation, and then improve program delivery (formative feedback).
2. To measure variability in program delivery for later statistical analyses of program effects. If outcome goals are not reached, conclusions about program effects can be related to the level of implementation.
3. To use as a source of dependent variables in modeling why delivery was or was not carried out as intended and what factors were related to the level of implementation.
4. To understand the potential for scale-up or replicability. If other sites are expected to follow the lead of the TNE sites, it is important for them to have data on how the program was structured, the challenges along the way, the factors that fostered or hindered the reform effort, and what components appeared to be crucial for achieving the desired outcomes.

Scheirer (1994, p. 65) points out "(t)he more that variation in program delivery is expected among multiple sites, the greater the need for process evaluation." The inherent and significant differences characterizing the TNE institutions underscore the importance of doing a systematic, careful, and comprehensive process evaluation.

Both the short-term and longer-term research should be useful for policymakers struggling with improving the quality of our nation's teachers and schools, for schools and districts attempting to hire, train, and retain teachers, for institutions preparing teachers, and for any future initiatives aimed at reforming teacher education.

The TNE grant requires each institution to set aside funds for a local site evaluation to be conducted by an agency external to the teacher education program. The site evaluations—unlike the national evaluation—are site specific and, at this stage, designed to provide formative feedback to the institutions as they implement the initiative. The national evaluation encompasses a cross-site design and is intended to draw lessons learned from attempting to implement the design principles outlined by Carnegie in its prospectus in four different institutions, cultures, and environments.

The Initial Phase of the Evaluation and Data Collection Activities

The first phase of the national evaluation was funded by Rockefeller in December 2002. The objectives of this first phase were to lay the foundation for the larger, longer-term evaluation, collect baseline and early implementation data on the programs and the institutions, and analyze the environments in which these four institutions were operating with respect to state policies. After they were selected, the sites were each asked to submit a design proposal to Carnegie documenting how they proposed to align their teacher education program with the TNE design principles (described in more detail in Chapter Two). Reviewing and revising the proposals took some time, and the sites did not receive their first-year funding until November 2002–January 2003. Carnegie required each institution to submit a progress report to Carnegie in the first week of October 2003 on the "first year" of implementation. Thus, although most of the sites had been implementing for between 8 and 10 months, the academic year (September 2002–August 2003) was adopted as the working definition of a "year." For our project and for purposes of this report, we adopted the same convention.

The data collection and analysis activities underlying this report include:

- Development of a baseline picture of each institution. We developed a detailed profile of the institution against which changes can be judged. These data included: description of the teacher education program; curricula of the teacher preparation program; type of degrees offered; nature and extent of the student teaching and other clinical experiences in the program; types of assessments of student performance; characteristics of students (performance on Graduate Record Examinations [GREs], state and professional qualification or certification exams, demographics); characteristics of faculty (demographics, educational attainment, awards and distinctions, number of full-time and part-time faculty); data on graduates, placement rates, and any follow-up of these graduates; internal and external evaluations of the program; relevant initiatives and/or research activities undertaken to improve the teacher education program; and evidence showing the depth of the institutional commitment to teacher education.

- An analysis of each institution's design proposal to understand the specific activities through which the institutions planned to implement the design principles.
- A site visit during the first year to monitor early progress of the TNE initiative. The site visits lasted two to three days and encompassed interviews with the project director; deans of the Colleges of Education and Arts and Sciences and the directors of the teacher education programs; and team leaders and key faculty working on aspects of the TNE initiative, including education, arts and sciences, and K–12 faculty. Other data collected included work plans, progress reports, and work products.
- A review of state regulations and policies governing teacher licensure and local teacher labor market conditions to understand the local policy environment.
- Two interviews with Daniel Fallon, Chair, Education Division, Carnegie Corporation of New York, who designed and launched the TNE initiative. Karin Egan and Barbara Gombach, Programs Officers in the Education Division, were also present at the second interview.
- An interview with two AED representatives.

The results of the first task were documented in McCombs et al. (unpublished), which provided a detailed profile of each institution just prior to the start of the initiative. This report documents the results primarily from the next three tasks, although we do provide a baseline summary profile excerpted from the earlier report.

Organizing the data was a challenge for several reasons. The sites were understandably concerned about being compared with one another, given the fundamental differences in the type, size, and capacity of the institutions. In addition, the sites needed to be situated in their particular state policy contexts. Both of these factors argued for organizing data by site. On the other hand, one of the goals of our national evaluation is to focus on cross-site data to draw together lessons learned from across the sites, which argued for organizing the data by topic across sites. Our organization of the material represents a compromise between these two goals. We organized the data by site but maintained comparability across the sites in terms of the structure and organizing principles, so readers can examine the approaches of the different institutions to a particular design principle. We then examined the data to understand lessons learned across the four sites.

Another issue that arose was how much material to provide with respect to the state context. This, after all, provides the backdrop against which the TNE reforms are carried out. Unfortunately, the sheer magnitude of the data quickly became overwhelming. For example, for each state, we collected data on the following topics: an overview of the state education system, the current fiscal condition of the state, teacher certification requirements, teacher education program requirements, additional routes to teaching, state-mandated new teacher induction requirements, requirements for continued professional development, and an overview of state recruitment and retention initiatives. These data were gathered from published reports and the state Web sites. As a result, we summarized the material, limiting the discussion to about 7 to 10 pages for each state. These data are presented in Appendix E. Each of the sections on the individual sites discusses the institution's perceptions of the influence the budget and policy context of the state had on implementation progress and the challenges the institutions face because of proposed or actual state policy changes.

Organization of the Report

Chapter Two provides an overview of the TNE initiative and the design principles that form the underpinning of the reform, the selection process by which the first four grantees were selected, and a brief description of the sites at baseline to set the context for the subsequent chapters discussing changes brought about by TNE. We then sketch the theory of change implicit in the prospectus and the selection criteria whereby Carnegie believed that the reform would lead to the desired outcomes of better-prepared teachers and eventually higher pupil learning. Technical assistance forms a key component of the intervention and it is important to understand the functions and role of the technical assistance provider. This is discussed in Chapter Three. Chapter Four is based on our site visits and materials provided by the institutions, including the institutions' first-year progress report to Carnegie. It presents an overview of how the sites structured the project in terms of leadership and work teams, the approach taken by the institutions to translate the design principles into practice and the progress they made in implementing the three major design principles. This chapter also discusses the perceived impact of state fiscal and policy context on the TNE initiative. Chapter Five reports findings across the sites. These findings are based on what participants reported during the interviews regarding their TNE experience and the perceived impact of TNE on their institution, and our own observations. Our findings lead to some recommendations regarding how implementation could be improved. These are discussed in Chapter Six.

There are five detailed appendixes. Appendixes A–D focus on the individual sites: Bank Street, CSUN, MSU, and UVa, respectively. Appendix E details the state policy contexts.

Purpose of the Report

It is important to be clear about what this report does and does not do. It provides a detailed look at first-year plans and implementation of TNE across the four institutions set against the state policy contexts. The report is meant to be a descriptive record of the unfolding of this initiative, based on qualitative data. As the initiative progresses, we hope to collect data on intermediate and final outcomes. But that is for the future. Our goals in this report are much more limited—to understand where the institutions were at the start of the reform and how they proposed to reform their programs, to track the progress they made in the first year of implementation, and to document the early lessons learned.

CHAPTER TWO

The *Teachers for a New Era* Initiative: Overview, Selection Process, and Theory of Change

This chapter presents an overview of the TNE initiative and the process that resulted in the selection of the first four grantees. The prospectus identified several factors that it recognized needed to be aligned for the theory of change to be implemented successfully. Many of these were embodied in the selection criteria. Using the prospectus and the selection criteria and process, we outline a theory of change that underpins the TNE initiative.

Teachers for a New Era

Rationale and Goals

Carnegie's goal is to provide funds and assistance to selected universities to develop excellent teacher education programs that will produce caring, competent, and effective teachers. In this way, it hopes to be able to develop evidence about the best way to produce effective teachers, and to add to the knowledge base for teacher education, a knowledge base that is sadly lacking at present.

In its prospectus (Carnegie, 2001), Carnegie offered a rationale for its focus on improving teacher education:

> New and convincing evidence that teaching is more important for schoolchildren than any other condition has been stunning in its clarity and exciting in its implications ... Now, recent research based upon thousands of pupil records in many different cities and states establishes beyond doubt that the quality of the teacher is the most important cause of pupil achievement. Excellent teachers can bring about remarkable increases in pupil learning even in the face of severe economic or social disadvantage. Such new knowledge puts teacher education squarely at the focus of efforts to improve the intellectual capacity of schoolchildren in the United States. More than ever, the nation needs assurance that colleges and universities are educating prospective teachers of the highest quality possible.

The ultimate goal of the TNE initiative is both bold and ambitious. The prospectus (Carnegie, 2001) states that

> At the conclusion of the project, each of these institutions should be regarded by the nation as the locus for one of the best programs possible for the standard primary route to employment as a beginning professional teacher. The benchmarks of success for this effort will be evident in the characteristics of the teachers who graduate from these programs. They will be competent, caring, and qualified, will be actively sought by school districts and schools, and will be known for the learning gains made by their pupils.

Carnegie also makes it clear that, as a result of the TNE grant, it is expecting radical changes in the way institutions organize themselves academically, allocate resources, evaluate participating faculty, and partner with K–12 schools.

Design Principles

The TNE prospectus outlined three broad design principles that Carnegie believes characterize excellent teacher education programs:

- **A teacher education program should be guided by a respect for evidence.** A culture of research, inquiry, and data analysis should permeate the program. Attention needs to be paid to pupil learning gains accomplished under the tutelage of teachers who are graduates of the program.
- **Faculty in the disciplines of the arts and sciences must be fully engaged in the education of prospective teachers,** especially in the areas of subject-matter understanding and general and liberal education. Faculty from the arts and sciences should also be engaged in supervision of student teachers, particularly in clinical settings.
- **Education should be understood as an academically taught clinical practice profession.** This requires close cooperation between colleges of education and actual practicing schools; appointment of master teachers as clinical faculty in the College of Education; and a two-year residency induction period for graduates of a teacher education program, during which graduates will be followed and provided mentoring and support (Carnegie, 2001).[1]

Previous reform efforts have emphasized the importance of a research-based teacher education curriculum, engagement of arts and sciences faculty, and a rich integrated clinical component (Barney, Eide, and Kirby, 2001). However, TNE differs from previous reform efforts in two ways: (a) the explicit emphasis on measuring the "value added" of the teachers prepared by the institution in terms of student achievement gains, and (b) an insistence that providing support and mentoring to graduates during their first two years of teaching (the two-year induction period) is the responsibility of both the teacher education and arts and sciences faculty.

In addition, the prospectus emphasizes a number of other areas that teacher education programs need to address as part of their program redesign:

- **Pedagogical Content Knowledge:** Faculties from both arts and sciences and education need to work together to ensure that teachers have a deep understanding of subject matter, as well as pedagogical content knowledge (PCK) that would allow them to teach imaginatively and productively.
- **Literacy and Numeracy Skills:** The program should ensure that teacher candidates acquire and demonstrate mastery of literacy and numeracy skills, and that they are prepared to teach them, irrespective of the level at which they will be teaching.
- **Academic Concentration of Elementary and Middle School Teachers:** Attention needs to be paid to the question of an appropriate academic concentration for a candidate intending to become an elementary school teacher (and perhaps a middle school teacher). This question should be addressed in a rigorous way, with close

---

[1] Scannell (1999) lists many of these same principles as characteristics shared by successful teacher education programs.

attention to credible evidence from the research literature, to ensure that elementary teachers learn the core structure of multiple disciplines and are prepared to teach content knowledge in a variety of subjects.

- **Use of Technology:** Knowing how to evaluate and use new technologies to facilitate teaching and learning is an essential skill in the teacher's repertoire and, therefore, programs need to integrate instruction about technology throughout the curriculum.
- **Cultural Considerations and Minority Recruitment:** Given the demographic and cultural composition of the nation's students, teachers need to be taught basic elements of the cultures in which students live, and how sensitivity to culture works as an ally to effective teaching. In addition, there is an especially pressing need for teacher candidates who represent minority communities, particularly in the areas of science and mathematics. Teacher education programs need to find ways to recruit more students from groups that are underrepresented in teaching.
- **Late Deciders:** Some students decide to become teachers late in their undergraduate careers and/or transfer in from community colleges. Therefore, specific provisions need to be developed within the program to ease the entry of qualified candidates who come to the program later than the normally indicated point of admission.[2]

TNE also makes it clear that it is expecting teacher education to be a **universitywide commitment**. Many previous and current reform efforts in the teacher education arena have also emphasized the importance of fully engaging the institutional leadership in reforming the teacher education program. To ensure that the institutional leadership is fully engaged in the reform effort, the TNE award is made to an officer in the president or provost's office whose administrative authority extends throughout all academic units of the institution, rather than to a school, college, or dean.

Institutions selected for awards are expected to become national exemplars of best practice in the field of teacher education. To fulfill this responsibility, they are expected to widely disseminate information about lessons learned, successful innovations, and difficulties encountered.

In talking with reformers, Carnegie found that what often keeps institutions from implementing ideas is the absence of time and money. In deciding the amount and period of the grant, Carnegie was determined to "get that excuse off the table" by making the grant as large as possible, given their available total budget. Carnegie decided that $1 million a year was large enough to get people's attention, and that reform of this magnitude required at least five years. Further, if programs could demonstrate their effectiveness in terms of the pupil learning gains made under the tutelage of their graduates, then they would be seen as exemplars and influence both other institutions and state policies.

The Selection Process

Early in the fall of 2001, Carnegie appointed a National Advisory Panel to help select institutions to be invited to submit proposals for funding under the terms of the TNE initiative and asked RAND to provide analytic assistance to the panel and Carnegie during the selec-

---

[2] These principles have their basis in a number of studies that are summarized in American Council on Education (1999).

tion process. Carnegie asked the panel members to consider the following criteria for selection:

- the quality of the teacher education program currently in place at the institution
- the capacity of the institution to serve as an exemplar or model for other institutions
- the effects of the institution on the enterprise of teacher education
- the local or regional public policy environment that most directly affects the institution
- the capacity of the institution to engage in leadership activities to persuade other institutions to adopt successful features of the design principles
- the quality of the faculty and administration
- other criteria that were deemed relevant.

After considerable discussion, such criteria as depth and breadth of leadership, stability of leadership, and commitment to change were included in the list of criteria to be considered during the selection process. In addition, Carnegie and the panel representatives were sensitive to selecting a group of institutions that represented the wide variety of institutions and programs that prepare teachers. The panel members and representatives from Carnegie and other foundations identified several teacher education institutions as meeting all or some subset of the criteria listed above. RAND developed comparable profiles of these institutions based on publicly available data. Based on these data and their own expert judgment, panel members and foundation representatives selected seven institutions as candidates for funding in the first year. Carnegie representatives, panel members, RAND, and, in some cases, other foundation members made site visits to these seven institutions early in 2002. RAND used the selection criteria and the core design principles as organizing principles for the data and provided site visit reports to Carnegie and the rest of the advisory group. Based largely on the data gathered during the site visits, panel members and foundation representatives ranked the institutions, although the final decision was Carnegie's. The Annenberg Foundation and the Ford Foundation decided to join Carnegie in funding one institution apiece in the first year.[3] This meant that four institutions could be selected for funding in the first round. The awards were announced in April 2002. The first four grantees were Bank Street College of Education; California State University, Northridge; Michigan State University; and the University of Virginia.

- **Bank Street College of Education, New York, New York:** Bank Street College of Education is an independent institution devoted entirely to improving the education of children and their teachers. The college comprises three divisions: Children's Programs, which runs the School for Children; the Division of Continuing Education; and the Graduate School of Education devoted entirely to teacher education. The Graduate School offers the M.S. and M.S.Ed. degrees and initial New York State teaching certification through a number of different programs that can be completed in as little as 12–15 months, although two years to completion is most typical. All applicants must have completed a bachelor's degree prior to their acceptance into Bank Street. Generally, Bank Street graduates about 250 teachers per year from programs leading to initial certification.

---

[3] The Annenberg and Ford Foundations have appointed Carnegie to represent the funders. As a result, the initiative is overseen and monitored by Carnegie through the technical assistance provider.

- **California State University, Northridge, California:** CSUN offers multiple paths to elementary and secondary teaching credentials, including undergraduate programs offered jointly by the College of Education and arts and sciences colleges (the Integrated Teacher Education Program [ITEP] and the Four-Year Integrated Teacher Credential Program [FYI]). In addition, it offers several versions of the post-baccalaureate program (fifth-year program). In 2000–01, CSUN issued a total of 1,554 initial credentials. Overall, a little less than half the graduates were minorities.
- **Michigan State University, East Lansing, Michigan:** MSU's teacher education program is a five-year route to a bachelor's degree and a Michigan teaching certificate. The Department of Teacher Education also offers an 18-month certification program for postbaccalaureate applicants. MSU prepares approximately 550–600 teachers a year.
- **University of Virginia, Charlottesville, Virginia:** At UVa, the Curry School of Education and the College of Arts and Sciences offer a five-year integrated Teacher Education Program, the culmination of which leads to both the baccalaureate (BA) and the Master of Teaching (MT) degrees, called the BA/MT program. In addition, the Curry School of Education offers a two-year postbaccalaureate program in which students with a completed BA degree in a noneducational field earn a Master of Teaching degree (PG/MT program). UVa graduated 124 teachers in 2002. Enrollment in the Curry School teacher education program has been growing in recent years.

The teacher education programs at the four sites were, to some extent, already aligned with the TNE design principles, which is not surprising given that alignment was weighted heavily in the selection process. All four institutions had an evaluation component in place and attempted to use data from assessments of students and the programs themselves to improve the way teachers were prepared in these institutions. However, none of the four had attempted to gauge the effectiveness of their graduates in terms of pupil learning gains. Three of the four institutions (Bank Street is the exception) showed some degree of collaboration between teacher education and arts and sciences faculty in designing and team-teaching courses for teacher education candidates.

All four institutions had strong relationships with K–12 schools and included K–12 faculty in their teacher preparation programs to some degree, largely in the clinical component of the program. Bank Street specifically looks for faculty with prior K–12 teaching experience. Collaboration between the institutions and the schools often extended beyond the teacher preparation programs to a broader-based effort to improve K–12 curriculum, content knowledge of teachers, and student learning.

None of the institutions followed their graduates systematically or had in place a comprehensive induction program to support their new graduates.

Theory of Change

Any new program or project could be thought of as representing a theory in that the decisionmaker hypothesizes that a particular treatment will cause certain predicted effects or outcomes.

The Design

The TNE prospectus outlines several key principles that characterize "excellent" teacher education programs. As described earlier, the following are the key design principles:

- decisions driven by evidence
- engagement of arts and sciences faculty
- integrated clinical component.

Other components emphasized in the prospectus include: PCK, appropriate academic concentrations for elementary and middle school teachers, use of technology, attention to diversity and cultural issues, and establishing pathways for late deciders.

Carnegie's thesis is that adoption and implementation of these design principles will result in an "excellent" teacher education program, whose teacher graduates will be well trained, capable, and qualified. Teachers trained by institutions well aligned with the Carnegie principles will be "high-quality" teachers, whose quality is measured by the learning gains made by their pupils.

Enabling Factors

For Carnegie's theory to work, institutions must fully implement the proposed reforms. Several conditions must be fulfilled before a major reform effort seeking a substantial departure from the status quo will achieve its objectives (Sabatier and Mazmanian, 1979). These enabling factors were recognized in the TNE prospectus and the selection process.

Figure 2.1 presents our depiction of the TNE "theory of change." The boxes on the left represent factors and actors that need to be aligned for coherent and effective implementation of the theory of change, recognized implicitly or explicitly in the prospectus and the selection process. The boxes on the right represent the causal linkage outlined in the prospectus and underlying Carnegie's vision. The two circles represent the desired outcomes specifically mentioned in the prospectus: well-trained, competent, and qualified teachers, and student learning and achievement. The dashed lines represent the feedback loops into the program—necessary if the program improvement is to be evidence based.

External Resources. The initiative rests crucially on the assumption that substantial external resources and technical assistance are needed for the reform to be successful in changing the way teachers are prepared in these institutions, and the TNE initiative is structured to provide both. TNE is providing $5 million per institution and is expecting institutions to provide matching funds, for a total of $10 million. This level of funding is unprecedented in the history of teacher education reform. In addition, AED has been asked to provide considerable hands-on assistance during the five years of the grant.

Universitywide Commitment. Given that TNE is expecting radical changes in organization, allocation of resources, and faculty evaluation processes, the prospectus explicitly recognizes that the buy-in and continuous support of top administrators, such as presidents and provosts, are crucial to the success of the effort.[4] Indeed, TNE insists that the grant be administered out of the provost's office, not the department of education, believing that this will cause TNE to be seen as a university endeavor and bring about greater faculty buy-in.

---

[4] This is borne out by earlier studies of reform. For example, see Sabatier and Mazmanian (1979); Wisniewski (undated); American Council on Education (1999).

Figure 2.1
Theory of Change Underlying the TNE Initiative

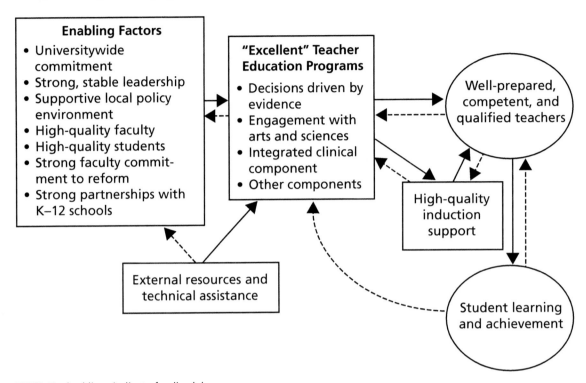

NOTE: Dashed lines indicate feedback loops.

RAND *TR149-2.1*

Strong, Stable Leadership. In any reform effort, strong, supportive leaders are critical. For example, Elmore writes:

> [T]he job of administrative leaders is primarily about enhancing the skills and knowledge of people in the organization, creating a common culture of expectations around the use of those skills and knowledge, holding the various pieces of the organization together in a productive relationship with each other, and holding individuals accountable for their contributions to the collective result. (2000, p. 15)

The evaluation of the BellSouth Foundation initiative to reform teacher education—which was brought to Carnegie and the panel's attention—showed that turnovers in top administrative positions and deanships often disrupted the changes under way (Wisniewski, undated). Recognizing this, Carnegie looked for both strength and depth of leadership during its selection process. Interestingly, TNE's requirement that the grant be overseen by an officer in the president or provost's office whose administrative authority extends throughout all academic units of the institution, rather than to a school, college, or dean fits well with Bardach's (1977) notion of a "fixer," an important official who controls resources important to crucial actors and who has the desire and the staff resources to monitor the process of implementation and to intervene when required.[5]

_____

[5] In RAND's work on New American Schools, we found that stability of leadership and centrality of the reform effort in the overall agenda of leaders led to higher implementation of comprehensive school reform (Berends, Bodilly, and Kirby, 2002; Bodilly, 1998; Bodilly and Berends, 1999).

Supportive Local Policy Environment. The initiative is meant to spur innovative, outside-the-box thinking on the part of the selected institutions; however, these institutions still need to comply with state rules and regulations governing teacher licensure and certification. These and other regulations may act to inhibit entry into the new programs or limit the ability of the programs to substantially change teacher education in some areas. For example, states often mandate specific course work for certification (Walsh, 2001; Prestine, 1991), adopt different types of licensure tests with different passing scores (National Research Council, 2001), and mandate induction requirements. In addition, the conditions of teacher demand and supply in states and districts might lead to various strategies that run counter to or undermine the institution's effort at reform. For example, alternative certification programs or emergency credentialing may seem easier routes into teaching for qualified candidates who do not wish to commit the time or the financial resources required to go through a more rigorous, structured program. Many of these district and state policies could run counter to what the institutions are attempting to do under TNE.

Carnegie explicitly recognized the importance of the state and local policy environment in its selection criteria, while acknowledging that the policy environments might change over time. Carnegie hopes that the universities will work with state and local officials to change policies that are likely to prove an obstacle to what they are trying to accomplish with the TNE funds. In addition, it plans to bring what leverage it can to bear on state and local policy.[6]

High-Quality Program Entrants. Program entrants need to meet quality entry standards if they are to become high-quality teachers with deep subject-matter and pedagogical knowledge. Research has shown that teachers who score higher on tests of verbal ability and other standardized tests produce greater achievement gains in students (Ehrenberg and Brewer, 1995; Ferguson, 1991; Ferguson and Ladd, 1996; Greenwald, Hedges, and Laine, 1996; Kain and Singleton, 1996).[7] Thus, the quality of the entering teacher pool will matter.

High-Quality Faculty. Equally clearly the quality of the faculty will matter in assuring the ability to implement the key design principles. What the redesign of the teacher education program calls for is faculty who are experts in their field; are familiar with the latest scientific research in the field; are able to impart this knowledge and expertise to their students; have had prior teaching experience and/or have significant involvement in K–12 schools; model good teaching practices; and are able to use feedback from students, other faculty, and teachers for continuous improvement of the program, curriculum, and their own teaching.

In its selection criteria, Carnegie emphasized the quality of the teacher education program and the quality of the institution as important enabling factors.

Strong Faculty Commitment to Reform. Implementation requires faculty who are not only high quality but committed to the reform effort undertaken by the institution. Mazmanian and Sabatier (1989) define "commitment and leadership skill of implementing

---

[6] It is not simply the state and local context that is important here. The federal government has raised the stakes with regard to teacher licensure tests through its Teacher Quality Enhancement Act (Title II) passed in 1998, and reauthorized in 2002, holding states and higher-education institutions accountable for the quality of teacher preparation and licensing. Based on graduates' performance on state teacher tests, federal funding could be reduced. The recently passed No Child Left Behind Act of 2001 also sets minimum standards for teacher quality and requires schools and districts to notify parents whose children are being taught by teachers who do not meet the quality criteria.

[7] The American Association of State Colleges and Universities (1999), in its call for teacher education reform, bluntly stated that at least 75 percent of each entering class in teacher education should be in the top 25 percent of the total student body.

officials" as the variable that most directly affects the policy output of implementing agencies. Without willing and able faculty who embrace reform and provide the necessary leadership, no reform can be enacted, no matter how effective it may be. Faculty are the "street-level bureaucrats" at the core of educational change (Weatherly and Lipsky, 1977) and educational change will depend on what faculty do and think. As Fullan points out, "it's as simple and as complex as that" (1991, p. 117). While faculty commitment to reform cannot be mandated, Carnegie attempted to ensure it in a variety of ways. During the selection process, Carnegie looked for depth of commitment to the reform at all levels, and a willingness to change; it tried to ensure that TNE would be seen as a universitywide endeavor by placing the oversight and administration in the provost's office; it provided substantial funding that could buy release time for current faculty and/or subsidize new faculty so they could devote considerable amounts of time to TNE.

Strong Partnerships with K–12 Schools. In common with previous teacher education reform efforts, the Carnegie prospectus identifies building supportive relationships between school- and university-based faculty as central to success. This idea is not new. For example, the Holmes Group reports develop the notion of Professional Development Schools as, among other things, clinical learning environments (Holmes Group, 1990). Their reports call for stronger relationships between university faculty and master teachers in the schools, including the development of "Career Professionals," or clinical professors. One of the National Network for Educational Renewal's (undated) postulates emphasizes that teacher education programs must provide a wide array of laboratory settings for their teacher education students where they can observe, participate in hands-on experiences, and see good teaching modeled (Holmes Group, 1990). However, few institutions have succeeded in establishing strong, collaborative relationships between university-based and school-based faculty. Holmes Group (1995) outlined some of the reasons that these relationships have not prospered. Briefly: (a) The cultures of school and university are often at odds with one another. University faculty fear becoming mired in the problems of the public schools, and often regard them as lowly places; (b) Collaboration requires time, often a major disincentive to both school and university faculty; and (c) Most important, the university reward structure, which favors publications over all other criteria, acts to strongly discourage involvement of university faculty in K–12 schools. Teacher union and district rules and regulations may also act as barriers.

Strong partnerships with K–12 schools are a key component of TNE's theory of change. Without these, it would be difficult to implement one of TNE's key design principles: having an integrated, clinical component. Varied and frequent student teaching experiences require the support of schools, and the support of cooperating or mentor teachers.

From "Excellent" to "Exemplary"

TNE's goals require teacher education programs to take the next step: to go from being "excellent" at what they do to becoming "exemplary" (Figure 2.2). Once they know what works, it is incumbent on them to help other institutions adopt similar programs, in part or in whole. This next step is a critical piece of TNE's vision. Ultimately, the legacy of the TNE initiative will be judged by whether the reform efforts last and to what extent they are emulated across the nation. Thus, it will be important to examine the steps that the grantees take to disseminate their practices and programs: presenting at professional organizations; assist-

Figure 2.2
Moving from "Excellent" to "Exemplary"

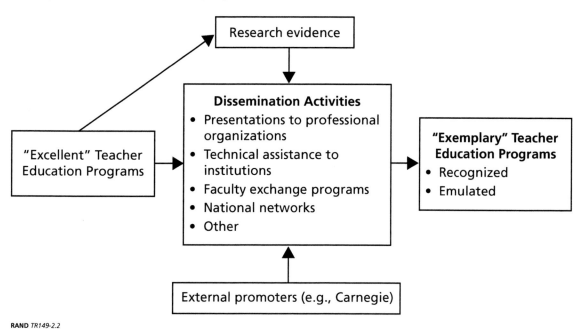

ing neighboring or peer institutions; and setting up exchange programs with other institutions to further inculcate their faculty into best practices and research, as well as providing extended venues for their own faculty to spread the word. It is not necessary that the programs adopted by other institutions be an exact replica of the grantee institution's program. Institutions need to and are likely to adapt their design to fit local conditions.[8]

To summarize, TNE's theory of change envisions "excellent" teacher education programs well aligned with the design principles and other components. These excellent programs will produce well-prepared, competent, and qualified teachers who, when fully supported by a high-quality induction program, will successfully make the transition into the classroom. These teachers will be grounded in best practices and will in turn produce pupil-learning gains. As a result of the evidence produced by these TNE institutions and wide dissemination, other institutions will be influenced to adopt these successful practices and states will be persuaded to codify these into licensure and certification requirements.

---

[8] It is interesting to note that the influence of earlier reform efforts on member and nonmember institutions has been uncertain. In their evaluation of the Holmes Group, Fullan et al. (1998) concluded that the most significant reforms across all universities included the development of overarching conceptual frameworks for curriculum guidance, the introduction of more rigorous program entry standards, and the development of improved preservice assessments. The least change came in articulating learning goals to teacher education candidates, emphasizing research and inquiry throughout the program, and evaluating teacher education programs internally. One problem may have been that the Holmes Group reports may not have provided enough guidance on "how" to make the needed changes. For example, Gideonse (1996) criticized the Holmes Group's *Tomorrow's Schools of Education* as offering little practical help to those trying to change.

Figure 2.3
Modeling Possible Outcomes of the TNE Initiative

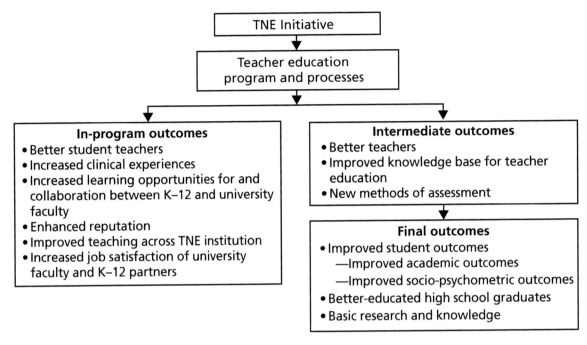

RAND *TR149-2.3*

Measuring the Outcomes of TNE

TNE is a complex initiative that requires radical institutional and cultural changes. A national evaluation of an initiative of this magnitude and complexity faces several challenges, chief among them that the outcomes of interest are not likely to be seen or measured until several years after the initiative ends. Answering the questions listed in Chapter One requires that several kinds of outcomes be tracked and measured over time as the initiative unfolds. It is useful to categorize these as in-program outcomes, intermediate outcomes, and final outcomes, as shown in Figure 2.3.

In-program outcomes can be thought of as those affecting various stakeholders during and because of their direct participation in the program. For example, the changes in program content and structure should improve the quality of student teachers, and this should directly benefit: the teacher education students themselves (greater confidence in the classroom), the teacher education program (decreased need for counseling, assistance, or intervention, and greater ability to provide productive supervision), the partner K–12 schools (increased ability to provide quality instruction and to provide targeted assistance to K–12 students), and the funders (who emphasize close relationships with schools and integrated clinical experiences). As another example, the TNE institutions plan to hold workshops or disseminate their findings regarding effective teaching to other faculty not directly involved in the initiative. This could bring about improved teaching across the university. This would benefit the university faculty and teacher education students and probably non–teacher education students as well; funders (who value effective teaching); and institutions of higher education (IHEs), both partner and non-TNE institutions, that might benefit if knowledge about how to bring about more effective teaching was widely disseminated.

Intermediate outcomes can be thought of as benefits that accrue later in the process and may themselves be valued, but are not seen as final outcomes. We define three types of intermediate outcomes, as shown in Figure 2.3.

First, the primary outcome of these programs will be to produce "better" teacher graduates, defined as competent, caring, well-educated, with a strong sense of self-efficacy, with a strong knowledge of content and pedagogy, who are likely to be sought after by districts and schools.

Second, each of the TNE institutions is making efforts to review the research base of teacher education and to collect evidence on what works and what does not. This presumably is likely to benefit a wide range of stakeholders (for example, teacher education faculty, who can use this to make the program better; partner institutions, to whom this knowledge is disseminated; non-TNE teacher preparation institutions, that could use the research to develop evidence-based teacher education programs; and funders, who may be interested in seeing such knowledge developed and disseminated).

Third, because assessment is a key component of the TNE initiative, each of the TNE institutions is examining different methods of assessment and thinking about developing new ones. These would be used to assess their teacher candidates and graduates and to improve the program. In addition, the institutions are looking to develop or improve diagnostic assessments that could be used to assess progress of K–12 students and to improve classroom instruction. These new assessments will add to the general knowledge base for teacher education and might have an effect on a wide range of beneficiaries.

Final outcomes are the end result of the change process. The ultimate goal of the TNE initiative is, of course, to improve K–12 student outcomes but this is likely to have longer-term and broader benefits as well. Better teaching and a more supportive class environment are likely to lead to improved conditions of learning and teaching in classrooms and schools. This could foster a greater interest in learning, a higher level of student engagement, and a greater student respect for cultural differences. Academic outcomes would include improved content knowledge, retention in school, and eventually better-educated high school graduates. Students could also meet proficiency standards sooner, thus freeing up their schedules to take more advanced and enrichment-type courses. This latter outcome is contingent on the other student outcomes taking place, i.e., students are indeed learning more, performing better, and have fewer behavioral problems. Having better-educated high school graduates has benefits across the board—it would benefit all IHEs in terms of having higher-quality freshmen and employers in having a higher-quality workforce. These benefits may well be reflected in terms of potential cost savings.

Linking Teaching Quality and Student Achievement

The ultimate outcome measure defined by TNE is pupil-learning gains. However, improving student outcomes depends on more than teacher quality—federal, state, and district policies, principal leadership, school contexts, community support. The list is daunting, and the best-prepared teachers could well be stymied by unsupportive school and home environments, poor or unstable leadership, and policies that could result in little or no pupil learning accomplished in their classrooms. The effect of teachers on student achievement will need to be measured carefully to account for these many factors. In this respect, value-added modeling (VAM), a collection of complex statistical techniques that uses multiple years of test score data on students to estimate the effects of individual schools or teachers, offers a potentially useful method for isolating teacher effects, but great care must be taken in including the proper controls and in making inferences from the analyses.[9] Much of this literature shows sizable, persistent teacher effects on student achievement.

None of these outcomes can be measured in the early years of the reform effort. Nonetheless, accounting for potential benefits of TNE in a cost-benefit analysis framework is useful because it shows clearly the kinds of data that need to be collected as the initiative unfolds. In the short run, we are limited to tracking implementation. However, as we pointed out earlier, this kind of process evaluation offers valuable data and insights that will both inform our longer-term, more summative evaluation of TNE and provide formative feedback to assist the sites.

We next turn to the role of the technical assistance provider in TNE.

---

[9] The literature suggests that teacher effects are large, accounting for a significant portion of the variability in growth, and that they persist for at least three to four years into the future (Wright, Horn, and Sanders, 1997; Rowan, Correnti, and Miller, 2002; Rivkin, Hanushek, and Kain, 2000; Sanders and Rivers, 1996; Rivers, 1999; Mendro, Jordan, Gomez, Anderson, and Bembry, 1998; Kain, 1998). McCaffrey et al. (2004) undertook a rigorous review of the literature on value-added models. Based on their reviews and original analyses, the authors concluded that although the studies reviewed all have shortcomings, together they provide evidence that teachers have discernable, differential effects on student achievement, and that these teacher effects appear to persist across years. They warn that the magnitude of some of the effects reported in the literature are overstated and that reported teacher effects are sensitive to assumptions underlying the statistical models, but this issue has been largely ignored in the literature. Kupermintz (2003) in a recent article also examined the validity of teacher evaluation measures produced by the Tennessee Value Added Assessment System (TVAAS). He points out several threats to the validity of the TVAAS teacher evaluation information, including the importance of correctly accounting for the ability and background characteristics of students.

CHAPTER THREE

The Role of the Technical Assistance Provider, Academy for Educational Development (AED)

It was clear to Carnegie from previous experience with the urban schools initiative that a reform of this magnitude could not be undertaken without substantial technical assistance. Carnegie contracted with AED, a nonprofit project management agency, to administer the project and to provide technical support to the institutions as needed. AED staff were teamed with an outside consultant with considerable expertise in teacher education and teacher quality issues, who serves as the principal investigator for the project. Carnegie asked AED to provide a full range of support to the grantees, without fully specifying what these services should be. At the time, Carnegie and AED believed that AED's primary function would be brokering technical assistance so that most of the assistance would consist of the grantees asking for help on a specific issue and AED linking them with an expert in that field. However, the kinds of assistance required by the sites during the first year turned out to be quite different from what had been originally conceived, and AED ended up spending considerable time consulting directly with sites on project management issues and clarifying the funders' wishes. This was partly due to the way the selection and proposal process was structured.

Assistance During the Proposal Phase

During the first year, Carnegie selected the grantees and then asked them to submit a design proposal outlining how they would implement the principles outlined in the prospectus. Carnegie requested that AED provide the sites assistance in writing the proposals. They paid site visits to or conducted conference calls with each institution and served as liaison between Carnegie and the sites regarding such questions as fungibility of funds, interpretation of the principles, etc. The proposals were all reviewed by a committee appointed by Carnegie, and each institution received a detailed commentary on its proposal asking for revision, clarification, or elaboration of specific points that the proposal had failed to address in a satisfactory manner. All four proposals needed substantial revisions, and budget issues required negotiation. AED was instrumental in helping the institutions during the rewriting and negotiation phase. AED noted that while the proposals were fairly specific on what the sites wanted to do, they tended to be somewhat vague about how they would implement the ideas. This gave rise to the idea of requiring each site to develop a work plan for each design principle detailing specific tasks, next steps, milestones, and two- and five-year goals. Some of the work plans were overly ambitious, setting short-term goals that seemed unlikely to be met, so AED worked with the sites to help them develop more reasonable time lines and milestones.

Assistance and Monitoring During the First Year of Implementation

AED's tasks during the first year consisted of

- **Project management and monitoring through biweekly phone calls with the site project directors and two site visits:** The biweekly schedule was flexible; AED tried to maintain contact with the project directors on a regular basis. Other individuals at the institutions, most notably staff from the budget office, often contacted them with questions about various aspects of the budget and reporting requirements of the grant.
- **Acting as TNE's fiscal agent:** This role came about by happenstance. The three funders preferred not to be seen as funding particular institutions; as a result, they pooled their funds together and AED disbursed the funds at Carnegie's request.
- **Convening the grantees twice a year for workshops:** The AED contract requires them to hold two institutes a year, focusing on specific aspects of the TNE initiative. The two workshops held in the first year focused on value-added modeling of teacher effectiveness, and teacher induction programs. Experts were invited to present papers, and facilitated workshops were held for teams of TNE staff from the four institutions. In addition, one of the purposes of the first institute was to provide the institutions with time to communicate with institutional teams both within and across institutions. Although some of the teams were less than enthusiastic about participating initially, AED reported that the sites found the team facilitation very helpful and were very positive about the institute.
- **Fostering intersite communication:** Carnegie, in its original meetings with AED, had asked AED to foster intersite communications through various means— meetings, email, Web-based meetings, and online newsletters. As mentioned above, the workshops also offered time for the site teams to get together. In addition, AED held periodic conference calls to facilitate learning across sites.
- **Brokering technical assistance when requested by the sites:** AED felt that the sites needed to be farther along in their implementation before outside experts could be helpful.[1] Instead, AED itself has been providing most of the technical assistance in terms of helping the sites with early implementation issues and making sure they make progress toward goals identified in their work plans. It is likely that the brokering service will be used more during the second and later years.
- **Disseminating information about TNE:** An important part of AED's role is to publicize and disseminate information about TNE. One of the ways AED performs this role is by creating opportunities for the institutions to make presentations to the larger professional and scholarly communities. For example, AED set up a forum at the annual meeting of the American Association of Colleges of Teacher Education (AACTE) at which Daniel Fallon, Chair of the Education Division of the Carnegie Corporation, who designed and is overseeing TNE, provided an overview of TNE and the institutions' projects. This was attended by about 85 to 90 people. More recently, AED set up panels at professional meetings of the American Educational Research Association and the National Board for Professional Teaching Standards.

---

[1] One of the sites reported that it relied on its own resources to find an expert in a needed area.

Staffing

AED's team is led by three key staff, each of whom has primary responsibility for one or two institutions. The project team consists of between seven and eight staff members. The project director spends about 40 to 50 percent of her time on TNE, and other principals spend about a third of their time on the initiative.

AED's Role: A Balancing Act

The fact that AED is both a "critical friend" and an agent of the sponsor requires the academy to maintain a careful and delicate balance between helping the institutions and monitoring them for early problems and issues. Each institution is monitored against its own goals and work plan. AED hoped the institutions would recognize that the work plan is a living document that will need revision as implementation continues, and thought that most did so. Because the four institutions have very different institutional cultures, some are more familiar or comfortable with the kind of role that AED has been asked to play. In some cases, the institution's needs play to AED's strengths—for example, MSU asked AED to facilitate some of the university's team meetings and to provide training in facilitation to the team coleaders. In addition, some sites are more willing than others to be open regarding problems and shortcomings. AED's philosophy is to build a long-term relationship with the sites based on trust and honesty so that it can help the institutions. If something goes awry, AED will help develop solutions to resolve the problem. AED feels that a problem would need to be intractable before the academy would formally ask Carnegie to address it. The academy does, however, keep Carnegie informed of progress on an informal basis.

AED noted that while all the institutions used AED in different ways, time expenditures over the first year had been somewhat equitable. Once the institutions start requesting outside experts, AED will attempt to balance resources among the institutions. In addition, AED sees its role as diagnosing the areas in which the sites need help and procuring it for them. If most of the sites need help with a particular issue or design principle, AED may hold a workshop for all the institutions rather than providing expert help to the individual institutions separately.

The next chapter focuses on implementation of the TNE initiative in the four individual institutions.

CHAPTER FOUR

Overview of Progress in Implementing TNE in the First Year

This chapter presents a summary of the progress the sites made in implementing TNE in Year 1 (November 2002–January 2003 through September 2003). Appendixes A–D present considerably more detail on the sites, their plans, and progress.

The chapter examines each of the sites in turn. For each site, we present an overview of the leadership structure and staffing of the project at the site, the basic approach to reforming the teacher education program to align with the TNE design principles, the progress in implementation, selected Year 2 activities, and the perceived impact of the state fiscal and policy context on the site's ability to implement TNE.

In discussing implementation progress, we present a summary of the progress each site made in implementing the three major design principles: decisions driven by evidence, engagement with arts and sciences faculty, and teaching as a clinical practice profession. In some cases, the sites also made progress in addressing other design principles; these are also discussed. Grouping activities by the design principles allows the reader to examine the range of activities undertaken by the sites, but it should be remembered that this grouping is somewhat artificial. Some of the activities listed under one design principle transcend the categorization and fit under several headings. For example, there was considerable collaboration between arts and sciences, education, and K–12 faculty in developing definitions of quality teaching and/or developing measures of what teachers need to know or do. This work would fit under all three design principles. However, we believe this categorization offers a useful way of looking at progress. In grouping activities under the various design principles, we were guided by the design proposals, the progress reports submitted by the sites to Carnegie, and our interview notes.

Bank Street

Project Structure: Leadership and Staffing

As shown in Figure 4.1, Bank Street recruited a full-time project director from outside the school to oversee and coordinate the TNE activities and formed a leadership team composed of the project director, the dean, and two education faculty members. In Year 2, a faculty member who was hired to oversee induction also became part of the leadership team. Bank Street established a Coordinating Council[1] that included representatives from the New York State Board of Regents, the National Board for Professional Teaching Standards, and the

---

[1] This was required by the TNE prospectus.

Figure 4.1
Project Structure and Staffing, Bank Street College of Education

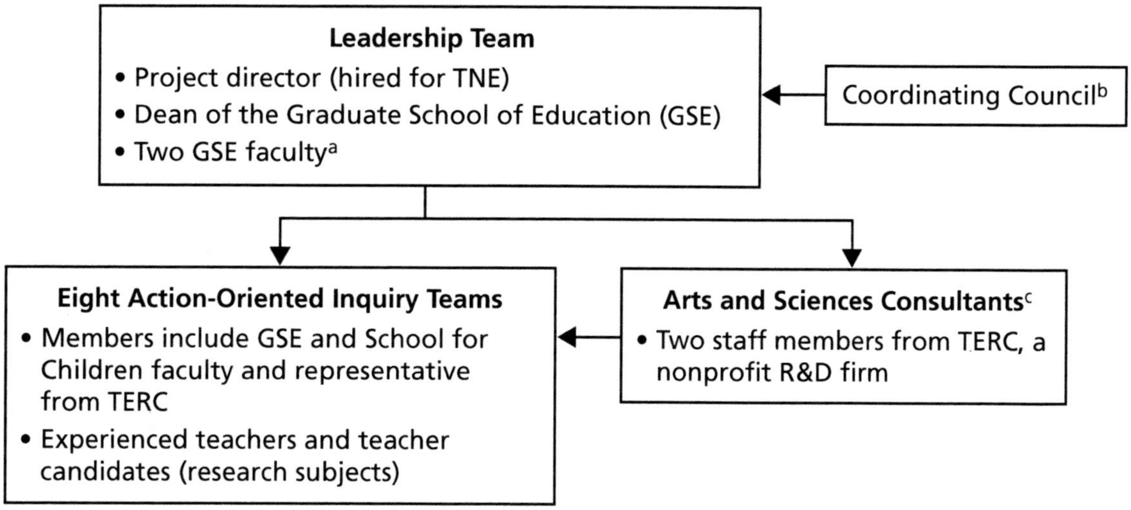

```
┌─────────────────────────────────────────────────┐
│                 Leadership Team                  │
│  • Project director (hired for TNE)              │◄──── ┌──────────────────────────┐
│  • Dean of the Graduate School of Education (GSE)│      │  Coordinating Council^b   │
│  • Two GSE faculty^a                             │      └──────────────────────────┘
└─────────────────────────────────────────────────┘
```

```
┌──────────────────────────────────────┐        ┌──────────────────────────────────────┐
│  Eight Action-Oriented Inquiry Teams  │        │    Arts and Sciences Consultants^c    │
│  • Members include GSE and School for │◄───────│  • Two staff members from TERC, a      │
│    Children faculty and representative │        │    nonprofit R&D firm                  │
│    from TERC                           │        └──────────────────────────────────────┘
│  • Experienced teachers and teacher    │
│    candidates (research subjects)      │
└──────────────────────────────────────┘
```

[a] Newly hired induction coordinator added to team in Year 2.

[b] Formed in Year 2 to disseminate information to external organizations.

[c] Partnership with Sarah Lawrence College in Year 2.

RAND *TR149-4.1*

New York City Department of Education. The role of the Council is to disseminate TNE information to external organizations and to help reflect on the project findings and their implications for teacher development policies and programs. The first meeting of the Coordinating Council will be in Year 2.

The project director works full time on TNE. The dean spends 25 to 50 percent of his time on TNE but is budgeted for 25 percent of his time under the TNE budget. The others on the leadership team are each covered 40 percent by TNE.

TNE work at Bank Street is carried out by action-oriented inquiry (AOI) teams. AOI research team members were education faculty from the Graduate School, except for one School for Children faculty member and a mathematics consultant from TERC, a not-for-profit research and development organization with expertise in mathematics, science, and technology education. A second TERC consultant provided guidance to all the AOI teams. AOI members who were College faculty were provided 15 percent coverage for their TNE work. Teachers were paid a small stipend.

Implementation Progress: Selected Highlights

The goal of the AOI component of the TNE initiative is to inform project renewal and ensure that it is evidence based. Bank Street plans to use the findings of the AOI projects to inform admissions, the induction program, and their teacher education and teacher leader programs. The AOI teams' process and findings also provide faculty with new ways to think about their work and develop data collection strategies to be integrated into their graduate course work.

Bank Street faculty formed eight AOI teams. In the spring, each AOI team studied one experienced teacher and one teacher candidate during a 2–3 week unit of mathematics or literacy instruction. Each team conducted a preinterview, observed classes, and collected

Table 4.1
Year 1 Implementation of TNE Design Principles, Bank Street College of Education

Design Principles	Year 1 Activities

Decisions based on evidence	• Developed framework for defining quality teaching, largely based on California Standards for the Teaching Profession, to serve as a framework for data to be collected by the AOI teams
	• Used work of AOI teams to begin developing a research base that could be used to guide program change and to provide faculty with new ways to think about their work
	  – Held training for AOI members on how to conduct research
	  – Each team studied an experienced teacher, novice teacher, and/or a teacher candidate over 2–3 weeks (interviews, observations, and student work), focusing on literacy and numeracy
	  – Integrated findings across teams
	• Worked with local evaluator to update and improve database for tracking graduates

Engagement with arts and sciences faculty	• Recruited two representatives from TERC to participate in the AOI work • Worked to establish institutional relationship with arts and sciences faculty from another university or college; will partner with Sarah Lawrence College in Year2

Teaching as a clinical practice profession	• Commissioned studies to inform induction plans
	  – Stevens Institute conducted focus groups with graduates and faculty members and did a review of electronic induction
	  – Hired graduate student to review state efforts to support new teachers in the classroom with a view to finding exemplary induction programs

student work. The teachers who were being studied were considered to be members of the AOI teams as well.

Because Bank Street is an independent college of education, involving arts and sciences faculty, and doing so in a meaningful way, is a tremendous challenge. Bank Street worked to form a partnership with arts and sciences faculty from another university and was successful in establishing an institutional relationship with Sarah Lawrence College as of the start of Year 2.

During Year 1, Bank Street laid the groundwork for its future induction activities by commissioning studies that would inform its induction plans. The information in the two reports will help Bank Street develop principles on which to base the induction program, which aims to provide a menu of options for candidates.

Looking Ahead to Year 2

Extend Work of AOI Teams. The cross-case analysis of the AOI teams' work will be used to inform revisions of the domains and the methodology used to conduct the research and as the basis for a database to inform program improvements. In addition to literacy and numeracy, the AOI teams will focus on science in Year 2. They plan to increase the number of AOI teams from eight to ten and to solicit wider participation from School for Children faculty, Continuing Education faculty, and arts and sciences faculty from Sarah Lawrence College. They will also introduce more flexibility in the team structure to allow faculty to work with more than one team.

Incorporate Student Assessment Measures into AOI Work. Bank Street will examine three levels of assessment: standardized tests, pre- and post-tests in literacy and numeracy with teacher candidates' students, and curriculum-embedded assessments.

Focus on Induction. The induction coordinator will form an induction committee that includes external partners. Representatives from TNE leadership will also meet with districts to see how best to align their induction plans with state requirements.

Impact of State Budget and Policy

While New York is facing lower than expected revenues, resulting in significant budget shortfalls and cuts to higher education, Bank Street, a private institution, has not been directly impacted by these cuts. The downturn in the economy, however, has led to a small reduction in private gift giving.

Bank Street recently reregistered all its teacher education programs with the state, making necessary changes to ensure compliance with wider new state regulations on the knowledge, skills, and dispositions required for certification to teach in New York state. However, Bank Street will need to consider how it will fit its induction program with the district first-year mentoring program that is now required by the state.

California State University, Northridge

Project Structure: Leadership and Staffing

CSUN's leadership team consists of the Vice Provost for Academic Affairs (project director), and two co–associate project directors: the Dean of the College of Education and the Interim Dean of the College of Social and Behavioral Sciences (Figure 4.2). The leadership team is assisted by a 14-member steering committee, made up of representatives from K–12 schools, the College of Education, the various colleges of arts and sciences, and one member from the Achievement Council (a community organization dedicated to improving achievement of low-income and minority students).

CSUN created a coordinating council to serve as an advisory body to the TNE project and to monitor progress, facilitate success, and publicize achievements of the TNE project. The group met for the first time in August 2003.

CSUN formed three committees linked to the design principles. The three committees, each chaired by one member of the steering committee, organized themselves into various work groups, each with its own focus and time line. Each group consisted of between five and twelve members, a mix of K–12, education, and arts and sciences faculty. In total, 83 university and K–12 faculty participated in the various committees and work groups that are implementing the CSUN work plan.

CSUN also hired five new faculty members whose salaries are covered by TNE funds and who are designated as TNE fellows. The advertised positions stressed direct experience in K–12 schools and/or demonstrated interest in pedagogy along with the more usual academic credentials and research. The appointments include half-time release from teaching for TNE work. New tenure-track faculty in the College of Education were also hired to help with the implementation of TNE goals. These include two new faculty in research and assessment and instructional technology, respectively. In addition to these new faculty, CSUN implemented a teacher-in-residence (TIR) program in partnership with the Los Angeles Unified School District (LAUSD). Two teachers were appointed for the past academic year, one a special educator and the other from secondary English. On campus, their primary roles were serving on the steering committee and assisting with partner schools.

Managerial personnel (deans, associate deans, and chairs) with 12-month appointments were not given release time. Thus, the TNE work was added on top of their normal responsibilities. The regular teaching load for faculty is 12 units per semester (generally four courses). Most faculty on nine-month appointments received 3–6 units of release time for

Figure 4.2
Project Structure and Staffing, California State University, Northridge

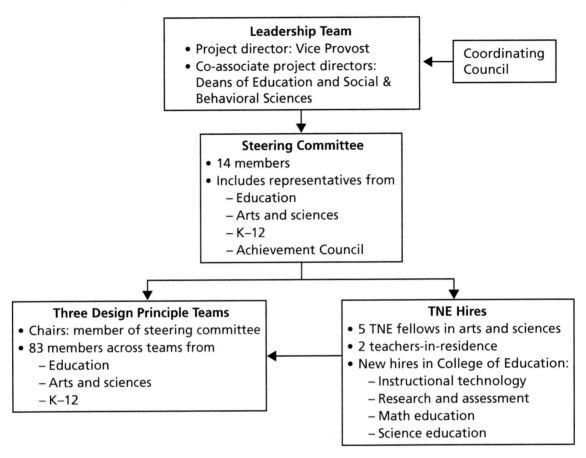

RAND *TR149-4.2*

TNE, although without exception, faculty estimated they spent considerably more time than this on their respective committees and work groups. Some university faculty and all K–12 faculty received stipends of $1,000.

Implementation Progress: Selected Highlights

As shown in Table 4.2, the first team—which focused on the first design principle regarding evidence—concentrated on several efforts aimed at identifying existing definitions and measures of excellent teaching, pupil learning, and the stages teachers go through in their development. The team examined the pathways to credentialing at CSUN and identified how skills and knowledge of teacher candidates were measured at each of these transition points in the various programs. Two other major efforts were data related. Because of the scattered and incomplete nature of the available data on students, CSUN is making a concerted effort to develop an integrated database on its students. Another major emphasis has been to understand and design a value-added assessment model for documenting the learning gains of pupils. CSUN is focusing on grades 4–8 and on mathematics and literacy. In collaboration with the LAUSD, it has designed a pilot to implement these models using data on a small number of teachers in schools that vary in performance.

Table 4.2
Year 1 Implementation of TNE Design Principles, California State University, Northridge

Design Principles	Year 1 Activities

Decisions based on evidence	• Reviewed literature to identify existing definitions and measures of excellent teaching and stages of teacher development
	  – Identified how knowledge, skills, and dispositions of teacher candidates at each stage of development are measured in CSUN's programs
	  – Used data on 40 CSUN students to evaluate the validity of these measures
	• Developed operational definition and measures of pupil learning
	• Developed partnership with LAUSD and designed pilot test to use value-added assessment modeling to measure learning gains of pupils, focusing on grades 4–8 and mathematics and literacy

Engagement with arts and sciences faculty	• Submitted proposal to Faculty Task Force on Roles and Rewards to expand the definition of "professional contribution"
	• Reviewed literature on PCK in mathematics and social science to develop a working conceptualization of PCK and good teaching
	  – Offered presentations on PCK to interested faculty and developed recommendations on how to establish communities of practice to study PCK
	  – Identified model programs and made site visits to two institutions
	• Worked on infusing PCK into the mathematics and science strands of the ITEP and will assess the impact of doing so
	• Observed four elementary mathematics classes in culturally diverse settings with the idea of creating a videotape library of effective instructional techniques

Teaching as a clinical practice profession	• Reviewed literature and conducted focus groups to understand characteristics of effective pedagogy • Reviewed other induction programs and state requirements and conducted small focus groups to examine components and design of effective programs, resources needed for implementation, and how to align with state induction requirements • Developed criteria for teachers on faculty appointment • Reviewed literature on professional growth of teachers and identified clinical sites to implement best practices

An example of how TNE is changing the culture of the institution is the proposal submitted by the team working on the second design principle regarding engagement with arts and sciences faculty to the Faculty Task Force on Roles and Rewards. This proposal seeks to expand the definition of "professional contribution" to include publications in leading teaching and education journals so that these would count for promotion and tenure decisions. Some members of this team reviewed literature on PCK in mathematics and social science and developed a working conceptualization of PCK and good teaching that was shared more broadly with faculty. Two task groups worked on the mathematics and science strands for the ITEP Multiple Subject credential program. The goal was to come up with plans to infuse PCK into the math and science courses in the ITEP program and to assess the impact of doing so. For example, for the mathematics strand, the university has developed new courses with different curriculum, in-class activities, and textbooks. CSUN is now offering three different classes—the new course; a hybrid of the old and new; and the old course—and plans to assess the PCK of the students under the three regimes. The science task group will be conducting the same experiment.

The third team focused on defining effective pedagogy and examining such issues as how best to use schools as clinics and how to define an effective induction program. This has led to conversations between, for example, Chicano Studies and the College of Education about how to create a joint master's program and how to provide for the needs of experienced teachers. A pilot induction program has been proposed that addresses new standards for induction.

Other Issues Identified in the TNE Prospectus

In addition to the activities described above, CSUN also made progress on two other issues. The first was the late-deciders issue. The staff of the Liberal Studies/ITEP undergraduate teacher education program at CSUN continued discussions with the local community colleges whose students transfer to CSUN regarding articulation agreements that would ensure that the course work was equivalent and up to standard. The second was with respect to infusing technology into the curriculum. CSUN revised its delivery approach to instructional technology learning to be in line with the new California teacher education standards.

Looking Ahead to Year 2

Increase Integration Across Project. As a result of CSUN's experience and feedback from others, a major focus of CSUN's work in Year 2 is ensuring integration across the project. To facilitate this, steering committee members will work across teams, and more flexible groupings and resources will be put in place. CSUN is doing away with the permanent committee structure so faculty can work on tasks and teams for short periods of time.

Establish Partnerships with Districts, Principals, and Teachers. A second focus is establishing partnerships that will be responsible for designing and implementing clinical models to promote best teaching practices that effect greatest pupil learning.

Select Clinical Sites. This will require obtaining district, teacher union, principal, and teacher cooperation, particularly with respect to such issues as increased workload and extra compensation for participation.

Compensate Faculty Through Reassigned Time, Rather Than Stipends. This will help alleviate some of the workload issues facing these faculty.

Impact of State Budget and Policy

CSU campuses are funded entirely on a full-time equivalent (FTE) basis. CSUN is currently funded for 22,000 students, although enrollment is over 24,000. To deal with this situation, the university will likely increase class sizes. CSUN, like the other CSU campuses, faces mandated nonfunded costs, such as risk insurance and conversion to new technology. Last year, CSUN had a 5 percent decrease in the budget, and for 2003–04, the decrease will likely be 6–7 percent. However, it has had the largest growth among all the CSU campuses for the last two to three years, cushioning the school from the cut in the budget. Overall, the state fiscal crisis has not had an effect on the TNE project at CSUN.

The University still plans to put approximately $200,000 into an endowment fund each year for five years and indeed, contributed $250,000 the first year. The College of Education raised an additional $800,000 that could be counted as matching funds, not including the major gift from the Eisner Foundation.

As discussed in Appendix E, many changes are under way in California with respect to teacher certification and licensure. Respondents expressed concern about the new testing and induction requirements and changes in the legislation that will require changes in already approved teacher education programs.

Testing. California's implementation of the new testing requirements under No Child Left Behind (NCLB) are a matter of concern for CSUN faculty. NCLB requires that teachers show subject-matter competency by passing state tests rather than by just graduating from an approved subject-matter program, as was previously the case in California. Currently, the state is determining how best to fit the exam requirement into the credentialing process. CSUN believes that the new testing requirements may impact the demand for its subject-matter programs because it believes that teachers may choose to take the test without going through a subject-matter program. This concern is compounded by the suspicion that the new state test, the CSET, is not as rigorous as the previous test that was in place. The passing rates on the previous tests required for candidates who did not go through an approved program to receive the credential were quite low—less than 20 percent. In contrast, early pass rates on the CSET have been substantially higher—ranging from 45 to 60 percent.

CSUN must also contend with the fact that some students already in the program and some recent graduates may be required to take the test as well, which will likely cause consternation among that group.

Additionally, the timing of the new CSET test for the multiple subject credential is an issue. The state believes it should be a requirement for student teaching; CSU is trying to determine whether it should be a precondition for entry into teacher education. The test incorporates some items on pedagogy, which suggests that it would be better if students took the test before student teaching and after some courses on pedagogy. However, some wonder what will happen to students if they do not pass the test at this later point in time.

Currently, the state requires students to be assessed on Teaching Performance Expectations (TPEs) with the Teaching Performance Assessment (TPA). TPEs are infused throughout the preservice program, and students must pass the TPA at the end of the program before being recommended for the credential. As a result, CSUN spent a great deal of time ensuring that its teacher education programs aligned with the TPEs and TPA. However, the role of the TPA is unclear at this point. Although the TPA is now in pilot testing and the original time line called for all teacher education programs to develop an implementation plan by June 2003, funding for implementing the TPA has not yet been received; therefore, a moratorium was placed on the submission of the TPA implementation plan.

New Induction Requirements. The state now requires that teachers go through an induction program or complete a fifth-year program to obtain a professional clear credential. CSUN will need to position its TNE induction activities within this context, and new teachers who are already overburdened may not feel they have time to participate in the new TNE induction on top of the district induction. Faculty also noted a few general concerns about the new requirements:

- The new standards are seen as burdensome and overly detailed so that it is hard to fit content into the framework, especially for the joint master's programs.
- The district is now responsible for recommending teachers for the clear credential, and there is some concern about the ability of districts to document and judge whether teachers have met standards.
- Faculty raised questions regarding the quality of mentors and how they will be supported and trained.
- Districts offer free courses and workshops to meet the induction requirements while teachers must pay to take fifth-year courses at the university.
- Due to state budget constraints, state funding for the mandated induction is in doubt.

Limitations on Number of Credits for Teacher Education. The proposed new legislation, SB81, seeks to limit the number of credits for teacher education; as a result, ITEP programs that had been approved earlier require too many credits under the new rules and will have to be redesigned. The CSU faculty across the campuses are working on the length of the integrated program and making suggestions to the state.

Michigan State University

Project Structure: Leadership and Staffing

The leadership team for MSU's TNE initiative consists of the Assistant Provost for Undergraduate Education and Academic Services, who serves as the project director, and two coprincipal investigators: the Director of Research in the College of Education and the Associate Dean for Science and Mathematics Education in the College of Natural Science, who holds a joint appointment in mathematics and teacher education (Figure 4.3). Each of the co–principal investigators receives one-quarter release time for TNE work, while the project director's time is contributed by MSU.

In addition to the overall responsibility for the project, the project director manages all data requests from MSU's TNE teams and is working with the State Department of Education on a database that will track all Michigan public school teachers (including MSU graduates teaching in Michigan public schools) over time. The coprincipal investigator from the College of Education has the primary responsibility for representing and ensuring effective involvement within the college. He also oversees all issues of budget, personnel, and evaluation. The other coprincipal investigator represents the Colleges of Natural Science, Arts and Letters, and Social Science, and is responsible for ensuring that arts and sciences faculty are involved with TNE and for ongoing communication with the different colleges. Oversight of the TNE teams (described below) is divided among the three leads.

Figure 4.3
Project Structure and Staffing, Michigan State University

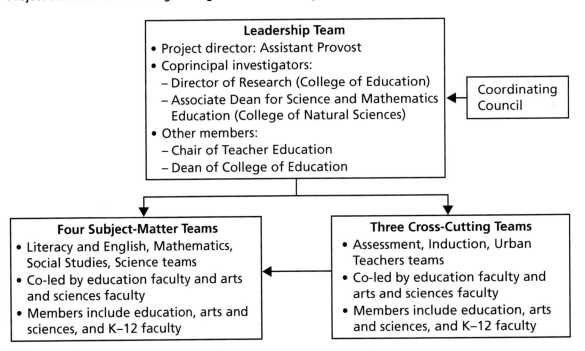

The two ex-officio members of the leadership team are the new Chair of Teacher Education and the Dean of the College of Education.

MSU formed a Coordinating Council that is headed by the provost and includes—in addition to the deans of the various colleges at MSU—the Michigan Superintendent of Public Instruction, the head of the school principals' association, representatives from the teachers' unions, the head of the middle schools initiative, representatives from business, the dean of Wayne State University, and the superintendent of the Lansing school district.

MSU hopes that the council will disseminate TNE information and provide information about potential changes in state policy directions that would impact the TNE efforts. The council will be meeting two to three times a year.

The overarching theme of MSU's design proposal is "making content and context central." To do this, MSU established seven groups organized thematically rather than by design principle. There are four subject-matter development teams—K–12 Mathematics, K–12 Literacy and English, K–8 Social Studies, and 7–12 Science—and three crosscutting teams: Assessment, Induction, and Urban Teachers. Each team comprises arts and sciences, education, and K–12 faculty and is co-led by faculty from the College of Education and from an arts and sciences college. The budget allocated release time and/or summer salary for the coleaders of each team. However, other faculty who are invited to participate in the teams are expected to do so as part of their regular workload.

Implementation Progress: Selected Highlights

Teacher knowledge standards (TKS) are a centerpiece of MSU's TNE work (Table 4.3). The standards map what teachers should know and be able to do across a seven-year career, divided into three stages: emergent (four years of undergraduate work), novice (one year of internship), and target (two years of induction). The TKS are linked to these developmental stages. The standards were largely developed by the Literacy team, which wanted a general framework before developing subject-specific standards, with strong input from Arts and Letters faculty. These standards will inform the assessment work and will help target changes and improvements in the program by clarifying expectations about what knowledge and actions can be expected at different levels. Once the framework was approved, the Literacy and Mathematics teams began creating the standards for disciplinary knowledge and teaching knowledge through the summer. A cross-team committee with members from the Literacy and Mathematics teams was charged with developing additional standards.

The two main efforts undertaken by the Assessment team include a transcript analysis and an examination of assessment in different courses. The teams are using the transcript analysis to study characteristics of students prior to admission to the teacher program, including their Accelerated Collaborative Teacher (ACT) scores, in hopes of identifying characteristics that would help predict success in the classroom. The subgroup is also attempting to obtain noncognitive interest inventory information collected as part of the ACT but not usually analyzed by ACT. The examination of assessment in the disciplinary majors and in the general education courses is an extension of work conducted under a grant from the Hewlett Foundation. Under this grant, MSU has identified some broad learning goals and is attempting to measure through pre- and post-tests whether students are making progress toward these goals. The Assessment team has also been considering ways of linking learning gains of pupils to teacher characteristics and training, including using data from the Michigan Educational Assessment Program (MEAP), the state assessment.

Table 4.3
Year 1 Implementation of TNE Design Principles, Michigan State University

Design Principles	Year 1 Activities
Decisions based on evidence	• Conducted a transcript analysis to identify characteristics that would help predict success in the classroom (including ACT and other data) • Examined assessment in the general education courses; as part of another grant, identified several broad learning goals and developed plans to assess students' progress toward goals • Examining preinternship field experiences to measure the nature and consistency of experiences • Developed plan to obtain systematic data on teacher graduates and examined how to link learning gains of pupils to teacher characteristics and training using the Michigan state test

Engagement with arts and sciences faculty	• Developed TKS as the centerpiece of TNE work
	  – Mapped what teachers should know and be able to do at each stage (emergent, novice, and target)
	  – Developed by the Literacy team; used by content teams to develop content-specific TKS, with input from the Assessment team
	  – Held workshop to unveil standards framework for all TNE participants to get buy-in
	• Jump-started work of Science and Social Studies teams because of changes in state certification requirements

Teaching as a clinical practice profession	• Started to examine different ways to provide induction and feasibility of building multiple credentials into induction program
	  – Studied cohort of 16 MSU graduates
	  – Focused on literacy
	• Developed one-page memo on what Michigan teachers need
	  – Feedback to teachers at a daylong retreat
	• Hired Web expert to design Web programs and platforms to support induction

Altogether there are 80 faculty, including education and arts and sciences faculty and graduate assistants involved in TNE. The directors of the integrative studies programs in social studies, arts and humanities, and general science held a crosscutting university seminar on general education issues. As mentioned earlier, the Science team started work earlier than expected partly because of the changing state rules for elementary science certification. The Social Studies team also started earlier than expected and is developing standards for social studies.

The Induction team and the Literacy team undertook an overview study of the preinternship field experience components of the education program with a view to measuring the nature and consistency of the experience. The Induction team is looking at the entire range of clinical experiences in the program and attempting to design an induction program for MSU graduates. Believing that induction has to be more than just mentoring, the team is examining multiple formats and the feasibility of building multiple credentials (such as a master's degree, a certificate, etc.) into the program. Schools and districts are intent on developing their own induction programs, so the Induction team is keenly aware that they need to work with the schools and districts to develop shared objectives.

Other Issues Identified in the TNE Prospectus

Recruiting teacher candidates from underrepresented groups is part of the Urban Teachers team's charge. The team faced several challenges that made progress difficult in the first year, including leadership changes, dearth of faculty expertise in urban education, and a lack of coherence in the tasks that caused uncertainty on the part of team members about how they could contribute to the project. The Urban Teachers team expects to make better progress under new leadership. MSU has been successful in obtaining funding for pieces of the urban agenda and believes that this extra funding will help move the work forward in the coming years.

Looking Ahead to Year 2

Map Standards to the Program, Identify Curricular Gaps, and Look at Needed Changes. The challenge in Year 2 is to map standards to the program and to look at the changes that are needed to fill holes in the program. Over the next year, MSU plans to finish the draft of the TKS and start a serious review process with multiple constituents. MSU needs to build in ample time to get people engaged, to obtain feedback, and to revise based on the reviews. In addition, it will review course work taken by teacher education students to measure opportunities to learn and to target areas for revision, based on data. It needs a clearer vision of what is realistically possible.

Get Buy-In From Undergraduate Chairs to Consider Program Revisions Based on the TKS. A serious issue likely to arise in the second year is the willingness of the undergraduate chairs to consider program revisions based on the TKS. Programmatic changes cannot be undertaken lightly because they affect the core courses that all students are expected to take. A real effort will be made to involve the undergraduate chairs to bring them into the loop and to get their support for the standards.

Make Progress with Its Urban Work. The Urban Teachers team's tasks will include an online review of what other colleges and universities are doing in urban education and conducting focus groups with teachers in small, urban areas to ask them about their teacher preparation programs.

Improve and Increase Communication both Within and Beyond the Project. MSU also plans to improve and increase communication both within and across the TNE teams and also with broader audiences outside of TNE. Among other efforts, this would include developing Web sites for the teams, holding small localized meetings and cross-university seminars, and cosponsoring events with different university leaders. As part of this effort, it will monitor political issues that might impact its current TNE plans.

Impact of State Budget and Policy

In 2003–04, state funding to MSU was reduced by 10 percent, bringing state support per student to the 1995–96 level. The budget cuts have hurt the university somewhat: They are leaving some open positions unfilled (for example, the College of Natural Sciences is down ten FTEs), eliminating some departments or combining them, and closing some centers. Further cuts seem likely in the next two years. However, the $1.2 billion capital campaign started in 1999 and expected to continue until 2007 is progressing better than expected. In terms of TNE, as mentioned earlier, the university has been very successful in raising over $10 million in matching funds.

By and large, TNE participants did not raise any major concerns with respect to state policy on teacher education. They had jump started the Science team because of the changing certification requirements for science teachers while the Induction team seemed sensitive to and willing to work in conjunction with the Michigan state-mandated induction program.

University of Virginia

Project Structure: Leadership and Staffing

The TNE project director is a faculty member of the English department who previously directed the Center for Liberal Arts, which provides professional development to teachers (Figure 4.4). The director works out of the provost's office and is assigned half-time to TNE and is assisted by an Implementation team, consisting of deans and faculty members from the Curry School of Education, deans and faculty from the College of Arts and Sciences, the head of the Faculty Senate, the associate director of the Teaching Resource Center, the holder of the Goldsmith Distinguished Teaching Professorship, the Director of University Outreach and Executive Assistant to the Provost, and representatives from local school divisions.

Selected members of the Implementation team form a core leadership group: the Project Director of TNE; the Director of Teacher Education; and three faculty from the Curry School: the Associate Dean for Academic Affairs; the Chair of Curriculum, Instruction, and Special Education; and a faculty member from the Department of Leadership, Foundations, and Policy Studies. With the exception of the director, none of these members holds an official TNE title. This core group is primarily responsible for the day-to-day implementation and planning of TNE. Apart from the director, only one leadership team member had summer salary built into the Year 1 budget and no other release time was offered to the core leadership group members.

Figure 4.4
Project Structure and Staffing, University of Virginia

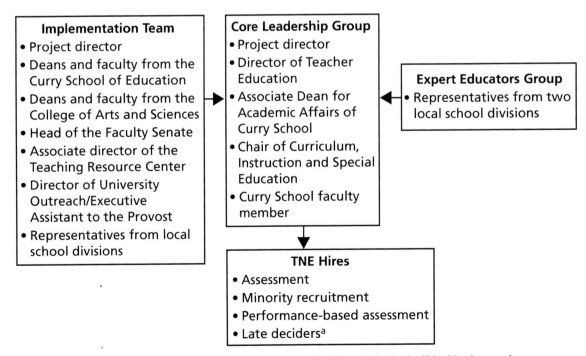

a Half-time postdoctoral fellow hired for late-deciders work; a full-time individual will be hired to work on this issue in Year 2.

RAND TR149-4.4

The Expert Educators Group comprises representatives from the two major local school districts. This group was established in the spring 2003 semester and functions as an advisory group, particularly in the area of induction.

UVa will form a Coordinating Council in Year 2 to help work with state agencies, the legislature, and accreditation groups to promote fundamental changes required for the success of the program. The council will include top officials from the Virginia Department of Education, the Virginia State Board of Education, the U.S. Department of Education, and various professional community and business organizations.

UVa hired a director for the Teaching Assessment Initiative to oversee the assessment work; a postdoctoral fellow to lead the performance-based evidence work; and a head of recruitment to focus on recruiting minorities into teaching. UVa was not successful in hiring someone to work on the late-deciders program in Year 1. In the interim, UVa hired a new Curry Ph.D. graduate to work part time on the late-deciders issue.

Implementation Progress: Selected Highlights

The major areas in which UVa has been working in its first year include assessment, the creation of new courses, strengthening of advising teams, and induction (Table 4.4). The Teaching Assessment Initiative has been in active communication with the state to obtain student test data that are linked to teachers. UVa is also considering more qualitative measures, such as motivation, in addition to state assessment scores. The center has funded 15 research studies examining a variety of assessment topics, such as the value added to public education by UVa teacher education as defined at the program level; specific teacher education courses or discrete features within the teacher education programs; attitudes and practices of in-service teachers and preservice teachers as they progress through the five-year teacher education program. A series of assessment seminars hosted by the provost is designed to raise awareness of assessment techniques, develop a culture of research and practice, and engage teacher education and arts and science faculty with one another. UVa piloted its elec-

Table 4.4
Year 1 Implementation of TNE Design Principles, University of Virginia

Design Principles	Year 1 Activities

Decisions based on evidence	• Established the Teaching Assessment Initiative under a new director
	  – Funded 15 research studies at approximately $3,000 to $5,000 apiece
	  – Worked to establish requirements for student participation in research studies that will track teacher education candidates' progress over time
	  – Contacted state to obtain student test data
	• Held assessment seminars hosted by the provost for 15 arts and sciences and Curry School participants
	• Piloted electronic portfolio system
	• Hired postdoc to work with faculty to collect performance-based evidence

Engagement with arts and sciences faculty	• Launched new courses and seminars
	  – Issued request for proposals (RFP) for development of TNE Common Courses
	  – Developed two counterpoint seminars linked to survey courses and designed to enhance PCK
	• Planned seven teams that will work to improve advising structure in their subject area, each consisting of one arts and sciences faculty; one teacher education faculty; and one K–12 teacher

Teaching as a clinical practice profession	• Induction for all teachers from local school divisions
	  – Expert Educators Group playing a key role
	  – Create community of educators that includes UVa faculty and K–12 faculty
	• Reconsidered initial plan to appoint TIR to make role more meaningful

tronic portfolio system in Year 1. The Open Portfolio contains data on all field placements, student evaluations, and student artifacts. UVa also hired a staff member to work on developing performance-based evidence.

UVa piloted two Common Courses in the arts and sciences to develop a model for future TNE Common Courses. These courses are large survey courses, often team-taught, with discussion sections led by graduate teaching assistants. One discussion section is to be devoted specifically to pedagogical issues and is intended for students enrolled in the BA/MT program or interested in the teaching profession. UVa solicited proposals from faculty to develop Common Courses but received few applications because the request was issued late in the year. UVa also developed two counterpoint seminars targeted at BA/MT students and designed to increase PCK. The courses are linked to a survey course that the students have taken and focus on how that course's content can best be taught in a middle school or high school setting.

UVa planned advising teams in seven major subject areas (English, mathematics, history, etc.). These teams have been tasked with developing an improved advising structure for teacher education students by creating better links among the departments and stronger ties with arts and sciences faculty. These teams consist of an arts and sciences faculty member, a teacher education member, and a K–12 member.

UVa plans to have a two-part induction system—one focused on its graduates and the other focused on all new teachers in the local area. As a first step, UVa formed its Expert Educators Group to assist in planning induction for all new teachers in the local school districts. Based on advice from the group, UVa is focusing initially on activities to help connect new teachers with their community and the university. Given that UVa's new single faculty members also have a difficult time getting settled in the Charlottesville community, they are developing a network of "new educators" that brings together new K–12 teachers and UVa faculty.

Other Issues Identified in the TNE Prospectus

UVa placed a lot of emphasis on recruiting teacher candidates from underrepresented groups. UVa has hired a new faculty member to build minority support on campus. She will work with arts and sciences faculty to make them aware of the BA/MT option so they can provide this information to students during initial advising and work with the local K–12 schools to help recruit and retain minority teachers.

Looking Ahead to Year 2

Fill Key Positions. UVa plans to make two key hires during Year 2: one to serve as coordinator of induction to lead the induction work for both the school divisions and the UVa graduates, and another to coordinate the late-deciders issues.

Foster Greater Involvement of Arts and Sciences Faculty. To involve more arts and sciences faculty in TNE activities, the TNE leadership has invited two associate deans from the College of Arts and Sciences to join them twice monthly at meetings. In addition, UVa seeks to recruit faculty who may be predisposed to participate in TNE. As a result, the university has hired a graduate student to help identify arts and sciences faculty with an academic or personal interest in K–12 education.

Expand Participation in Assessment Seminars. These will continue to be hosted by the provost in Year 2, and the number of arts and sciences faculty who are invited to attend will expand. The Year 2 seminars will focus on the research studies that are funded by TNE through the Assessment Center.

Increase Communication Between School Districts and the University. UVa plans to have school division representatives speak to groups of faculty in Year 2 as a way of increasing communication between the two.

Impact of State Budget and Policy

In 2002–03 UVa's state funding was cut $24.5 million in the academic areas. UVa instituted a midyear tuition surcharge in spring 2003 and raised tuition in the fall. It has been dedicated to avoiding staff cuts because layoffs lower morale and hurt the school's ability to move forward. It has taken a tiered approach to cuts, first asking all departments to bear the burden equally and then taking a more strategic approach, with a greater impact on auxiliary units. It has cut faculty travel, money for copiers, telephones, etc. This is not a sustainable situation, but helps preserve faculty slots. UVa preserved funding for teacher education, but noted that the program has grown by almost 50 percent over four years (100 graduates in 2000 to an expected 151 graduates in 2004) and has not received any increases in funding.

The state cutbacks in university funding have had an impact on the TNE work in that university faculty are more stretched and TNE is asking them to do additional work. There is simply no extra time in faculty members' workloads due to the budget cuts on the arts and sciences side. The proposed TNE seminars were derailed by budget cuts, but UVA is planning to offer a university seminar about minorities in education in 2003–04.

UVa Curry School faculty expressed concern about some of the state initiatives and proposed changes in state policy:

- **New majors for elementary education:** Virginia is considering requiring one of five majors for elementary education: English, history, mathematics, science, or an interdisciplinary degree consisting of all four of the majors. Regardless of state policy, such an interdisciplinary degree is not likely to happen at UVa, as there would be too little content in any one of the disciplines to suit any of the departments. There is some concern that the elementary education program might lose some students because psychology would no longer be considered an acceptable major; however, these students might be attracted to special education, which would still retain psychology as an acceptable major.

  UVa has been exploring the possibility of creating a mathematics and science major for students seeking to become elementary school teachers. These new certification regulations would make such a major unlikely. Faculty members are planning on presenting their ideas to the state legislature in the hope of gaining approval for their plan.

- **Alternative licensure:** Respondents expressed concern about the effect of any expanded alternative licensure provisions on the five-year program and on late deciders. Even now, each year, more than 100 UVa graduates who are not graduates of the Curry School seek teaching positions after graduation.

Summary

As mentioned earlier, the first "year" got off to a late start—the sites only received their funds in November 2002–January 2003. In Year 1, the sites focused on planning and setting up structures to carry out the TNE work; these structures were tailored to their individual contexts. Despite the late start, the sites appeared to have made progress in implementation and used the experiences gained in the first year to reconfigure what they wanted to focus on in Year 2. We saw evidence of institutional culture change in the form of increased involvement of arts and sciences faculty on issues related to the teacher education program. There is also evidence that the faculty are overburdened, but all the sites are attempting to recruit new faculty and staff members and are trying to leverage extra funding to help support TNE work. It is also evident that the state policy environment has the potential to affect the ability of the sites to be faithful to the TNE vision.

Asked about progress in the first year, Carnegie reported being encouraged by the depth of commitment and interest at each of the institutions, and noted successes and evidence of changing cultures at all the institutions. Carnegie is aware that the challenges posed by the TNE initiative are profound and that the consequences of many of the changes now being implemented in the sites may not appear for a generation. Carnegie believes that the sites are just turning the first corner of what is a very long road.

CHAPTER FIVE

Cross-Site Observations on First-Year Implementation

The data that we gathered from the sites both during baseline and the first site visit and our analysis of the design proposals were useful in understanding where the four institutions were at baseline, how they proposed to reform themselves to align their teacher education programs with the TNE design principles, and the progress they made in the first year. In addition, participants' reflections on the first-year experience offered insights into some of the successes and challenges. This chapter integrates impressions and lessons learned across the four sites. We found a remarkable similarity in the experiences reported by the sites—all the more remarkable given how different the institutions are with respect to type, size, capacity, and mission. We also relate these observations to the theory of change outlined in Chapter Two. In addition, we provide comments that reflect the funders' perspective, when relevant.

The sites have made progress over the past year in implementing their work plans, especially given that their "year" really consisted of between eight and ten months. They have overcome challenges and appear to be moving ahead with commitment and enthusiasm.

Recognition by Top-Level University Administrators and Strong Project Leadership Enhanced the Credibility of TNE

The insistence of the funders that the leadership for TNE should rest in the provost or president's office helped the projects gain visibility and prestige. The open and vocal support of university leaders has attracted arts and sciences faculty into the TNE fold. Appointing senior and well-respected faculty from both arts and sciences and education to head the projects has helped facilitate dialogue across the campus departments and fostered implementation. Clearly this speaks to some of the enabling factors mentioned earlier in Chapter Two. Universitywide commitment and strong, stable leadership help foster implementation and also promote strong faculty commitment to reform.

Institutions Varied in Their Project Structure and Ways of Compensating TNE Participants, but All Recognized the Need for New Faculty and Staff to Help with TNE

The institutions varied in the way they set up the project structure and staffing for TNE and the way they chose to underwrite the time costs of TNE participants. For example,

- Bank Street hired a full-time project director and paid for one-quarter of the dean's time and 40 percent of the time of the other two members of the leadership team. In addition, AOI team members were provided with 15 percent time.
- CSUN and MSU both set up a tripartite structure with two named coleaders under the project director, who is a senior member of the provost's office. However, while MSU covered one-quarter of its coleaders' time, CSUN chose not to provide release time for senior faculty who were on 12-month appointments. Thus, the coleaders were expected to add the TNE work on top of their already heavy workloads. In contrast, CSUN offered a stipend or release time to all its team members, whereas MSU expected its associates to do this on a voluntary basis as part of their "service" obligation.
- UVa provided funds to cover the project director half time but did not budget any coverage or release time for the other senior members of the leadership team, with the exception of summer salary for one member. In addition, there was no formal recognition of the role of the other leaders. Participants reported that this meant that the TNE work could not be formally acknowledged in faculty curriculum vitae and occasionally led to confusion among other participants about the relative roles and responsibilities of the leaders.

To some extent, all the institutions are aware of the limitations of attempting to undertake such a large reform with faculty who are already overburdened with teaching, research, and service duties. As a result, the institutions searched for or made new faculty hires that will work for significant portions of their time on TNE. For example, Bank Street hired an induction coordinator to oversee the induction work, CSUN hired new TNE fellows and provided them with half-time coverage to work on TNE, and UVa hired three individuals to lead work on assessment, minority recruitment, and performance assessment and was looking for staff to help develop late-deciders programs. The sites hired many of these faculty under different criteria than those applied to typical academic hires—for example, CSUN emphasized interest in and/or experience with K–12 schools in its position-open notices for the TNE fellows, along with the more usual emphasis on teaching and academic research. All the institutions also provided coverage for or hired administrative staff to provide support for the project.

In this context, the importance of external resources in fostering reform is clear. Given the complexity of the reform and the number of players that are involved (many of whom are already overburdened), the ability to provide compensation for time spent on TNE work is crucial. Obviously, the manner in which these resources are used to support the faculty will have important implications for faculty commitment to the reform and long-term sustainability. With external resources, the sites have been able to hire new faculty and/or staff to help with TNE. These new appointments will help alleviate some of the pressures on the current faculty and move the reform along at a faster pace than would otherwise have been possible.

Junior Faculty and Those Close to Promotion Points Were Concerned About Time Spent on TNE

Junior faculty worried about refusing to participate, given the high visibility of the project—indeed, many were excited about participating and were committed to teaching and K–12 schools—but felt they paid a heavy price for taking on this work. Some arts and sciences deans openly spoke of their concern about the publications records of junior faculty engaged in TNE, while some faculty members who were close to tenure points expressed fears about whether they had sufficient time to put their tenure review packages together and whether what they had was sufficient. This again, if not addressed, may have implications for faculty commitment to the reform and to making such commitment university wide, both of which are important to implementation.

Sites Selected Different Strategies Tailored to Their Institutional Culture

The sites displayed perspicacity in choosing their overall approaches. Because CSUN and MSU already had a fair degree of overt and explicit collaboration between arts and sciences and education faculty, they chose to establish implementation teams with leaders from both colleges. Playing to the research interests of its faculty, UVa offered funding to arts and sciences and education faculty for research focused on assessment issues and the opportunity to teach new, integrated courses. UVa also attempted to reach out to local school districts and to be sensitive to "turf" issues. Bank Street, realizing that it had the farthest to go in terms of educating its faculty regarding assessment and collaboration with arts and sciences, chose to establish small teams with some limited arts and sciences involvement and to help train them in research methodology and the use of data.

Changing Culture Is Challenging, but Progress Is Evident

Changing institutional culture and making the project a cross-university endeavor, however, was uphill work. We heard this sentiment over and over again. As mentioned earlier, while in theory the idea of having groups from various departments and from K–12 schools is a good one, the learning curve for these members was steep and required patience, time, and willingness to learn from each other. For example, despite its new partnership with Sarah Lawrence College, including arts and sciences faculty at Bank Street required a sensitive integration that did not devalue the expertise of its own staff. There is clear recognition on the part of both the funders and the institutions that TNE demands a radical culture change across all the institutions and that this will take time and effort.

However, there were clear signs of progress, and the sites should take credit for the innovative ways in which they have involved faculty from different departments. The leadership teams drawn from different colleges worked collaboratively and the work teams—despite the burdens on time noted above—seemed to be enthusiastic and working hard at developing a common language and contributing to teacher education. Indeed, most faculty reported that this was a learning experience, and that they "did intellectual work together," stepping outside the boundaries of their own discipline and learning to see through different lenses.

Involving K–12 Faculty in Meaningful Ways Proved Harder Than Expected

Having strong relationships with K–12 schools is both an enabling factor and a key component of the TNE theory of change. Because the sites had existing relationships with districts and schools, they were able to appoint some K–12 faculty to work with them in a number of areas (especially in induction). Respondents from several sites reported that involving K–12 faculty was harder than expected. Some of this was due to logistical issues and some due to substantive issues. For example, although CSUN was relatively successful in involving K–12 faculty in its teams, the incompatibility among the teaching schedules of arts and sciences faculty, College of Education faculty, and K–12 partners led to many scheduling difficulties and logistical problems. Some K–12 members dropped out of the group; they found it difficult to get to meetings and were unsure of their roles. UVa has successfully used K–12 educators in an advisory capacity on the induction component but faced logistical issues, such as providing parking for its K–12 partners, as well as substantive issues in hiring K–12 faculty as teachers-in-residence (TIRs).

Some of the difficulty, however, arises because the sites have not yet determined how best to involve teachers. For example, MSU's literacy team chose to develop standards without involving K–12 faculty, while the mathematics team integrated them successfully into its work. Both MSU and UVa have shelved the TIR idea temporarily until they can give more careful thought to the position. CSUN has appointed TIRs, but there is some concern about the role of these teachers with respect to the program and TNE. Both MSU and CSUN also face recruitment challenges because salaries of experienced local teachers are considerably higher than those traditionally offered assistant professors.

Sites Recognized the Need for Improving Communication Both Within and Outside of TNE

TNE is large and complex and involves large numbers of participants. Obviously, communication became an issue both within TNE and between TNE and non-TNE faculty, and all the sites mentioned this several times. The leadership teams were particularly cognizant of this and emphasized that clear and frequent communication of the vision, process, and progress is needed to get the buy-in necessary for promoting universitywide commitment to reform from both internal and external audiences.

However, the sites faced a tension between wanting to bring the teams together to communicate and work together to avoid duplicated effort, and trying to prevent the teams from becoming so large as to be unwieldy. As pointed out by the CSUN site evaluator, the three CSUN committees for the design principles lacked coordination and often ended up going over the same ground. The larger sites are considering establishing different Web sites for each team with different levels of password protection so that team members can communicate with one another while cross-site teams also can access work products.

There Is Some Redundancy in the Work Being Done by the Sites

Assessment is front and center in the TNE prospectus, and the funders are committed to using student learning as the eventual outcome by which the quality of teacher graduates should be judged. This requires sophisticated technical expertise and access to high-quality data, both of which may be harder to come by in some institutions and some states than others. The funders clearly recognize that the assessment component using pupil-learning gains to measure the effectiveness of teachers and teacher education programs is the most taxing and alien part of the reform for teacher education programs. However, Carnegie feels the time is right for this kind of emphasis and that there is a climate change in higher education that will push more and more departments to provide evidence of the value they add to students' learning. The growing pressure from accrediting agencies to measure and demonstrate student learning is also spilling over into the teacher education realm.

CSUN has made progress in gaining access to high-quality data but would welcome collaboration, while MSU has considerable expertise in assessment. All the sites seem to be going over the same ground—learning about value-added modeling and examining different ways of measuring the learning of both their teacher candidates and the pupils taught by their graduates. The sites expressed a desire for collaboration in this area, which is challenging for all of them.

Induction is another area in which current efforts have been marked by a great deal of redundancy. For example, Bank Street, CSUN, and MSU all conducted literature reviews of induction programs and attempted to define best practices. In both of these areas, faculty felt there was a lot of duplication of effort across the sites ("no need to reinvent the wheel"; "self-discovery is good but there is no need to be provincial").

Technical Assistance Played an Important Role in Facilitating Implementation

As envisaged in the TNE theory of change, the role of technical assistance is to facilitate implementation, provide tools with which to translate the reform into reality, and provide external oversight and accountability to move the sites forward. In almost all respects, AED staff received uniformly high marks for their technical assistance role. They helped the sites translate their proposals into specific work plans with time lines and concrete goals that can be used both to keep the teams focused and to monitor progress. In general, the leadership and faculty teams seemed to appreciate the discipline imposed by the work plans, although developing and revising them took a lot of time. The work plan was seen as a roadmap and an important referent. TNE is a large, complicated enterprise, and the work plan helped it focus on where the teams need to be by a certain time. Furthermore, as group membership changed, the work plan gave faculty leaders a way to introduce new members to the TNE work. They saw the work plan as a living vehicle and found revising the work plan helpful, as it allowed the leaders to see the progress they were making on different pieces. AED has been helpful in reminding them to be realistic when setting goals.

Perhaps the most important role of AED has been to represent the funders, relaying questions brought up at the sites and seeking clarification, as well as helping negotiate budgets. In addition, AED also offered advice on a variety of issues, ranging from identifying institutions that could provide guidance on developing productive and close working relationships with community colleges to forging closer relationships with arts and sciences faculty. For two of the institutions, AED facilitated off-campus retreats or other meetings.

AED has been a conduit for learning about other TNE institutions, and the project leaders appreciated the chance to talk with the other sites during the cross-site conference calls and workshops set up by AED. The workshops on the whole were well received and seen as helpful and well organized. The sites reported that the assessment session was substantive and interesting.

There were a few complaints. A small number of participants complained about the amount of work that a site visit from AED entailed. The work plans generated the most dissent, but even there, the dissenters were in a minority. Some of the faculty asserted that the work plan was so "ridiculously" detailed that the bigger picture was lost; they reported that it did not show clearly the end goal and instead focused on shorter-term outcomes, leaving one uncertain as to how the larger, longer-term goals would be accomplished. Others observed that AED's focus on so much detail and insistence that the teams follow the tasks faithfully led to checking off boxes to the detriment of the larger project ("a checklist mentality"). The lack of connectedness in the work plan may actually encourage "stovepiping," with work of various teams not well coordinated.

AED maintains weekly or biweekly contact with the sites, although it has more frequent email contact with the site leaders. The site leaders estimated that, on average, one-quarter of the time they spent on TNE was spent working with AED in Year 1. AED tracks progress and reports back to Carnegie. From all that we heard, it is clear that thus far, AED has managed to balance both supporting and monitoring the institutions.

Carnegie was also pleased with the technical support provided by AED and impressed with the level of energy it brought to the task. AED was able to serve as an intermediary between the funders and the sites to make sure that the sites were not too intimidated to ask questions, to interpret and spell out the details of the design principles, and to operationalize the prospectus's broad intellectual perspectives within the local culture of the sites. Carnegie noted that it does not foresee a reduction in the need for or the level of technical assistance that AED is providing. The challenges are overwhelming, and AED will be required to both support and push the institutions farther along the road to reform.

State Policy Environments Have Important Implications for TNE Implementation

Supportive state and district environments are crucial to the ability of the sites to carry out the TNE work. Induction and teacher licensure requirements both have a direct influence on the way the institutions design their programs, something the sites are already facing. State (and federal) policies regarding teacher licensure and induction requirements are already affecting all four institutions. In particular, all four sites are struggling to align their TNE induction programs with those administered by the district and/or mandated by the state. The changes already occurring or under consideration in California and Virginia (for example, with respect to teacher testing, new approved majors, and alternative licensure) may have implications for TNE implementation in both institutions.

As we noted earlier, the reduction in state funding has not thus far affected the teacher education programs in the three public institutions. However, with further cuts, institutions might not be able to continue to protect their teacher education programs. Reductions in faculty and/or support are likely to affect future TNE implementation.

These cross-site observations lead naturally to some recommendations that might help foster greater buy-in and facilitate implementation in later years. We discuss our recommendations in the next chapter.

CHAPTER SIX

Recommendations and Next Steps

The first year was a learning year for the sites. All the sites made progress on implementing the design principles, and learned what worked well and what did not. We present below some recommendations, based on our observations and early lessons learned that might help further implementation in later years. A second section looks ahead to Years 2 and 3.

Recommendations for Future Implementation

There are several lessons that we can draw from the first-year experience in implementation, and these should prove helpful not merely to the sites themselves but to the new sites just starting implementation of TNE, the funders, and others considering similar reforms. Several of these lessons delineated below echo what others have found in similar reform efforts, and many of our sites offered similar thoughts in their progress reports to Carnegie. Nonetheless, what is useful about the lessons we note below is that they are based on a cross-site analysis and not on the experience of an individual site and that they display remarkable consistency across sites.

- **Provide Tangible Support and Clear Recognition of TNE Leaders and Participants.** We believe it would be helpful to provide formal, explicit recognition of the role of TNE leaders and tangible support in the form of release time for both leaders and participants. Even when release time was provided, it often did not appear to be sufficient for the work that had to be done. Most faculty reported that they worked many more hours on TNE than had been allocated. Providing more generous support would help ease the workload and maintain faculty commitment to the project. This is particularly important in the public universities, in which faculty are also squeezed by department budget cuts.
- **Encourage Recognition of TNE Work in the Promotion and Tenure System.** While we fully appreciate how difficult this is to implement, explicitly recognizing TNE work in promotion and tenure decisions and wide dissemination of these changes would go a long way in allaying fears of junior arts and sciences faculty and increasing their participation. This is an area in which CSUN has taken the lead, although the other universities are aware of this issue. This is, of course, not an issue with Bank Street.
- **Ensure That New TNE Faculty Understand the Criteria for Promotion.** As mentioned earlier, new faculty are often hired for TNE under criteria that seem different from those used for typical academic hires. It is important to ensure that these faculty

have contracts that spell out explicitly the criteria on which they will be judged. The experience of other universities in this respect—where faculty members hired for nontraditional roles ended up leaving because the promotion and tenure rules were too rigid to recognize their contributions—offers a cautionary tale.

- **Pay Attention to Involving K–12 Faculty More Directly in TNE.** The sites need to give some thought to ways in which they can integrate K–12 faculty into their TNE work and/or provide substantive roles for their teachers-in-residence.
- **Collaborate Across Sites to Do Joint Work on Assessment and Induction.** The two main areas in which cross-site collaboration would be helpful are assessment and induction. In Year 1, there was a great deal of redundancy in the work undertaken by the sites. The sites could benefit from more frequent communication and meetings on this topic, and some joint work on modeling issues. In addition, the work on induction perhaps could have been centralized—this would have been more efficient and would have led to less variability in the quality of products. One of the suggestions for AED that came out of our site visits was in this area of collaboration. Faculty felt that AED could do a lot more to facilitate dialogue and cooperation among the sites. In addition, the assessment piece requires a lot of technical assistance that AED could help broker.
- **Maintain a List of Technical Experts.** When asked about whether they had availed themselves of AED's brokering function, the sites said they had not, partly because they did not know whom to ask for. AED could be more proactive in maintaining a list of technical experts in the areas relevant to TNE and disseminating this list to the sites so they would have been aware of the kinds of help that were available.

Next Steps

The short-run objectives of the evaluation are to answer the first two research questions we posed earlier:

1. To what extent did the grantees implement Carnegie's design principles (including the induction program) and other principles laid out in the prospectus? What did the grantees attempt to do with the Carnegie funds?
2. What factors fostered or hindered implementation?

As we pointed out in Chapter One, answering these questions is crucially important for the evaluation. If implementation is weak or fails to occur, then the larger, long-term questions become moot to a large extent. In addition, the inherent and significant differences characterizing the TNE institutions underscore the importance of performing a systematic, careful, and comprehensive process evaluation.

In Year 2, the sites face greater challenges in that Carnegie has upped the stakes in the assessment arena, while still expecting the sites to continue moving forward with the rest of the TNE agenda. In a memorandum to the sites dated November 13, 2003, Daniel Fallon stressed the importance and urgency of the assessment component, and urged that it be assigned an immediate high priority. While being careful to say that Carnegie was not specifying the measures, research designs, or theoretical models to be used, the memorandum made it clear that the methods chosen "must be consistent, meet basic canons of scientific practice, especially reliability and validity, and be useful in your local culture. In most cases, therefore, the measures will be particularly convincing if they are expressed in ways that relate clearly to the standards imposed by the local school district, or the state or federal government. This suggests that measures coordinated with local testing will play some part in the value-added assessment strategy you devise."

Carnegie listed two kinds of activities that the institutions need to begin immediately:

- The first is designing and implementing a framework that will lead ultimately to evaluating the performance of teacher graduates by assessing the degree of learning growth accomplished by the pupils they teach.
- The second is selecting a group of practicing teachers (who may or may not be graduates of the program) who are willing to share data on pupil learning growth and information about their teaching practices.

The four institutions are expected to administer their first round of pupil assessments by fall 2004, and to report preliminary empirical findings in spring 2005 when they will be up for renewal of the TNE grant.

As the initiative unfolds, we plan to continue to monitor the progress of the TNE sites through annual site visits to understand the progress the TNE sites are making in implementation and the factors that foster or hinder implementation. As the sites ramp up their work and seriously address assessment issues, we plan to observe them closely to understand the kinds of data they are collecting and their modeling efforts to measure pupil learning gains, as required by Carnegie. In addition, we plan to interact with the sites to understand the kinds of data and evidence they are collecting on the effectiveness of their redesigned courses as measured by the learning of their teacher candidates. Given the importance of the state policy environment, we will continue to track state fiscal and policy contexts to monitor their effects on TNE through Web sites, interviews with state officials, and perceptions of TNE leaders and key faculty.

This is a crucial time for teacher education reform. Because we are the national evaluator for TNE, one of our longer-term goals is to provide a cogent history of the initiative, from inception to implementation and beyond, to document how such an initiative unfolds and the changes it brings about in selected and other associated institutions, set within the context of what is happening elsewhere in the field of teacher education, the labor market for teachers, and the standards-driven, test-based accountability systems introduced to K–12 schools. This report represents an important first step in this direction.

Bank Street College of Education: Profile at Baseline and Year 1 Implementation

Overview of the Teacher Education Program at Baseline

General Description of Programs

Bank Street College of Education is an independent institution devoted entirely to improving the education of children and their teachers. The college comprises three program divisions: Children's Programs, which runs the School for Children, an on-site demonstration school for children aged three to thirteen, and the on-site Family Center for infants and toddlers; the Division of Continuing Education, which provides outreach and professional development to schools, districts, and other educational agencies; and the Graduate School, which prepares postbaccalaureate students to serve as teachers, administrators, or in other professional roles in education, such as museum education, educational TV and multimedia, writing for children, and curriculum development. Two other divisions—External Affairs and Finance & Administration—provide support for the program divisions.

The work of Bank Street is primarily guided by the ideals set forth by its founder Lucy Sprague Mitchell, a leader in progressive education. The college's credo (Bank Street, 2002a, p. 4) states:

> What potentialities in human beings—children, teachers, and ourselves—do we want to see develop?
>
> A zest for living that comes from taking in the world with all five senses alert.
>
> Lively intellectual curiosities that turn the world into an exciting laboratory and keep one ever a learner.
>
> Flexibility when confronted with change and ability to relinquish patterns that no longer fit the present.
>
> The courage to work, unafraid and efficiently, in a world of new needs, new problems, and new ideas.
>
> Gentleness combined with justice in passing judgments on other human beings.
>
> Sensitivity, not only to the external formal rights of the "other fellow," but to him as another human being seeking a good life through his own standards.
>
> A striving to live democratically, in and out of schools, as the best way to advance our concept of democracy.
>
> Our credo demands ethical standards as well as scientific attitudes. Our work is based on the faith that human beings can improve the society they have created.

Bank Street's Graduate School offers the M.S. and M.S.Ed. degrees and initial New York state teaching certification and certificate extensions through a number of different programs. Students may complete programs in early childhood, childhood, or middle school education, with the option to specialize in bilingual education and/or to pursue a dual certification in general and special education. Bank Street also offers a dual degree program in special education and social work for each of the three age levels, in cooperation with the Columbia School of Social Work. Additional programs leading to initial teaching certification include Infant and Parent Development and Early Intervention/Early Childhood Special and General Education, Teaching Literacy and Childhood General Education Dual Degree, and Museum Education with a specialization in Childhood or Middle School Education. Programs can be completed in as little as 12–15 months, and must be completed within four years; two years to completion is most typical.

All applicants must have completed a bachelor's degree prior to their acceptance into Bank Street. Applicants for all programs must demonstrate, through previous study, a breadth of knowledge in the subjects they will teach, as well as a solid foundation in the arts and sciences, including course work on artistic expression, communication, information retrieval, concepts in history and social studies, humanities, a language other than English, scientific and mathematical processes, and written analysis and expression.

Application materials include transcripts from previous undergraduate and graduate study, three letters of recommendation, an autobiographical sketch, and essay responses to questions regarding experience working with children and professional ambitions. Candidates also complete a spontaneous "program essay" during their visit to the college, and have a formal interview with a program faculty member. Admissions decisions are made on a rolling basis from September through June.

In assessing applicants through written materials and interviews, admissions committee members look for such qualities as depth of thinking, self-reflection, good communications skills, a history of personal growth, attention to the individual needs of children, and other traits in accordance with the admissions criteria. Academically, applicants are generally expected to have an undergraduate GPA of 3.0 or higher, although it is possible for applicants to demonstrate strong academic abilities in other ways.

In 2001–02, Bank Street received 656 applications for all programs and accepted 79 percent, or 515 candidates. Of these, 393, or 76 percent, enrolled the following fall or spring.

Clinical Component

A full year of Supervised Fieldwork and Advisement is considered the center of the Bank Street experience. Each teacher candidate is assigned to a graduate faculty advisor and becomes part of a cohort with five to seven other candidates also assigned to the same advisor. The advisor visits and observes each of his or her advisees at least half a day each month in their fieldwork setting, and works closely with the students' cooperating teachers if they are interns or student teachers. The advisor meets individually with each candidate twice monthly for in-depth consultation, including goal setting, reflection, and planning, and has regular meetings with the candidate and the cooperating teacher. Formal feedback is given at the end of each placement. The entire cohort meets for a weekly two-hour conference group to collaborate on the challenges they face in their field placements, share experiences, and help each other to examine their assumptions and question their practice. The advisor is responsible for "guiding [the advisee's] integration of theory and practice; ensuring coherence across the components of his or her master's level program; encouraging the habits of inquiry, reflection, connection, collaboration, and advocacy; and assessing each student's progress including his/her own capacity for self-assessment" (Bank Street, 2001, pp. 9–10).

Students work three to five days a week in a field setting appropriate to their programs. Students who are new to the field of education are placed as student teachers, completing three separate placements over the course of the advisement year with at least two different age groups. Student teachers work three days per week in the classroom, and are unpaid. Students who have experience working with children in structured settings may apply for a limited number of internships. Interns generally complete two placements in the same school, with different age groups. Interns work four days per week in the classroom, and receive a stipend. Students who are already employed as assistant teachers or head teachers complete their advisement year in their own classrooms, under the supervision of their faculty advisor. The advisement year typically occurs after the candidate has taken classes in child development and mathematics or reading, but is nearly always taken concurrently with further course work.

Bank Street does not consider field experiences and clinical practice to be the "culminating" portion of its degree programs, but rather emphasizes that fieldwork may take place at any time during the first and/or second year of a candidate's program. Course-related field experiences prior to the Supervised Fieldwork and Advisement may include classroom observations, recording and analysis of children learning in a variety of educational settings, tutoring, and interviewing or shadowing families or education professionals.

At the conclusion of the advisement year, advisors help their advisees develop plans for professional development during their initiation into the teaching profession. The advisor-advisee relationship often continues beyond the student's time at Bank Street, with prior students seeking the advice and counsel of their advisors long after they have graduated.

Bank Street has recognized that in the past, some candidates, particularly current practitioners seeking a master's degree, were unable to experience a wider range of students in their fieldwork than those in their own workplace. In addition, the state requires field placements with students in high-needs schools, students with disabilities, English language learners, and socioeconomically disadvantaged students. As a result, Bank Street arranges specific after-school, weekend, and other supplementary experiences to provide all teacher candidates with experiences working with diverse students in K–12 schools.

Faculty

A total of 116 faculty members taught in Bank Street's Graduate School in 2002–03. The organization of Bank Street's faculty is unusual, as there is no tenure and no system of professional rank. All full-time faculty are on one-year contracts. Nearly all faculty workloads are based around a 40 percent commitment to advising. One must serve as an advisor to become a faculty member. No matter how many courses taught or years teaching at Bank Street, if an instructor has not been an advisor, she or he is called (and paid as) an adjunct. Teaching a two- or three-credit course counts for 15 percent of a faculty member's annual workload, while teaching a one-credit course or coteaching a two- or three-credit course counts for 8 percent of workload. A full-time workload may include advising and teaching four courses a year. Faculty also may engage in a variety of other types of work in place of teaching, such as program administration, research and professional work, or staff development in local schools and districts.

In recent years, approximately 50 percent of credit-bearing courses in the graduate programs have been taught by faculty on 90–100 percent workload contracts, with the balance taught by part-time and adjunct faculty. Data on Bank Street's faculty in 2000–01 show that 15 percent were non-Hispanic black, 9 percent Hispanic, and 1 percent Asian. These proportions seem to be relatively stable across recent years.

In making personnel decisions, Bank Street places special emphasis on previous teaching experiences and special competencies that will enable its faculty to work effectively to improve high-need urban schools. Of the 11 most recently hired members of the 2002–03 Bank Street faculty, ten had previously been employed in New York City public schools or other urban educational settings.

Data on Students

In 2002–03, Bank Street had 564 students across all the programs. Bank Street's Graduate School serves a number of different types of students, including currently practicing teachers and career changers in addition to those who have just completed their undergraduate degrees. In 2002–03, incoming students had an average undergraduate GPA of 3.23, and 26percent came to Bank Street from outside New York State. Matriculated students in programs leading to initial teaching certification averaged 30 years of age. The vast majority of Bank Street students were female (97 percent) and 79 percent were non-Hispanic whites.

Data on Graduates

Bank Street graduates about 250 teachers per year from programs leading to initial certification. In 2001–02, 216 candidates completed the program and were eligible for teacher certification. During that same school year, 156 candidates registered for and took the Liberal Arts and Sciences Test (LAST) or the Praxis II Communications Skills Test and General Knowledge Test, one of which is required to demonstrate content knowledge for certification in New York state. Bank Street graduates had a 97 percent pass rate, slightly higher than the statewide pass rate of 95 percent. In addition, 154 students registered for and took the Assessment of Teaching Skills–Written (ATS-W) or the Praxis II Professional Knowledge Test, one of which is required for demonstration of professional knowledge and pedagogy for certification in New York state. They had a 100 percent pass rate, higher than the statewide pass rate of 96 percent.

Evaluation Component
Evaluation of Students. Bank Street employs multiple assessments in evaluating students. Examples of types of assessments used in the program include observations, journals, logs, case studies, interviews, lesson plans, research papers, critical literature reviews, policy analyses, curriculum plans, portfolios, video- and audiotapes, Web pages, peer response, student work samples, self-assessment, group projects, role plays, online discussions, multimedia presentations, artistic endeavors, and standards-based analyses. As the 2001 institutional report notes, "The diversity of assessments represents [Bank Street's] commitment to the idea that learning can occur and be expressed in a variety of formats" (Bank Street, 2001, p. 45). According to course syllabi, at least three forms of assessment are used in every Bank Street course to model and instruct candidates in using multiple types of assessment.

Evaluation of Graduates. A 1995–96 NCTAF study surveyed a broad sample of public school teachers, questioning them about the effectiveness of their teacher preparation program. The sample included a number of graduates of Bank Street programs. In 33 of 36 areas covered on the survey, Bank Street graduates felt better prepared than their comparison group peers did, and significantly better prepared in 25 areas. The difference between the groups was largest in areas dealing with development of curriculum; ability to create a positive, productive learning environment for all students; teaching for higher-order thinking and performance; and being prepared to use research and other colleagues to improve their practice. Bank Street graduates felt less well prepared than their peers to use technology in the classroom. In the same study, more than 90 percent of surveyed principals working with Bank Street graduates found them to be "well or very well prepared" in comparison to teachers from other teacher education programs, and most found them well prepared in all areas (Darling-Hammond and Macdonald, 2000).

A second study (Darling-Hammond et al., 2002, p. 4) that focused more narrowly on teacher preparation in New York City found Bank Street to be an outlier program with significantly higher mean ratings than other teacher preparation programs on a number of items designed to probe teachers' perceptions of their preparation.

While Bank Street keeps in touch with many of its graduates informally, particularly through the advisor-advisee relationship, at baseline it did not formally track its graduates.

Program Evaluation. Bank Street's plan for program assessment features a system of administrative structures and faculty committees reviewing a number of internal and external indicators. The college uses advisor evaluations of students, student transcripts, and external testing for state licensing to assess the progress and competencies of current students. Additional indicators including periodic surveys of graduates, course evaluations, and accreditation reports also help to inform the faculty and administration on the effectiveness of Bank Street's programs. In recent years, Bank Street has focused much of its program evaluation efforts on National Council for Accreditation of Teacher Education (NCATE) and New York state accreditation visits. Currently engaged in Middle States Review, the college sponsors two program reviews annually, with the programs cycling through on a five-year rotation.

Collaboration with Arts and Sciences Faculty: Selected Examples

Because Bank Street is an independent college of education, the Graduate School of Education has no direct institutional links to a college of arts and sciences. The college instead relies on its admissions process to ensure the academic preparation and subject-matter knowledge of teacher candidates.

Despite the lack of institutional links to arts and sciences faculty on campus, Bank Street has made efforts to collaborate with content-area experts in the New York area:

- Historically, the college has collaborated with the American Museum of Natural History, Columbia School of Social Work, Parsons School of Design, and the Urban Education Semester program—a theory and practice introduction for liberal arts undergraduates. The Urban Education Semester program represents a collaboration among: Bank Street College, K–12 New York City Schools, Bates College, Brown University, Connecticut College, College of the Holy Cross, Swarthmore College, Vassar College, and Wesleyan University.

- The college established a partnership with the Lincoln Center Institute in an effort to integrate a range of arts-based pedagogical, curricular, and assessment techniques in graduate and public school classrooms. This partnership includes workshops for Bank Street faculty; joint planning sessions for deans, principals, and arts administrators from the school districts and Lincoln Center Institute staff; partnerships between teaching artists and classroom educators; and professional development support for faculty and classroom teachers in such areas as evaluation through portfolios and using the arts to support learning standards across the curriculum.

Collaboration of University Faculty with K–12 Schools: Selected Examples

Bank Street runs the on-site private PK–8 School for Children. The school models progressive education teaching and provides a site for teacher preparation students to student teach and observe. Students who apply to the School for Children are selected for their interest in the school and with an eye to maintaining diversity within the student population reflective of the population of New York City. Financial aid is available for low-income parents. Bank Street also runs an on-site full-inclusion family center for infants and toddlers. Each classroom has a fully certified teacher and teacher aides, many of whom are Bank Street graduate students.

Midtown West is a K–8 public school that contains three smaller schools: two elementary (one monolingual and one dual language) and one middle school. Midtown West was created as a collaborative effort by Bank Street and the New York City Board of Education and is run by an advisory board that includes administrators, teachers, parents, and a Bank Street liaison. The school has a diverse student and family population from 52 cultures, speaking 16 languages. The dual language school is often used for student clinical placements.

New Beginnings, a collaboration between Bank Street and the Newark, N.J. public schools, is an initiative designed to support Newark's educators in creating classroom experiences and environments that are responsive to the needs of the students. Bank Street faculty provide intensive professional development to teachers, paraprofessionals, administrators, and parents in nine Newark preschool and primary grade schools. Over the five years of the project, the program has comprehensively restructured Newark's early childhood classes and created models for effective teaching.

The Training for All Teachers grant is a collaboration with Central Harlem's Community School District 5. Under this grant, Bank Street is working to redesign some of the teacher education courses so that they include more attention to issues related to English language learners and to offer direct preparation to District 5 teachers so that they can better serve the needs of English language learners in their classrooms.

This was how Bank Street looked at the time it was chosen for the TNE grant. We now turn to the design proposal describing how Bank Street proposed to transform itself into a TNE institution embracing and institutionalizing the TNE design principles.

Design Proposal

As mentioned in the introduction, each institution developed a design proposal for Carnegie that outlined its plans for how TNE would be implemented. This section outlines the major activities that Bank Street proposed in its design proposal. Obviously, these were plans and, as such, will undergo revision during the implementation process. However, they do provide an idea and vision for how TNE will be implemented in the institution. We present the information in narrative form around major categories of activities—action-oriented inquiry teams, assessment, recruitment, program improvement, and induction—that Bank Street planned to undertake to produce high-quality graduates who produce better pupil outcomes. We also present this information organized under the design principles in Table A.1.

Action-Oriented Inquiry Teams. Bank Street proposed to start by establishing action-oriented inquiry (AOI) teams to develop an empirically based set of content knowledge used by exemplary elementary teachers in three areas: literacy, numeracy, and social studies and later expanding to include science. The teams would consist of faculty members from Bank Street, a content specialist, and a teacher candidate or graduate who would be observed in her/his classroom. The inquiry team would collect student work on three students in 16 classrooms as a starting point. The classrooms would be selected to ensure diversity among the student body in terms of age and student demographics and among school contexts (progressive schools, high- and underachieving schools, etc.). The data collected by the teams would be the basis for program assessment and redesign. The proposal (Bank Street, 2002b, p. 10) noted that

> [b]y the end of year two, we will have a faculty steeped in the existing literature, constructed our own understandings of the professional literature by creating our own study, and used the elements of rigorous inquiry and the findings of our inquiries to inform our program work.

Bank Street's program rests on its credo, which describes education as both a moral and political undertaking. As such, the program attempts to foster both ethical standards and scientific attitudes in its graduates, to ensure that they have the knowledge, skills, and dispositions necessary to become advocates for children and for the teaching profession. As part of its early work, Bank Street planned to clarify and operationalize its credo, to assess its candidates' development toward becoming embodiments of its values, and to improve the program based on these data to ensure that its goals are met.

Assessment. In terms of assessment and pupil learning, Bank Street noted that the relationships between teacher opportunities for learning and pupil learning are indirect at best. It proposed to focus on understanding how teacher graduates learn and how best to increase such opportunities in the first two years after graduation. These data would be used for program improvement. Bank Street is a member of the Delta Project (as are the other three TNE sites), an initiative funded by the Carnegie Foundation for the Advancement of Teaching. The Delta Project aims to develop a teacher educator's toolkit incorporating a broad repertoire of assessments to measure the depth and breadth of content and pedagogical content knowledge (PCK), as well as the growth of professional skills, understandings, and dispositions among prospective teachers. Drawing on its work with the Delta Project, Bank Street proposed to develop a variety of assessment techniques to evaluate the learning of its own teacher education candidates and the learning done under the tutelage of its teacher graduates. A particular focus would be the ability of Bank Street's candidates to integrate technology into classroom instruction. In addition, the college proposed to examine student work samples and other types of innovative classroom-based assessments to document the

Table A.1
Major Proposed Activities, by Design Principle, Bank Street

Design Principle A: Decisions driven by evidence	*Drawing on Research*
	• Form AOI teams, consisting of candidates and teachers, Bank Street college faculty, and content specialists, to
	  – Review research in three areas initially—literacy, numeracy, and social studies, later expanding to other subjects
	  – Observe classroom practice to develop initial definition of teaching and establish goals
	  – Develop and pilot instruments for gathering data linked to goals for candidates and goals for candidates' pupils, and continuously collect and analyze data. Instrumentation and data will serve as analytical tools for program assessment and redesign.
	
	The Role of Pupil Learning
	• Measure teacher opportunities for learning and instruction and use these data for program improvement.
	• Study student opportunities for learning across contexts and develop instruments to measure pupil learning.
	• Help candidates learn to use assessment techniques to support their own teaching.

Design Principle B: Engagement with the arts and sciences	*Subject-Matter Understanding* • Examine, through AOI teams, the content knowledge teachers actually need to help students learn in order to generate an empirically based set of content knowledge in several areas and use this knowledge to develop assessments, adjust admissions criteria, revamp content-specific pedagogy courses, and shape the induction program. • Forge deep relationships with other IHEs and content-area experts (e.g., Stevens Institute, TERC, American Museum of Natural History). • Establish the Kerlin Institute for Science and Environmental Education with help from other IHEs, TERC, museums, or other specialists to create a science emphasis in the middle school program. *General and Liberal Education* • Foster the knowledge, skills, and dispositions necessary to engage in advocacy for children and the profession in teacher candidates. • Clarify and operationalize the Bank Street credo and values of advocacy; assess candidates' development; and improve program based on assessment results.

Design Principle C: Teaching as an academically taught clinical practice profession	*Pedagogy*
	• Develop and use instruments to measure changes in candidates' knowledge, skills, and dispositions and teach faculty how to use the data to inform and improve individual practice and programmatic policies, building on the work done by Interstate Teacher Assessment and Support Consortium and the NBPTS.
	
	Schools as Clinics
	• Building on the already strong relationships with schools, improvement efforts to be directed toward
	  – Improving linkage between research efforts and work in schools by involving K–12 teachers in AOI teams
	  – Involving K–12 faculty in program improvement through representation on coordinating council
	  – Linking work to schools' visions for improvement with a special focus on use of technology.
	
	Teachers on Faculty Appointment
	• Bank Street already recognizes excellent K–12 teachers as faculty colleagues with faculty and adjunct faculty appointments. Thus, in this area, it has already met the goal set by TNE.
	
	Residency (Induction)
	• Provide support for graduates in three locales: in their schools, online, and through programs at Bank Street, culminating in an appropriate document acknowledging completion of the induction program.
	• Develop an induction program that will be flexible, sustainable beyond the initiative, and applicable across multiple contexts where graduates live and work. It will be based on clear evidence of effectiveness, include a subject-matter component, and will be continually updated based on input of AOI teams.
	
	Preparation of Candidates for Professional Growth
	• Inform programmatic improvements through work of AOI teams and empirical data on the roles graduates play in schools, districts, and professional organizations; and the supports they need for continuous professional growth.

Table A.1—Continued

	• Work with Bank Street's Division of Continuing Education, the regional NBPTS center at Bank Street, professional organizations, and policymakers at all levels to offer multiple sources of support for its graduates, feedback from districts, and address the strengths, interests, and needs of graduates.
Additional issues to be addressed jointly by faculties in education and in arts and sciences	*Pedagogical Content Knowledge* • Work through AOI groups to illustrate what exemplary teachers use to support student learning in particular content areas. • Make initial programmatic changes (e.g., Kerlin Institute, development of case studies in mathematics, etc.) aimed at enhancing candidates' opportunities for learning, practicing, and assessing the development and use of PCK. • Investigate and redesign specific pedagogy courses. • Design an induction program that includes a focus on PCK. *Literacy and Numeracy Skills* • Focus on improving candidates' writing skills. • Share AOI findings on literacy and numeracy with appropriate committees on campuses from which Bank Street draws its students and/or arts and sciences partner IHEs for consideration. *Elementary and Middle School Education* • Share relevant findings and assessments from AOI teams with partner IHEs as part of the design of their undergraduate programs. *Technology* • Invest in selected schools' use of technology to create better locations for candidates to practice and assess their use of technology during field experiences. • Develop and implement use of technology assessments to measure the knowledge and skills set as the goals for candidates' use of technology to support student learning. *Cultural Considerations in Teaching and Learning* • Define "diversity" broadly to include culture, ethnicity, language, race, disabilities, gender, and sexual orientation. • Develop a self-assessment tool for candidates and an external assessment to be used by advisors to document candidates' growth over time in their capacity to use differences in effective teaching. • Build partnerships with additional K–12 schools to expand opportunities for all candidates to experience diversity in classrooms and school and community contexts during their clinical practice. • Continue to provide opportunities for Bank Street faculty to enhance their knowledge, skills, and dispositions in this area. *Recruitment of Underrepresented Groups in Teaching* • AOI groups to identify support needs of underrepresented groups at Bank Street through careful sampling of classrooms. • Redesign scholarship procedures to offer early and large fellowships targeted to candidates from underrepresented groups. • Undertake new efforts to get special funding for scholarships and supports targeted toward underrepresented groups. *Late Deciders in an Undergraduate Program* • This design principle is not applicable to Bank Street because it only offers graduate programs.

learning of the pupils being taught by its graduates. By year five of the TNE effort, the college's candidates would be well versed in using assessment techniques to support its own teaching.

Recruiting Teacher Education Candidates. Bank Street recognized the need to link recruitment and support to ensure that it can both increase the number of candidates from underrepresented groups and help them succeed. By year two, it planned to redesign scholarship procedures, add new funds, and provide earlier and larger fellowships to candidates from underrepresented groups, look for funding to provide enhanced professional and personal support to these candidates once they are admitted, and identify more specifically what is needed to support them in the program. The college's goal was to maintain or increase the percentage of candidates of color in the school by the end of five years (depending on economic factors).

Program Improvements. As mentioned above, the data Bank Street proposed to collect would be used to revise courses, curriculum, and clinical experiences to align with research. A particular focus would be content-specific pedagogy courses. The college planned for one of its foci to be science in the middle school program. Because Bank Street does not have arts and sciences faculty, it planned to be very aggressive in forging partnerships with institutions of higher education, such as Stevens Institute of Technology. The college planned to establish an Institute for Science and Environmental Education, which would offer an intensive science-centered experience during the summer followed by a full year of work in both science and pedagogy to translate this newfound content knowledge into constructive learning opportunities for students.

As part of its attempts to forge deeper relationships with other institutions of higher education (IHEs) and to foster wider dissemination, Bank Street proposed to consider offering residency programs for faculty from partner IHEs to spend a week at Bank Street and vice versa in Years 4 and 5 of the grant. The college also planned to disseminate findings on the numeracy and literacy skills of its candidates (that will now be tied to what teachers need to know and be able to do) to partner IHEs to assist institutions in better preparing their undergraduates. While good writing skills are a prerequisite for admission to Bank Street, the college also planned to develop programs to improve the writing skills of its candidates to help increase recruitment of underrepresented groups into teaching.

Bank Street itself has considerably upgraded its technological infrastructure and faculty expertise because of generous grants. It proposed to invest in selected K–12 schools to enhance their use of technology to support student learning. To develop a more systematic approach to assessing its candidates' skills in this area, the college would appoint faculty working on technology initiatives to the AOI teams so that the assessments would overlap and be integrated.

One of the strengths of Bank Street is the fact that it already has a number of K–12 faculty on its staff. In addition, it planned to have greater and earlier involvement of K–12 faculty in program improvement, especially through the coordinating council and the inclusion of K–12 faculty on the action-oriented inquiry teams, and to link its work in schools with the schools' own vision for improvement.

Bank Street adopted a broad definition of diversity to include culture, ethnicity, language, race, disabilities, gender, and sexual orientation. The AOI teams would supplement existing strengths by developing a self-assessment tool to be used by candidates and an external assessment to be used by the advisor to document candidates' growth over time in their capacity to use acknowledge, draw on and employ differences as resources in effective teaching. They also would explore building partnerships with additional K–12 schools to expand opportunities for all candidates to experience diversity in classrooms and school and community contexts during their clinical practice and to continue to provide opportunities for Bank Street faculty to enhance their knowledge, skills, and dispositions in this area.

Induction Program and Support. As part of the induction and mentoring program, Bank Street proposed to offer support to graduates online, at schools where they teach, and on campus through special events and workshops on content and pedagogy. They planned to start with small numbers of graduates at three schools and then scale up the program, to cover a large number of (but not all) graduates. The program would include several options from which graduates could design a program appropriate for their needs; these could include a subject-matter option, lesson-study options, development of case studies, provision of different experiences (for example, in partnership with the Lincoln Center Institute), and use of teaching portfolios. The induction work with graduates would help Bank Street understand teacher needs in the area of professional growth and leadership. This continuing support would be offered through its Division of Continuing Education, its regional center for the National Board for Professional Teaching Standards (NBPTS), and through partnerships with professional organizations and districts and states.

The next section discusses implementation of the TNE proposal in the first year. We begin by describing the project structure and staffing and the budget. We then examine progress in implementing the design principles. The next subsections report participants' views about TNE and the first year experience and some thoughts about implementation in the second year.

First Year Implementation

Project Structure and Staffing

Leadership. Once the TNE funding came through in December, Bank Street quickly hired a full-time project director from outside the school to oversee and coordinate the TNE activities and formed a leadership team composed of the project director, the dean, and two education faculty members. An induction coordinator was added to the leadership team in Year 2.

Bank Street established a coordinating council to reflect on the project findings and their implications for teacher development policies and programs both internally for Bank Street and externally for New York and the nation. The coordinating council includes representatives from the New York State Board of Regents, the NBPTS, and the New York City Department of Education. The first meeting of the coordinating council will be in Year 2. Originally, Bank Street conceived of the coordinating council as having a local focus and including a number of K–12 school representatives. However, the president of Bank Street urged the leadership team to broaden the membership and scope of the council and focus it on policy work. Bank Street also expects its newly formed coordinating council to provide a method of disseminating TNE information to external organizations.

The leadership team met weekly throughout the school year to discuss progress and met with teams of faculty working on TNE research activities on a weekly basis as well. The project coordinator works full time on TNE. The dean spends 25 to 50 percent of his time on TNE, and is budgeted for 25 percent of his time under the TNE budget. However, before Bank Street hired the project coordinator, the dean spent approximately four days a week on TNE. He reported that it was difficult to separate his TNE responsibilities from his general responsibilities as dean.

The project director is assigned to work half time with the AOI teams, one-quarter on the induction component and one-quarter on working with content and research specialists, project communications, and management and coordination. The TNE budget covers two faculty members of the leadership team 40 percent. Bank Street also set aside funds to cover the time of faculty who were actively involved in TNE research through AOI teams (discussed in detail later). These faculty members received 15 percent coverage from TNE.

New Faculty. As mentioned earlier, Bank Street hired a full-time project coordinator to guide Bank Street's TNE efforts. The project coordinator is responsible for coordinating the leadership team, monitoring the teacher sample in the field, assisting the AOI teams in their research reports, putting together the cross-case analysis of their results, and monitoring the work plan. She "keeps everybody marching down the street."

In spring 2003 Bank Street hired an induction coordinator to lead its induction activities.

Budget

About half Bank Street's TNE budget for Year 1 was allocated to the AOI teams. This included half-time for the project coordinator, 40 percent time for the three leaders, and 15 percent time for each of the 21 team members. It also included funds for local travel and some equipment. About $45,000 was targeted for work on induction and primarily included time for the project coordinator (25 percent) and for the induction leader (40 percent). About $125,000 was allocated for the content and research specialists and most of this was for a contract with arts and sciences consultants and travel. Cross-program expenses included one-quarter time for the dean, a full-time administrative assistant, $40,000 for conference participation and travel, and a little over $20,000 for telephones, computer services, and supplies. About $50,000 was set aside for evaluation, for which Bank Street contracted with an outside expert.

Matching Funds and University Contributions

Bank Street is making efforts to raise the matching funds, and the trustees and the president are actively involved in this fundraising effort.

Implementation Progress

Bank Street's first year implementation efforts focused on the areas in which its leadership believed it had the most work to do to achieve its TNE goals—creating evidence through research and involving the arts and sciences.

Design Principle A: Decisions Driven by Evidence. Bank Street's work to establish a research base for its program focuses on the work of the AOIs. The goal of the AOI component of the TNE initiative is to inform project renewal and ensure that it is evidence based. Bank Street plans to use the findings of the AOI projects to inform admissions, teacher education programs, the induction program, and their teacher leader program (i.e., aspiring principals). The AOI teams' process and findings also provide faculty with new ways to think about their work and develop data collection strategies to be integrated into their graduate course work.

Year 1 was the pilot year for AOI team work. To recruit AOI team participants, Bank Street issued an open call for applications from faculty members. There were more applicants than needed, so preference was given to individuals with expertise in literacy and numeracy, the two subject-matter foci of the pilot year.

Bank Street formed eight AOI teams. The AOI team researchers worked in pairs and studied an experienced teacher and a teacher candidate. Bank Street considered the teachers who were being studied to be members of the AOI teams as well. All the AOI research team members were education faculty from the Graduate School, except for one School for Children faculty member and a mathematics consultant from TERC, a not-for-profit research and development organization with expertise in mathematics, science, and technology education. They had hoped to have a linguist from City College participate in the effort, but the arrangements fell through, leaving one AOI team member short a partner. This AOI team member worked with the TNE leadership team.

The AOI teams met as a group every other week from November to March for two-and-a-half-hour meetings to discuss and refine the structure for their research. As a first step in the AOI work, the teams developed a draft framework for defining teaching drawn largely from the California Standards for the Teaching Profession. This framework defines six domains that describe the fundamental aspects of teaching practice:

- **Planning instruction and designing learning experiences for all students:** The teacher plans learning experiences for the needs of both the whole group and the individual. Student learning experiences are planned taking into consideration the students' background, interests, and developmental learning needs. Development is understood to include cognitive, social, emotional, and physical growth, as well as interactions among these aspects of development. Instructional plans are modified, when necessary, based on the needs of the students.

- **Understanding and organizing subject-matter knowledge for student learning:** it is through the teacher's deep understanding of subject-matter knowledge that he or she is able to organize the curriculum for student learning and help students integrate knowledge across the disciplines.

- **Creating and maintaining an effective environment for student learning:** Fairness, respect, equity, and democratic processes characterize the learning environment for students. Through classroom materials, procedures, and routines, students can learn, feel safe, and are able to use their instructional time together productively.

- **Engaging and supporting all students in their learning:** Students learn subject matter, problem solving, critical thinking, and skills through a variety of experiences. Students are encouraged to engage in a variety of kinds of learning, including self-directed, collaborative, reflective, structured, and sequential. Students have opportunities to interact with materials and people both in the classroom environment and the wider world. Teachers draw on knowledge of their own learning as one source to help them understand children's learning.

- **Assessing student learning:** Student learning should be assessed by the students themselves, along with the teacher, using multiple types of evidence. For example, evidence from the parents, gathered over time. Close observation and documentation of children provides a significant resource of evidence. Teachers engage as responsive partners in the learning process and share the results of learning assessments with students, families, and the learning community and use assessment to guide further student learning.

- **Developing professional responsibilities:** The teacher develops and articulates a view of good teaching that expresses the values, assumptions, and beliefs that inform his or her practice and pedagogical decisionmaking. Teaching is a lifelong endeavor that requires teachers to grow and renew continually as professionals, integrating a sense of personal and professional identity. It is through this renewal that teachers learn of new resources in the community and school and to support student learning. Professional teachers not only enhance their own practice, but also contribute to the development of others through their participation in a community of learners. Understanding how teaching deeply affects the lives of children and their families, the teacher is an advocate for children, promoting democratic principles and social justice (http://www.bankstreet.edu/tne/domains.html).

In addition, the AOI teams developed a seventh domain, initially called the "Habits of Hearts and Minds" to operationalize the Bank Street credo.

These domains establish a working definition of quality teaching that Bank Street will test and refine through AOI work. Bank Street used these domains to guide the data-collection efforts of the AOI teams and will inform future work on establishing subdomains in literacy and numeracy.

The leadership team developed a set of training materials that was used to train the AOI team members on methods for conducting their research projects. In the spring, each AOI team studied one experienced teacher and one teacher candidate during a two- to three-week unit of either literacy or mathematics instruction. Each team conducted a preinterview, observed three classes (each with a mini pre- and postdiscussion), collected student work for three students (representing a range of ability levels), and then conducted a postinterview with each teacher.

Each team coded interviews, observations, and student work. These coded documents were entered into a database, created by a consultant to the leadership team, which allowed the leadership team to analyze the data by domain. The leadership team then worked with faculty on developing a cross-case analysis to be presented to AOI team members and the rest of the Bank Street faculty.[1]

Bank Street maintains a TNE project Web site that includes information about TNE, the AOI team work, and the six domains of teaching, as well as a discussion tool to encourage dialogue outside of project meetings and across the faculty. To further disseminate findings and progress, Bank Street has produced articles on the TNE initiative for the faculty newsletter and hosted brown bag discussions to solicit faculty members' feedback. In addition, the leadership found that the AOI team members informally disseminate their activities to their fellow faculty members. Bank Street hopes all these activities will increase awareness of TNE among the faculty and help faculty become more familiar with research and how to use data.

To expand Bank Street's dissemination efforts with respect to TNE activities, project staff met with staff from Bank Street's Division of External Affairs to develop a comprehensive communications plan for the project that will encompass all its efforts in a systematic fashion. The plan will cover broad communication and discussion with respect to policy and practice, both internal and external to Bank Street.

In addition to the work the AOI teams have done to create a research base to inform the program, Bank Street has been working with its local evaluator to update and improve its database for tracking graduates. This database will allow the college to feed information about its graduates back into the program for improvement.

Design Principle B: Engagement with the Arts and Sciences. Because Bank Street is an independent college of education, involving arts and sciences faculty, and doing so in a meaningful way, is a tremendous challenge. Bank Street worked to form a partnership with arts and sciences faculty from a college or university that would include more than merely subsidizing time of selected arts and sciences faculty members. An early attempt to develop a

---

[1] Work on the cross-case analysis continues in Year 2.

collaborative relationship with City College was unsuccessful, but Bank Street was successful in establishing an institutional relationship with Sarah Lawrence College as of the start of Year 2.

In addition to seeking these institutional partnerships, Bank Street was successful in involving two representatives from TERC in the AOI work. One TERC representative served as an AOI team member, and another acted as a resource by facilitating the teams' conversations about their work.

Design Principle C: Teaching as an Academically Taught Clinical Practice Profession. During Year 1, Bank Street laid the groundwork for its future induction activities by commissioning studies that would inform its induction plans. The leadership team hired the Stevens Institute to study the strengths, interests, and needs of the college's students and graduates. The Stevens Institute conducted focus groups with graduates and faculty members and gave a preliminary presentation to the faculty on the results. The institute also produced a literature review and conducted a review of electronic induction.

In addition, Bank Street hired a graduate student from the University of Maryland to write a comprehensive report on exemplary state induction programs and to review state efforts to support new teachers in the classroom. The information in the two reports will help Bank Street develop principles on which to base the induction program, which aims to provide a menu of options for candidates.

Participants' Views on Year 1 Implementation

Comments we heard during our site visits from participants regarding their experiences and impressions during the first year of implementation offer some useful lessons learned. We grouped participants' views into the following categories:

- **Importance of leadership**
  - There appears to be a genuine respect for the leadership team and a lot of confidence in them.
  - Having a full-time project director is helpful in keeping the project moving forward.

- **Problems with timing and scheduling**
  - The timing of the grant made all parts of the process rushed. For instance, AOI teams had to rush through their work; the induction coordinator was not hired until spring; and there was not as much time as expected to forge relationships with institutions with arts and sciences expertise.
  - The dean had to carry the majority of the workload before Bank Street received the funding and a project director could be hired, which placed a considerable burden on him.

- **Culture changes resulting from focus on research and evidence**
  - Bank Street does not have a strong research presence, so research of the kind undertaken by the AOI teams is professionally challenging for the faculty and the institution. However, most feel that the experience is also rewarding and enriching. It is also a great opportunity for those being studied (candidates and teachers) to improve their own practice.

- Faculty report that conversations at Bank Street and relationships among faculty members have changed this year. Faculty are talking more about subject matter and evidence of good teaching.
- Involving a School for Children faculty member in the work of the Graduate School's AOI teams helped build connections between these two divisions of the school. Bank Street faculty members from both divisions see these connections as a way to disseminate the work of the TNE initiative and an opportunity for formal cooperation that previously did not exist.

- **AOI team process**
  - Participants in the AOI team process noted the difficulty in ensuring reliability with respect to the way collected data are analyzed across teams. There is the issue of reliability between teams and the problem of making sure that AOI teams and team members make similar coding decisions when analyzing data. Some respondents felt the need to be more systematic about what student work samples are gathered.
  - The group of all AOI team members may have been too large to work effectively in meetings.
  - There is a lot of interaction among the AOI team members and the TNE leadership and AOI activities are structured to be collaborative and support interactive decisionmaking.

- **Collaboration among arts and sciences, education, and K–12 faculty**
  - Including arts and sciences faculty will be a challenge to Bank Street even once partnerships are established. It will be necessary for institutional partners to find reciprocal benefits in their collaboration, to see it as an opportunity and not solely as an obligation. The dean of the partner institution may need to be a "cheerleader" for enlisting faculty, and it is hoped that Bank Street faculty members can make direct appeals to the partner institution's faculty.
  - Bank Street is still working to determine how best to use outside content expertise. The role of arts and sciences faculty gets slightly confused and will need to be clarified. In addition, the college wants to use the content experts in ways that do not devalue its own faculty members' expertise.
  - Collaborating with K–12 faculty and institutions on TNE is a natural extension of Bank Street's pre-TNE activities. On the AOI teams, the K–12 teachers who are being studied are considered members of the research team. Further, almost all Bank Street faculty have K–12 experience and bring that perspective to their work.

- **General concerns about TNE**
  - Given the nature of Bank Street's program and the focus on authentic assessments to monitor student learning, there is apprehension on the part of Bank Street faculty about the perceived emphasis in TNE on standardized test scores as a measure of teacher effectiveness. They understand why assessment and evidence is needed and why it is part of the initiative but "the devil's in the details."

Looking Forward to Year 2

The work of the AOI teams produced some valuable information and interesting insight for participating faculty members; however, the leadership noted that the information gained in the first year does not constitute enough evidence to inform program improvements. The cross-case analysis from the AOI teams' work will be used to inform revisions of the domains and the methodology used to conduct the research.

The AOI teams' work will continue in Year 2. In addition to literacy and numeracy, the AOI teams will focus on science in Year 2. Bank Street plans to increase the number of AOI teams from eight to ten, with a mix of faculty. It wants to solicit the participation of additional School for Children faculty, Continuing Education faculty, Education Leadership faculty, and arts and sciences faculty from its new arts and sciences partner, Sarah Lawrence College.

The TNE project will incorporate student assessment measures into the initiative. Bank Street plans to examine three levels of assessment: standardized tests, pre- and post-tests in literacy and numeracy with teacher candidates' students, and curriculum-embedded assessments.

Bank Street also will focus on induction. The induction coordinator will lead an institutional induction committee whose members are appointed by the college president. Representatives from TNE leadership will also meet with officials from the New York State Department of Education to discuss their induction plans.

Effect of State Policy Context

Budget

While New York is facing lower than expected revenues, resulting in significant budget shortfalls and cuts to higher education, Bank Street, being a private institution, has not been directly affected by these cuts. However, the institution did experience lower-than-projected gift giving due to the overall slump in the economy.

Policy

Bank Street recently reregistered all its teacher education programs with the state, making necessary changes to ensure compliance with new wider state regulations on the knowledge, skills, and dispositions required for certification to teach in New York state. However, Bank Street will need to consider connections between its induction program and the district-based first-year mentoring program that is now required, though not funded, by the state.

California State University, Northridge: Profile at Baseline and Year 1 Implementation

Overview of the Teacher Education Program at Baseline

General Description of Programs

The College of Education at California State University, Northridge (CSUN),[1] consists of six departments, which offer a variety of degree, credential, and certificate options. This report focuses only on the programs that are linked to three initial teaching credentials.

CSUN offers a number of postbaccalaureate and undergraduate programs that lead to three major teaching credentials:

- **Multiple Subject (MS) Credential:** Credential for elementary school teachers offered by the Department of Elementary Education
- **Single Subject (SS) Credential:** Credential for secondary teachers offered by the Department of Secondary Education
- **Education Specialist (ES) Credential:** Credential for special education teachers offered by the Department of Special Education. CSUN offers this credential in four specializations: Deaf and Hard of Hearing, Early Childhood, Mild to Moderate Disabilities, and Moderate to Severe Disabilities.

Many of the programs were revised as a result of the new standards for teacher credentialing, issued by the California Commission on Teacher Credentialing in fall 2001 following the passage of Senate Bill (SB) 2042, including the MS and SS credentials and the subject-matter program for the MS credential.

Postbaccalaureate Programs. CSUN offers three versions of the postbaccalaureate program (fifth-year program): a traditional program, an internship program, and the Accelerated Collaborative Teacher (ACT) Preparation Program. Most postbaccalaureate students go through the traditional or intern programs (CSUN issued over 1,600 credentials to students from these programs in 2001–02), while the relatively new ACT program is CSUN's smallest postbaccalaureate program, graduating 94 students in 2001–02.

Candidates for all these programs must have an overall GPA of at least 2.67 or 2.75 in their last 60 semester units. In addition, they must verify that they have attempted or registered for the California Basic Educational Skills Test (CBEST), a test of basic literacy in reading, writing, and mathematics.

---

[1] The college was renamed the Michael D. Eisner College of Education after CSUN received a major gift in May 2002 from the Eisner Foundation to establish the new Center for Teaching and Learning, with the idea that it will become a premier center for the nation on how best to support children with learning differences in the classroom. The initial focus of the center will be on the work of Mel Levine and the implications of his theories for teaching and learning. A part of the gift was used to establish the first endowed chair in the college to oversee the work of the Center for Teaching and Learning.

The traditional MS/SS program is designed as a fifth year of study. While it can be completed in one calendar year, it offers students flexibility in the scheduling of their course work and the choice of full- or part-time attendance.

The Internship Credential Program is a two-year, part-time course of instruction that is offered in partnership with local school districts. It provides an opportunity for candidates with full-time employment as public school teachers to complete a preliminary credential while on the job. To enter an internship program, candidates must have a bachelor's degree and demonstrate subject-matter competence by either completing a state-approved subject-matter program or passing a test.

The ACT program is a structured full-time, academic-year-long program offered in partnership with District B in the Los Angeles Unified School District (LAUSD). The program comprises two semesters; each semester includes a common core designed for all credential candidates; course work in an appropriate credential area; and field experiences. Courses are taught collaboratively by university faculty and classroom teachers. ACT students take courses during the evening and are available for fieldwork and student teaching during the day.

Undergraduate Programs. In 1999–00, CSUN began a new undergraduate program for students pursuing a teaching career: the Integrated Teacher Education Program (ITEP)–Freshman Option. Two years later, in 2001–02, CSUN began offering the ITEP–Junior Option and the Four-Year Integrated (FYI) Teacher Credential Program. These programs allow students to earn a B.A. and a preliminary credential in four years and one summer. ITEP is designed for students who want to become elementary or special education teachers. These students earn a B.A. in liberal studies and obtain either an MS or ES credential. The FYI program is designed for future secondary teachers. Currently, the FYI program is offered in two content specialties, English and mathematics, so FYI students obtain a B.A. in either English or mathematics and an SS credential in their content area.

These programs were developed jointly by faculty from the Colleges of Education and Arts and Sciences and K–12 schools. They feature a curriculum of blended, paired, and team-taught courses; early and ongoing field experiences in local schools linked with subject-matter course work; an emphasis on diversity and the literacy needs of urban children; a cohort approach; an infusion of technology, writing, and computation; and ongoing professional growth through a collaborative peer support system and a virtual professional development center. ITEP was recognized by the U.S. Department of Education as an innovative urban teacher education program and funded under the Title II Teacher Quality Enhancement program. Students enter these programs during their freshman year; however, ITEP also offers a Junior Option that allows for later entry into the program.

In the spring of 2002, 86 students were enrolled in the ITEP or FYI program; however, CSUN expects that enrollment in these programs will grow over time. Freshmen qualify for entry if they pass the CBEST and have completed each of the courses in the comprehensive pattern of college preparatory subject requirements with grades of C or better.

Clinical Component

In the traditional MS/SS credential programs, students must complete 20 hours of participation and observation in a school prior to student teaching. Students in ITEP gain field experience throughout the program, including observing students and teachers in the first several semesters and progressing to planning and teaching lessons to individual students and small groups of students and assessing literacy skills of students.

Candidates in the MS/SS credential programs complete field experiences as either student teachers or interns. The student teaching assignments provide candidates with the opportunity to experience all phases of a school year and one or more grading periods. MS candidates report to the classroom on a daily basis for a minimum of 15 weeks. They are required to complete two assignments at two of the following grade spans: K–2, 3–5, and 6–8. SS candidates participate in 32 weeks or more of field experience and practicum, with the exception of interns (those who are already teaching full-time on an internship credential), who complete one assignment at the middle school level and the other at the high school level. Emergency permit candidates (teachers earning a credential on the job) work with students in their own classrooms.

CSUN requires that all teacher education candidates have one assignment in a classroom with English language learners and teach under the supervision of a teacher with appropriate preparation. Also, they must have one assignment in a classroom where 25 percent of the pupils represent an ethnicity that differs from the candidate's. At least one of the two experiences takes place in a public school. ES candidates participate in a variety of field experiences across disabilities and age and grade ranges including supervised full-day teaching or intern practicum.

All MS and SS student teachers work with two master teachers, ES student teachers work with either one or two master teachers, and each intern is assigned a support provider. Clinical faculty are carefully selected and regularly evaluated.

The Beginning Teacher Support and Assessment Program (BTSA) is a major statewide initiative striving to create a coherent and meaningful induction program for first and second year teachers throughout California. The CSUN BTSA program is a collaborative effort between the university, LAUSD, and United Teachers Los Angeles (UTLA) that provides induction support to all new teachers in local districts A and C of LAUSD. The major work of BTSA is creating mentorship relationships between new classroom teachers and support providers, who may be members of a Cadre of Retired Educators (CORE) or on-site colleagues. Support providers meet one-on-one with their assigned new teachers throughout the year and offer support through observation, coaching, assistance, and role modeling. Additional services provided by BTSA include, among others, release days to allow observation of exemplary teachers and associated seminars; practical workshops offered through a professional development series; and the California Formative Assessment and Support System for Teachers (CFASST), a self-assessment tool to help new teachers create their own ongoing professional growth.

Faculty

In 2001–02, there were about 88 full-time faculty in the College of Education. Of the 58 tenured and tenure-track faculty who teach in the initial teacher preparation programs, almost all hold doctoral degrees. About 25 percent of the full-time College of Education faculty are minority.

Although the numbers vary by semester, of the 198 part-time faculty in the fall of 2001, 19 percent were minority, and 36 percent were male. Nearly all part-time faculty are either currently employed in or recently retired from school districts. Part-time faculty in initial certification programs are selected for specific courses and field supervision. All are credentialed and have experience in the specialization in which they teach or supervise.

Data on Students

At baseline, CSUN did not compile data on student quality indicators, such as average GPA, SAT scores, etc.

Although we do not have specific data on the gender and ethnic makeup of the College of Education students, as an entire institution, CSUN is quite diverse. In the fall of 1998, 37 percent of students identified themselves as non-Hispanic white, 22 percent identified themselves as Hispanic, 14 percent as Asian, and 8 percent as non-Hispanic black.

CSUN has undertaken a number of initiatives to increase the diversity of its teacher education candidates, including strengthening ties with local community colleges; offering scholarships in ITEP; providing scholarships to candidates with Hispanic, Filipino, Armenian, or Southeast Asian backgrounds to prepare them for state certification; and offering exceptional admissions for up to 15 percent of the candidates in the MS/SS/ES programs.

Data on Graduates

In 2000–01, CSUN issued a total of 1,554 initial credentials. Overall, about half or more of the graduates receiving the MS or SS credential were non-Hispanic whites, as were about two-thirds of those receiving the ES credential. The percentage of minorities has increased over time. In the academic year 2000–01, 81 percent of the graduates were female and 19 percent were male.

CSUN has limited teacher test data for their graduates because in California, until recently, teacher candidates who successfully completed the elementary subject-matter portion of the Liberal Studies major (for MS credential) or the subject-matter option of the degree major (e.g. English, mathematics) did not have to take a pedagogy test. Further, students who received a Liberal Studies major (for MS credential) or a subject-matter credential (for SS credential) did not have to take Praxis–Multiple Subjects Assessment for Teachers (MSAT) or the appropriate Praxis–Single Subject Assessment for Teachers (SSAT) examinations. California's teacher testing requirements have changed since baseline. As of 2004–05, all candidates applying for a preliminary credential will be required to take a subject-matter test. Consequently, a baseline on the measures will not exist.

Candidates in the MS and ES credential programs are required to take a state-mandated exit exam, the Reading Instruction Competence Test (RICA). In 2001–02, of the 590 candidates who took the RICA, 582 passed (99 percent).

Evaluation Component

Evaluation of Students. CSUN uses multiple sources of data to evaluate students and graduates. These include admission interviews, admission essays, and academic transcripts; state-mandated tests; candidate performance in required courses, including performance on a basic computer skills test and performance in technology methods courses; candidate performance in field experience, as determined by the university and field supervisors; and candidate portfolios. Candidates are required to maintain a portfolio throughout the credential program, in which they collect portfolio artifacts and develop reflective statements for each portfolio entry. These are used to assess the candidate's proficiency in meeting the 13 Teaching Performance Expectations (TPE) and six California Standards for the Teaching Profession

(CSTP). Candidates for Special Education credentials must also meet the Early Childhood Special Education (ECSE) Standards.

Evaluation of Graduates. CSU conducted a systemwide evaluation of teacher preparation programs across all of its campuses in 2001. About 70 graduates of CSUN and 59 principals and supervisors of these graduates participated in this evaluation. Without exception, CSUN graduates were rated higher by their principals and supervisors than were graduates from other CSU campuses. However, CSUN graduates rated themselves lower than did other graduates in terms of subject-matter knowledge and communicating with parents, perhaps as a result of greater self-awareness or because they tend to work in more challenging school districts than other graduates.

Program Evaluation. Each college, as part of its university program review, has been asked to develop goals and objectives of learning, to examine whether these objectives are being met, and to develop a plan and assessment protocols to gather data on its students. Partly as a result of this effort and partly as a result of the revised NCATE standards, the College of Education formed a Performance Assessment Task Force with representatives from various colleges, P–12 district representatives, and community college representatives in July 2001. A new Unit Assessment Plan was finalized in August 2002.

Collaboration with Arts and Sciences Faculty: Selected Examples

- The development, implementation, and refinement of ITEP featured a great deal of ongoing collaboration between faculty in education and faculty in the arts and sciences. Arts and sciences and education faculty who teach in the program continue significant collaborations in creating team-taught or linked courses across subject-matter disciplines and education.
- Faculty from the English department work with education faculty in preparing students for the single subject credential in English. English faculty teach courses, advise students, and design curriculum for the FYI program in English.
- Faculty in the Geography department teach earth science courses for teacher education students, with a particular emphasis on applying the principles to K–12 students.
- The Anthropology department teaches courses in the teacher education program that address the role of culture and ethnicity in the classroom. The goal is to help the teacher candidates understand and appreciate the multicultural setting in which they will work.

Collaboration of University Faculty with K–12 Schools: Selected Examples

CSUN is active in its community and has had partnerships with the local school districts and other community organizations for several years. The College of Education has over 35 collaborative projects with the LAUSD and the university has many more. Included are three Gear-Up initiatives, two Academic Improvement and Achievement projects, the BTSA program, and partnership sites through ITEP, ACT, and the Professional Development centers, including one at the Polytechnic High School in LAUSD B, which is used for ACT candidates.

- In cooperation with LAUSD, CSUN will build a new high school on the CSUN campus. This high school is designated to become a teacher academy and will serve as a laboratory school for CSUN.
- The CHIME charter school is designed as a professional development school in collaboration with CSUN and LAUSD. CHIME is an all-inclusive K–8 school that serves children with various needs—typical children, deaf and hard of hearing children, children with physical disabilities, and children with a range of learning and emotional disabilities.
- The Collaborative Academic Program Initiative is designed to uncover deficiencies in English and mathematics content knowledge among high school students. To evaluate reading skills, students are given a reading assessment in the 11th grade. The findings are shared with university faculty and K–12 schools and teachers to help them improve instruction.
- K–12 teachers worked with CSUN faculty to develop the ITEP and FYI programs.
- CSUN has constituted an Induction Program Planning Committee that includes arts and sciences and education faculty to help develop a two-year SB 2042 Induction Program with several school districts that would comply with the new state requirements under SB 2042.

Design Proposal

As mentioned in the introduction, each institution developed a design proposal for Carnegie that outlined their plans for how TNE would be implemented. This section outlines the major activities that CSUN proposed in its design proposal. Obviously, these were plans and, as such, will undergo revision during the implementation process. However, they do provide a vision for how TNE will be implemented in the institution. We present the information in narrative form around major categories of activities—evidence teams, assessment, recruitment, program improvement, and induction—that CSUN planned to undertake to produce high-quality graduates who produce better pupil outcomes. We also present this information organized under the design principles in Table B.1.

Evidence Team. CSUN proposed to establish a system of continuous evaluation and refinement of the teacher education program based on current research and on evidence of program effectiveness in raising the performance of CSUN graduates and their K–12 pupils. An evidence team would lead faculty and administrators from the arts and sciences and education, along with partners from K–12 schools, in a review of existing literature and data on effective practices, methodological issues, and K–12 student achievement. The team would develop a set of criteria to systematically evaluate both internal and external evidence on an ongoing basis. A research base on effective practices would be developed based on the literature review, professional and state standards, and eventually on evidence of the effects of the program on graduates and their pupils.

CSUN planned to use the research base to develop a system for evaluating its teacher education programs based on evidence of best practice. The system would be institutionalized in policies, processes, and procedures to ensure that evidence serves as the basis for important program decisions including those concerning curriculum, budgeting, personnel hiring and evaluation, and program approval.

Table B.1
Major Proposed Activities, by Design Principle, California State University, Northridge

Design Principle A: Decisions driven by evidence	*Drawing on Research* • Conduct review of existing literature and data to assess alignment between best practices and CSUN programs. • Undertake a cost-effectiveness analysis of various pathways to credentials and degrees. • Develop criteria for evaluation of evidence on teacher and pupil performance, and technology-based assessment system for applicants, candidates, and graduates. • Use early TNE work to develop an institutionalized system for program evaluation based on evidence of best practice and K–12 achievement. • Establish a clearinghouse of information on best practice for faculty, students, and school partners. *The Role of Pupil Learning* • Align existing methods of determining teacher competency by both CSUN faculty and school districts with indicators of competency identified by research on best practices. • Develop a program for collecting and analyzing data from multiple measures that can be used to explore relationships between the teacher education program and teacher and student performance. • Establish a process for modifying the teacher education programs based on evidence of performance and implementation in partner schools. • Improve methods of training teacher candidates to collect and use data from multiple types of assessment effectively in their teaching.
Design Principle B: Engagement with the arts and sciences	*Subject-Matter Understanding* • Engage curricular bodies, particularly the Center for Excellence in Learning and Teaching (CELT), in discussing alternatives to the current system. • Design new gateway and capstone courses and assess their effectiveness. • Recruit and train arts and sciences faculty to supervise student teachers. • Hold a series of workshops addressing topics related to shared responsibility for teacher preparation for arts and sciences, education, and K–12 faculty. • Involve arts and sciences faculty in refining the curriculum and testing pedagogical innovations in the on-campus academy high school. • Review and develop policies on tenure and promotion to encourage all faculty to be involved in teacher education. *General and Liberal Education* • Strengthen articulation agreements with community colleges to ensure the quality of transfer students' general education. • Increase writing across the curriculum. • Strengthen the information literacy program, which provides an array of learning experiences to students, including instruction in online research.
Design Principle C: Teaching as an academically taught clinical practice profession	*Pedagogy* • Review research literature on effective pedagogy along with California's standards for teacher preparation. • Develop a faculty professional development plan designed to facilitate self-reflection and peer support and provide greater rewards to faculty for good teaching. • Conduct workshops and colloquia related to pedagogy, linked to the work of CELT. • Assess how best to evaluate candidates' and eventually graduates' mastery of pedagogy. *Schools as Clinics* • Develop a consortium of Schools for a New Era, featuring strong relations between K–12 and university faculty. • Identify and develop roles of K–12 and university faculty, including faculty liaisons, team teaching, common professional development, and incentives for collaboration. *Teachers on Faculty Appointment* • Expand and improve upon the teachers-in-residence (TIRs) program by creating new supports for the program. • Appoint some TIRs to the TNE fellows group. • Expand opportunities for arts and sciences and education faculty to work in K–12 schools. *Residency (Induction)* • Develop an induction program that includes conferencing and mentoring, observation and supervision, a peer support system, and a summer institute. • Create an electronic support system that includes grade-level and subject-

Table B.1—Continued

	specific chat rooms and message boards, a clearinghouse of teacher resources, and a video library. • Survey recent graduates to learn more about how induction can meet their needs. • Develop tools to assess the effectiveness of the induction activities. *Preparation of Candidates for Professional Growth* • Study and create a community of teacher scholars on campus. • Tailor professional development to help graduates learn how to adapt their teaching to new environments over time by conducting research on the effectiveness of their own practice.
Additional issues to be addressed jointly by faculties in education and in arts and sciences	*Pedagogical Content Knowledge* • Recruit and appoint faculty in science and mathematics education to act as liaisons with arts and sciences. • Appoint six teachers as TNE fellows in the arts and sciences to provide leadership on PCK in their disciplines. • Examine teacher education programs to make sure they integrate subject matter and pedagogy. • Use Beck Grants for classroom projects to build PCK. *Literacy and Numeracy Skills* • Design pilot sections of general education courses in mathematics and writing tailored for teacher candidates. • Develop a numeracy assessment instrument to be administered after the completion of 60 units of course work. • Institute an intervention program for teacher education candidates with inadequate writing or numeracy skills. *Elementary and Middle School Education* • Identify relevant evidence, evaluate current program, and work with design principle teams to address issue in larger work. *Technology* • Revise curricula to address teacher education candidates' mastery of using technology to support learning. • Develop additional online courses to enhance candidates' ability to learn online. • Develop assessment programs for pupil learning that can be supported technologically. • Develop technology-focused professional development courses for faculty teaching in teacher education programs. *Cultural Considerations in Teaching and Learning* • Identify relevant evidence, evaluate current program, and work with design principle teams to address issue in larger work. *Recruitment of Underrepresented Groups in Teaching* • Identify relevant evidence, evaluate current program, and work with design principle teams to address issue in larger work. *Late Deciders in an Undergraduate Program* • Add two-year programs in additional subjects for single-subject secondary teachers transferring to or entering at the junior level. • Engage community colleges in the design of the lower division portion of transfer programs. • Improve advising for transfers and late deciders.

Assessment. CSUN proposed to improve on existing systems used by CSUN faculty and K–12 partners to measure the competency and performance of teacher candidates and graduates. New formative and summative evaluations based on best practices would be developed and implemented, along with new assessments of pupil performance and achievement. The Achievement Council would serve as an important link to pupil learning data in the LAUSD. While value-added analysis of standardized test scores would be explored as an important source of pupil learning evidence, CSUN noted that multiple measures would be needed to assess teacher and pupil performance. An important part of the focus on assessment would be training teacher candidates and graduates to collect and use multiple sources of data on student learning to inform instructional strategies. Assessment data would also be used to conduct a cost-effectiveness study of the various pathways to credentials and degrees at CSUN. The study would focus on determining the most effective use of resources to prepare teachers who use best practices, evidence, and current research to improve K–12 student achievement.

Recruiting Teacher Education Candidates. CSUN noted that the majority of its teacher candidates come from area community colleges, and that the transition is often difficult for students. Within the first two years, CSUN planned to draft model articulation agreements with three community colleges that would align lower-division work in teacher preparation. A special campuswide committee, as well as faculty from each community college, would develop the agreements and present them for review and discussion. These plans would be used as the basis for discussions with the other primary "feeder" institutions.

CSUN recently developed a junior option for the four-year integrated teacher preparation program for elementary teacher candidates to accommodate late deciders and community college transfer students. Junior options are under development for candidates wishing to teach English or mathematics in middle or high schools. Programs in other subjects are to follow.

Program Improvements. State standards and evidence from research and literature would be used as the basis for reviewing and revising courses and curriculum. The first review would be led by the CELT and will engage various curricular bodies in an attempt to balance depth with breadth in courses and curriculum. The focus would be on developing lifelong skills for intellectual inquiry. As part of the new approach to curriculum, gateway and capstone courses would be developed and piloted for teacher education programs, beginning with the ITEP.

An important part of the TNE initiative at CSUN is an expansion of the role of arts and sciences faculty in the preparation of teachers. Arts and sciences faculty would first be provided with professional development activities to prepare them to work more closely with teacher candidates, interact with K–12 faculty, and understand research and assessment strategies. The increased role of arts and sciences faculty would include service as faculty supervisors of interns and work with K–12 faculty to track discipline-based knowledge into the K–12 curriculum and classroom activities. The new on-campus academy high school would facilitate these efforts. CSUN had begun a review of promotion and tenure policies and procedures to provide appropriate acknowledgement of faculty contributions to teacher preparation and K–12 education that fall under a broad view of scholarship. The system should honor collaboration for curriculum development, school reform efforts, field-based teaching and research, and service.

CSUN proposed to expand the recruitment and appointment of TIRs, allowing more current K–12 teachers and administrators to join the faculty. Roles and responsibilities would be clarified and support structures, such as the faculty mentoring program and the faculty orientation program, would be used to assure that TIRs are fully integrated into the university culture and work life. In addition, TIRs would be appointed to TNE task groups and would develop relationships with faculty from both the College of Education and the arts and sciences.

CSUN noted that TNE provides an opportunity to revitalize its program for improving the writing skills of teacher candidates. While there is a universitywide program in place, the teacher education faculty have recognized that transfer students in particular would benefit from additional help. CSUN proposed that the Center for Excellence in Learning and Teaching would assist faculty in incorporating development of writing skills into courses in general education, the disciplines, and the teacher preparation program.

Induction Program and Support. Teacher certification standards in California now include detailed requirements for a two-year induction program that must be completed by new teachers. CSUN planned to augment these induction programs and exceed state standards. While the induction program would capitalize on geographical proximity and strong relationships with the LAUSD, opportunities would also be provided to graduates working in other districts to connect through online networks, email, etc. A pilot program would be developed and tested by a committee of faculty from the College of Education and the arts and sciences, along with K–12 personnel. Services would likely include mentoring, observation, supervision, peer support, and summer institutes. Possible services could include teacher resources, a video library, and online discussions organized by grade and subject.

The next section describes the progress CSUN made over the first year in implementing the TNE initiative.

First Year Implementation

Project Structure and Staffing

Leadership. CSUN appointed the Vice Provost for Academic Affairs as the TNE project director. Early in 2003, the Dean of the College of Education and the Interim Dean of the College of Social and Behavioral Sciences—who were deeply involved in TNE—were appointed deputy project directors to help provide overall leadership to the project. Later they assumed co–associate project director roles.

CSUN also faced other leadership changes. The provost retired during the summer of 2003 and an interim provost was appointed. CSUN's president hopes to appoint a new provost by January 2004 and has reiterated her own commitment to TNE and her desire to look for a provost who would be equally committed to TNE.

In the spring, a full-time administrative support staff member was hired for the TNE project, to assist the project directors and the work of the steering committee.

A 14-member steering committee was established under the direction of the project director. The steering committee was made up of representatives from K–12 schools, the College of Education, and the various colleges of arts and sciences, and one member from the Achievement Council. Over the first five months (September 2002 to January 2003), the main task of the steering committee was to develop the Year One Work Plan.

CSUN created a coordinating council to serve as an advisory body to the TNE project. The council will monitor progress, facilitate success, and publicize achievements of the TNE project. The group met for the first time in August 2003.

Team Structure. CSUN decided to use a committee structure to implement the Year One Work Plan, linked to the design principles:

- Design Principle A Team: Decisions Driven by Evidence
- Design Principle B Team: Engagement with the Arts & Sciences
- Design Principle C Team: Teaching as an Academically Taught Clinical Practice.

These are often referred to as teams A, B, and C, respectively. The three committees, each chaired by one member of the steering committee, organized themselves into various work groups, each with its own focus and time line. Each group consisted of between five and twelve members, a mix of K–12, education, and arts and sciences faculty. The selection of work groups was done informally by the deans of the various colleges. They recommended faculty from their colleges for the various work groups based on four criteria: experience with teacher education, ability to deliver what was needed, level of influence within the department, and commitment to K–12 education and teacher education. The president went to each of the eight colleges and stressed the importance of TNE to the institution. Perhaps as a result, very few of those selected for the work groups declined; those who did decline primarily cited lack of time as the reason. A very few also indicated that they felt they were not placed in the right group. In total, 83 K–12 and college faculty participated in the various committees and work groups that implemented the CSUN work plan.

There were weekly meetings among the three directors lasting about two to three hours. They also met twice a month with the steering committee for three hours and held meetings with the chairs of the work groups monthly or more often as seemed appropriate. Most teams met weekly or biweekly for a couple of hours.

New Faculty. This past year CSUN advertised for six new tenure-track faculty positions paid for by TNE funds and designated as TNE fellows. These fellows were expected to teach in their disciplines while assisting in leading the efforts to integrate arts and sciences and education in teacher preparation. The appointments include half-time release from teaching for TNE work in the areas of curriculum redesign and review, assessment, faculty development, and school and college partnerships.

The advertised positions stressed direct experience in K–12 schools and/or demonstrated interest in pedagogy along with the more usual academic credentials and research. For example, the notice for the faculty position in History clearly stated that the department was seeking someone with "evidence of teaching excellence and strong research potential and with the ability and desire to apply their scholarship and teaching skills to teacher preparation" (faculty position opening notice provided by CSUN). As a way of getting buy-in from the arts and sciences departments and colleges, the departments had control over the area and specialization for which the TNE fellows were to be recruited and the selection process.

Departments had to apply to have one of these faculty lines assigned to them and to demonstrate that they had a vision of how the new hire would fit into the department and be integrated with the rest of the faculty and the work the new hire would undertake. TNE provides extra money for these fellows, the teaching they do is free labor to the department, thus providing an incentive to the departments to participate in the process. The provost and the TNE project director met with the departments to clarify the work that these new hires were expected to do, and to ensure that this would be counted toward tenure and promotion. For example, the new faculty are expected to make contributions to their field but this is more broadly defined to include journals of teaching and learning.

The six positions that were advertised were in the Biology, English, Geography, Geological Science, History, and Sociology departments.[2] Five TNE positions were filled in Year 1. Two positions were filled in History because the candidates were so strong, while no candidates were hired for Sociology because the candidate pool was weak. The candidate that was put forward by the Biology department had traditional academic credentials but lacked experience with K–12 schools or demonstrated interest in pedagogy. As a result, the position

---

[2] The university has authorized a search that will start this year for a TNE position in the Mathematics department.

was not filled. Three of the new hires come with K–12 teaching experience; one taught at a summer teaching institute; and another codirected a research project in a public school system.

The TNE fellows are being mentored by the Interim Dean of the College of Social and Behavioral Sciences (Geography and History fellows) and by the Vice Provost for Academic Affairs (English and Geological Sciences fellows). The TNE fellows meet as a cohort on a regular basis and met twice this past year. Another specialist in assessment is also included as part of the cohort.

Some concerns were expressed by department faculty about the TNE fellows: faculty members who are both strong in the traditional discipline and are also interested in education may be hard to find; second, what if these TNE fellows are hired and/or get tenure and then later find they are not interested in TNE work? In addition, there appeared to be some resentment about being forced to look for faculty members with interests in education rather than research in the traditional discipline areas.

New tenure track faculty in the College of Education were also hired to help with the implementation of TNE goals. These include two new faculty in research and assessment, one in instructional technology, one in science education, and one in math education.

In addition to these new faculty, CSUN implemented a TIR program in partnership with the LAUSD. Two teachers were appointed for the past academic year, one a special educator and the other from secondary English. On campus, their primary roles were serving on the Teachers for a New Era Steering Committee and assisting with partner schools. Additional roles for TIRs include teaching courses, serving on committees, supervising field experiences, and serving as a resource for CSUN faculty. There was some feeling on the part of faculty that perhaps more thought should have been given to roles and responsibilities of TIRs and to better integration of these TIRs into scholarly research or team teaching. Simple things like not having a clear code that identified these TIRs as new faculty led to some administrative glitches. On the whole, TIRs were made to feel that their voices and contributions were welcomed. They felt excited about working to bring about the large organizational changes.

An additional six TIRs are proposed for next year.

Budget
By far, the largest item in the CSUN's proposed budget for Year 1 was faculty compensation, including release time for key faculty on the design principle teams (approximately $150,000), stipends for 35–40 additional faculty to help implement the project ($150,000), and payments to K–12 faculty ($75,000). Other big-ticket items were related to data collection, including $75,000 to the Achievement Council for help with LAUSD data and other assistance and $75,000 for designing and creating a longitudinal database on student achievement and teacher performance with the help of CSUN's Office of Institutional Research. The budget also set aside $75,000 for the local site evaluation.

Managerial personnel (deans, associate deans, and chairs) did not receive reassigned time. Thus, the TNE work was added on top of their normal responsibilities. For example, the two deans who are the associate project directors estimated they spent about 50 percent of their time on TNE over and above their regular jobs as did the Associate Dean of Education, who was one of the steering committee members and also a cochair of one of the design principle committees.

The regular teaching load for faculty is 12 units per semester (generally four courses). Most faculty on nine-month appointments got 3–6 units of release time for TNE, although without exception, faculty estimated they spent considerably more time than this on their respective committees and work groups. Some college faculty and all K–12 faculty received stipends of $1,000.

The financial report to Carnegie shows that CSUN spent approximately half what was budgeted in the first year (through August 2003). As CSUN points out, this pattern of expenditure was somewhat atypical. The costs from September 2002 to January 2003 were largely stipends paid to steering committee members (CSUN faculty and K–12 partners). Most of the work groups did not begin work in earnest until February 2003. In addition, the late start meant that not all faculty that might be interested in working on TNE were available and the committees were perhaps smaller than they previously had envisaged. Only about one-third of the funds allocated for K–12 faculty were spent; none of the funds allotted for data collection were spent in Year 1. In addition, a large proportion of the funds allotted for travel, conferences, graduate assistants, and the administrative assistant remained unspent.

CSUN was able to establish a good working relationship with LAUSD to obtain student achievement data. As a result, the college plans to use the $75,000 allocated for the Achievement Council to hire an assistant project director in Year 2 and additional staff to help the Office of Institutional Research with data collection.

The remaining funds have been carried forward and the school anticipates that in subsequent years they will fully use the allocation as specified. CSUN 12-month employees, who—as mentioned earlier—are not eligible for financial reimbursement, did much of the initial work. CSUN is anxious to find ways in which these faculty can be reimbursed in the following years.

In its budget, the university listed cash and in-kind contributions of approximately $1.5 million:

- Cash contributions included 100 percent of the project director's time; $50,000 toward travel expenses; $35,000 for the purchase of books and materials; $250,000 for the endowment fund; funds from three existing grants amounting to about $640,000; and funds from the Eisner Foundation. As mentioned before, CSUN received a major gift from Michael Eisner. Part of the Eisner gift was used to start the Center for Teaching and Learning (CTL) within the College of Education, and establish an endowed chair. Some of the research that will be done under the aegis of the center will undoubtedly have relevance for the TNE work. In addition, some of the funds will be used to establish an assessment center to integrate all kinds of assessment efforts at the university, including the literacy center (in which children with difficulties in learning are assessed and helped); counseling center; family focus center; etc. The idea is to develop a comprehensive assessment center that will also serve TNE purposes of collecting data on the program, students, and graduates. In addition, the university created and furnished an office suite devoted to housing the TNE project.
- In-kind contributions included 15 percent of a dean's time and release time for faculty team members.

Implementation Progress

Because CSUN organized itself into teams around the design principles, we discuss the progress made by each of these teams separately. The end of this section discusses progress made on other fronts as well.

Design Principle A: Decisions Driven by Evidence. Team A had two central foci (CSUN Design Principle A Team, 2003, p. 1):

1. Developing and piloting an operational definition of excellent teaching which includes as central elements (a) K–12 pupil learning and (b) a developmental model of teachers as professionals

2. Developing an operational definition of K–12 pupil learning and designing a value-added assessment plan for piloting the definition and initial measures.

Team A divided itself into several work groups. One work group undertook a selective review of available literature to identify existing definitions and measures of excellent teaching and the stages teachers go through in their development. They made several visits ("learning walks") and clinical supervision visits to K–12 schools, during which they interviewed over 40 teachers and conducted interviews with six LAUSD supervisors. A second group was tasked with establishing milestones in teacher development and establishing indicators of progress. The group identified the following transition points: admission to professional preparation; entry to initial clinical practice; exit from initial clinical practice; entry into professional clinical apprenticeship and induction; and entry into professional clinical practice. A third group worked on mapping the pathways to credentialing to the transition points and identifying how knowledge, skills, and dispositions of teacher candidates were measured at each checkpoint in these various programs. Data for a sample of about 40 CSUN students were used to evaluate the feasibility of the checkpoint measures.

Yet another group was asked to use data to assess the CSUN pathways. They first worked on developing a detailed description of pathways to the teaching credential at CSUN and then examined what data existed on students in these various pathways. The idea is to eventually design a plan for conducting a cost benefit analysis (CBA) of primary pathways.

In the process of collecting data, the team realized that considerable work needed to be done to develop a database that could identify and track students longitudinally. They decided to work with the Office of Institutional Research on database development and to postpone thinking about the CBA until later when data were available. The director of the Office of Institutional Research has had substantial involvement with TNE. In Year 2, in recognition of the central role of data in the TNE project, she has been appointed a member of the steering committee to work with the professor who is leading the assessment and data effort. Currently, CSUN has a historical database going back to 1995 with Social Security numbers. These data are used for tracking and projecting enrollments and grade reports. Problems arise because the Admissions and Records (A&R) database is separate from both the institutional research (IR) database that tracks the progress of students and the credentialing database. The limitations of the CSUN's system first came to light when SRI, its local evaluator, asked for some data. In addition, the multiple pathways and the high rates at which students drop in and out of cohorts make a cohort approach difficult to implement. CSUN's hope is to develop an integrated database, which none of the CSU campuses has. This fits well with what it needs to do for accreditation purposes, which will now require the university to focus on assessment. It already administers alumni surveys as part of program review. These surveys have a set of standardized questions to which departments can add their own more targeted questions. To help with this work, CSUN is combining funds from various grants, including TNE, to hire more people for the office.

Another of the work groups of team A was tasked with developing an operational definition of pupil learning. They defined it as "a relatively permanent influence on behavior, knowledge, and thinking skills that comes through experience" (Santrock, 2004, p. 210) after an extensive review of the literature, consultations and interviews with teachers, and site visits to schools. This definition led them to establish several indicators that could measure pupil learning in these areas. For example, behavior can be measured through student attendance, time on task, task completion, graduation rates; knowledge through standardized tests and constructed writing assignments; thinking skills through several measures outlined by the Institute for Learning (2003), such as the ability to evaluate feedback from others, anticipating learning difficulties and assigning time accordingly, and self-evaluation of progress made toward a learning goal.

A major emphasis for some members of the team has been to understand and design a value-added assessment model for documenting the learning gains of pupils. They reviewed the literature and consulted with other TNE institutions and other experts on best practices and with the research team from the California State University Chancellor's Office. The team found the site visits and focus groups with teachers very helpful in understanding that teachers were overburdened and that it would be best not to add to the burdens by imposing new assessments on their students. Thus the team adopted the principle of "no further harm" and decided to leverage the current testing situation. The group decided to focus on grades 4–8 and on assessing pupil learning in mathematics and literacy. In collaboration with LAUSD, they have tentatively sketched out a design for a pilot to implement these models using data on 18 teachers teaching in three elementary and three middle schools that rank low, medium, and high on California's standardized Academic Performance Index (API) score. The design calls for collection of data on teacher preparation, student demographics and prior test scores, teacher professional socialization (participation in professional development activities, such as the beginning teacher support and assessment program and state sponsored continuous professional development), and pupil achievement measures. They sought the advice of content experts and K–12 data personnel on the feasibility of their design and measures. They recognize that other assessments will be needed in the future in addition to gains on standardized tests to provide a more robust picture of student learning, but, as of now, they are focusing on the current California test.

Design Principle B: Engagement with the Arts and Sciences. There are seven colleges at CSUN apart from the College of Education: Social and Behavioral Sciences; Humanities; Arts, Media, and Communication; Health and Human Development; Science and Mathematics; Business & Economics; Engineering and Computer Science. The first five are currently involved with the College of Education. The TNE co–associate project director, who is also the interim dean of the College of Social and Behavioral Sciences, spent a good deal of time getting buy-in and promoting TNE to the arts and sciences faculty. She spent time talking one-on-one with them and also holding faculty meetings at which she would show them how many teacher education students were in their classes. Her close working relationship with the Dean of the College of Education, who is the co–associate project director of TNE, helped show faculty that collaboration can work. The new Dean of Business and Economics is interested in meeting to discuss TNE and the hope is that some of the economics faculty might help with the cost-effectiveness analysis of the multiple pathways to the credential. The Mathematics department is split ideologically, with a small but vocal minority against involvement in teacher education. Interestingly, there has been some resistance to collaboration from the College of Education, with some faculty feeling that "outsiders" were telling them what to do.

This collaboration between arts and sciences and the College of Education is changing culture at various levels. For example, departments writing vision statements pointing out their relationship to teacher education represents a big culture change. Another example is the proposal submitted by team B to the Faculty Task Force on Roles and Rewards to expand the definition of "professional contribution" to include publications in leading teaching and education journals so that writing in these areas would count for promotion and tenure decisions.

One work group of team B reviewed literature on PCK in mathematics and social science and developed a working conceptualization of PCK[3] and good teaching that could be shared more broadly with the faculty. They collaborated with the CELT to offer presentations on PCK and discuss alternative models in curricula.

Another team identified models of teacher preparation curricula that integrate PCK, application of technology, writing competencies, attention to disciplines, and context for K–12 teaching. They developed a structured protocol for site visits to institutions to meet with faculty working on PCK. Faculty visited colleges in South Dakota and Colorado. (This is an ongoing process.)

Two task groups worked on the mathematics and science strands for the ITEP Multiple Subject credential program. Their goal was to come up with plans to infuse and assess PCK into the math and science courses in the ITEP program. For example, for the mathematics strand, they are changing curriculum, in-class activities, and textbooks and offering three different classes: the old course, the new course, and a hybrid of the old and new. The plan is to assess PCK of the students under the three regimes. The science task group will be conducting the same experiment.

Some of the faculty observed four elementary mathematics classes in culturally diverse settings to plan for the creation of a videotape library of effective instructional techniques.

One work group developed recommendations on how to establish communities of practice in which arts and sciences and education faculty will study PCK and how to infuse PCK into current course work. The following were some of their recommendations:

- Broaden the scope of the Beck grants that are offered for instructional improvement to include projects that focus on how to infuse PCK into course work; Beck grants offer a stipend and/or release time and grantees will be required to report to TNE work groups, particularly the assessment group.
- Start a TNE speaker series to offer colloquia for arts and sciences to engender interest
- Offer sessions during faculty retreats
- Start discussion groups consisting of education, arts and sciences, and K–12 faculty around PCK in a particular subject; the mathematics group has started one that meets twice a month and the history group is considering doing so.

---

[3] This was based largely on Ball (2003) and Schulman (1987).

- Begin examination of how arts and sciences faculty can best be integrated into pre-service clinical practice.

Others identified current gateway courses in mathematics and proposed modifications to them along with ideas about how to assess learning. They also gathered data on the Writing Proficiency Exam (WPE) that students take during the first semester of the junior year. The goal is to make recommendations regarding the timing of the exam and assistance that could be given to students having difficulty passing the exam. This process is ongoing. Some faculty looked at the entrance-level mathematics exam, a state-mandated mathematics test that establishes mathematics placements for students entering CSU campuses. Many students fail this test and are required to take remedial mathematics courses before entering credit-bearing college courses. CSUN is considering different options to recommend to the state, such as moving the test to 11th grade, so students do not forget mathematics in later years of high school. In the same vein, to assess the general education that many of CSUN's transfer students receive at community colleges, relationships with local community colleges were examined including current curriculum articulation agreements and transfer agreements.

An important first task was to develop recommendations for revision of promotion and tenure criteria. These are now under consideration by the Faculty Task Force on Roles and Rewards.

Team B ran out of time on some of the tasks that they had hoped to undertake, such as an examination of issues related to general and liberal education received by their teacher candidates. They also decided to approach the issue of revising curriculum somewhat more slowly to get buy-in from faculty.

Design Principle C: Teaching as an Academically Taught Clinical Practice Profession. Team C focused on defining effective pedagogy and examining such issues as how best to use schools as clinics and how to define an effective induction program. The first task was to conduct a literature review on the characteristics of effective pedagogy, schools as clinics, induction models, and professional growth. For pedagogy, they reviewed various kinds of pedagogical models and conducted focus groups of faculty, classroom teachers, and administrators. The goal is to come up with a working definition of effective pedagogy and assess current practices at CSUN in that light.

Another big emphasis during this first year was to examine the literature on induction programs so that they could better understand the components and design of effective programs and the resources both financial and other that would be needed to implement such a program. The work group asked various institutions about their programs and reviewed those from whom they received materials.

They met with a small group of graduates to ask about what types of support they found helpful during their first year of teaching. The short report summarizing the results emphasizes the following: good mentors can be very helpful and can act as an emotional safe haven; it is better if the mentors are in the same subject, same grade, and in close proximity to the beginning teacher; professional development that focused on practical, hands-on material was more useful than more theoretical-based courses; there is a real need for PCK; students would like a combined master's program that would fulfill induction requirements. This has led to conversations between, for example, Chicano Studies and the College of Education about how to create a joint master's program and how to provide for the needs of experienced teachers. A pilot induction program has been proposed that addresses new standards for induction.

CSUN is also considering piloting, in Year 2, an online help system, so teachers can email faculty with questions.

One of the real concerns with respect to induction is that TNE induction will be in addition to state-mandated district induction, which teachers, mentors, and the district are already involved in and in which participants will be required to engage in so that they can obtain their professional clear credential.

Team C drafted a description of the attributes and characteristics of schools as clinics based on a literature review of best practices, state and national standards, and other universities' programs. The team then developed criteria for teachers on faculty appointment and three K–12 teachers were appointed as TIR faculty in the College of Education.

The literature review on professional growth of teachers focused on components of professional development; how to implement and sustain learning communities; responsibilities of administrators; importance of site culture; and how to transform mentoring relationships into collegial ones. The work group defined induction as the first two years of teaching; postinduction as three to five years; beyond that, a continuum with doctoral programs and national board certification. The current Secondary Education English and Math M.A. programs have national board standards infused throughout the course work. CSUN is interested in developing support for elementary education teachers to become board certified.

In Year 2, team members are beginning to work on identifying clinical sites for professional development and communities of practice and inquiry groups that would involve both classroom and university faculty. They hope to work in three clinical sites, one each from districts A, B, and C, or three sites in one district that form a feeder pattern (elementary, middle, high school). One concern is that it will be hard for all teams to use the sites at the same pace. Another is that, to do this, CSUN needs to get buy-in from both the superintendent and the teachers union. The university will need to develop a memorandum of understanding with both to allow the teachers to participate fully in the clinical sites and to do the required extra work.

Because of state requirements and the implications for TNE, CSUN established a task force to develop a teaching performance assessment implementation plan.

Progress on Other Issues Identified in the TNE Prospectus. In addition to the activities described above, CSUN also made progress on the following two issues:

- **Late deciders:** The staff of the Liberal Studies/ITEP undergraduate teacher education program at CSUN continued discussions with the local community colleges whose students transfer to CSUN regarding articulation agreements that would ensure that the course work was equivalent and up to standard.
- **Technology:** CSUN revised its delivery approach to instructional technology learning to be in line with the new California teacher education standards.

Participants' Views on Year 1 Implementation

Comments from participants regarding their experiences and impressions during the first year of implementation offer some useful lessons learned. We grouped participants' views into the following:

Lack of Time and Problems with Scheduling. Because the TNE funds were received well after the start of the fall 2002 semester, the teaching schedules of many CSUN faculty were already set. Thus, they could not be provided with release time (they were given stipends as compensation). Given the heavy teaching load at CSUN, many faculty felt overburdened.

This was a particular problem for faculty who were close to tenure or promotion points. Many of them felt they had given too much time to the project at the cost of publications and other work that might carry greater weight in these decisions.

Three to six units of release time did not appear to be sufficient for the work that had to be done. Most faculty reported they worked many more hours on TNE than they had been allotted. It was even more burdensome on senior faculty who were on 12-month appointments and so not eligible for release time. The TNE work was simply added on top of their already heavy workload.

The incompatibility among the teaching schedules of arts and sciences faculty, College of Education faculty, and K–12 partners also led to many scheduling difficulties and logistical problems. Although each work group was able to compromise and arrange meetings at various times of days, evenings, and weekends, scheduling difficulties remain a matter of concern. As is usual with every group, some members of teams only attended sporadically, some worked harder than others, and often the burden fell heavily on a few members, largely education faculty (especially untenured faculty). Some K–12 members dropped out of the group; they found it difficult to get to meetings and were unsure of their roles. Some cochairs had very heavy schedules and often could not attend the meetings.

Collaboration Among Arts and Sciences, Education, and K–12 Faculty. Most faculty felt that the work was definitely worth the time and effort. It was a learning experience and faculty were committed to the project. The arts and sciences faculty, despite their lack of knowledge about education vocabulary and content, were full participants with lots of questions. The K–12 faculty were equally vocal for the most part. Most faculty on the various teams felt they "did intellectual work together," stepped outside the boundaries of their own discipline, and learned to see through different lenses. One respondent commented that the "work was interesting and the group worked well. There was lots of cross-disciplinary sharing; we melded as a community and the work influenced the ways we thought about teaching."

A small number of participants, however, reported that while in theory the idea of having groups from various departments and from K–12 schools is a good one, the fact that several group members knew nothing about education meant a steep learning curve for them. It sometimes took two to three months to work with these faculty members enough to get them to understand work products and language. This was very challenging and a lot of time was spent bringing people up to speed. Some faculty criticized the CSUN culture that requires buy-in from "everyone," calling it "our biggest strength and our biggest weakness." They felt that trying to get everyone involved often led to long and unproductive discussions and prevented the group from making timely decisions.

The proposal to expand the definition of professional contributions to include publications in teacher education journals and work on TNE is more likely to pass now that more arts and sciences faculty are behind it. The fact that the CSU system is also pushing to recognize the role of teacher education as central to the mission of CSU also helps.

The new collaborations with the CSU chancellor's office and LAUSD also seem to be energizing the group.

A few arts and sciences faculty reported that participation in TNE changed their teaching and gave them a new focus on PCK. They have incorporated more group work and board work and also have a greater recognition that struggle is part of the process of learning.

TNE helped develop a small nucleus of faculty in different departments (for example, mathematics, in which the chair is very supportive) with interest in and now knowledge about teacher education who can help get buy-in from others. Overall, participants reported a greater recognition on campus with many more faculty acknowledging the presence of TNE.

Lack of Integration and Coordination Across Teams. According to project leaders, both AED and the local evaluator noted that the three committees for the design principles duplicated effort and lacked coordination. At first, because this was a foundation year, it seemed rational to design it around principles. The three groups had the same ends but saw through different lenses. Unfortunately, the TNE structure in Year 1 divided work in an artificial way. There was no clear recognition that there was (or needed to be) considerable overlap across the work of the teams. The work ended up being stovepiped.

General Concerns About TNE. The prospectus was criticized as too broad ("leaves nothing out"), with a lot of uncertainty and developmental work. TNE has lots of tasks but the size and complexity of a large university make it difficult to carry these out.

One respondent felt that TNE has an exaggerated belief in the importance of evidence and the feasibility of actually showing that pupil learning is due to teachers being better trained, given that the environment is not controlled. Others said measures need to be broader. If pupil test scores do not increase, can we say that this was "bad" teaching?

Looking Forward to Year 2

As a result of CSUN's experience and feedback from others, the main focus of CSUN's work in Year 2 is integration across the project. To facilitate this, teams will be better integrated, steering committee members will work across teams, and more flexible groupings and resources will be put in place. CSUN is doing away with the permanent committee structure so faculty can work on tasks and teams for short periods of time.

A second focus is establishing partnerships that will be responsible for designing and implementing clinical models to promote best teaching practices that effect greatest pupil learning. One of the main tasks is to select the clinical sites and obtain district, principal, and teacher cooperation.

A third change that has been implemented, as a result of CSUN's experience in Year1, is that all probationary faculty will be compensated through reassigned time rather than stipends. This will help alleviate some of the workload issues these faculty members face.

Effect of State Policy Context

Budget

The state fiscal crisis has not had an effect on the TNE project at CSUN. CSU campuses are funded entirely on a full-time equivalent (FTE) basis. CSUN is currently funded for 22,000 students but is teaching over 24,000. To deal with this situation, they will likely increase class sizes. CSUN, like the other CSU campuses, faces mandated nonfunded costs, such as risk insurance and conversion to new technology. Last year, CSUN had a 5 percent decrease in its budget and for 2003–04 the decrease will likely be 6–7 percent. However, CSUN has had the largest growth among all the CSU campuses for the last two to three years, helping to cushion the school from the cuts in the budget.

The university still plans to put approximately $200,000 into an endowment fund each year for five years, actually placing $250,000 into the fund the first year. The College of Education has raised an additional $800,000 that could be counted as matching funds, not including the major gift from the Eisner Foundation.

Policy

As discussed in Appendix E, there are many changes under way in California with respect to teacher certification and licensure. Respondents expressed concern about the new testing and induction requirements and changes in the legislation that will require changes in already approved teacher education programs.

Testing. The new testing requirements under NCLB are a matter of concern for CSUN faculty. NCLB requires that teachers show subject-matter competency on tests rather than by just graduating from an approved teacher education program, as was previously the case in California. Currently, the state is determining how best to fit the exam requirement into the credentialing process. CSUN believes that the new testing requirements may affect the demand for its subject-matter programs because teachers might choose to take the test without going through a subject-matter program. This concern is compounded by the suspicion that the new state test, the California Subject Examination for Teachers (CSET), is not as rigorous as the previously required test. The passing rates on the previous tests (required of candidates who did not go through an approved program) were quite low—less than 20 percent—while early pass rates on the CSET have been substantially higher ranging, from 45 to 60 percent.

In addition, CSUN must contend with the fact that some students already in the program and some recent graduates may be required to take the test as well, which will likely cause consternation among that group.

Additionally, the timing of the new CSET test for the multiple subject credential is an issue. The state believes it should be a requirement for student teaching; CSU is trying to determine whether it should be a precondition for entry into teacher education. The test incorporates some items on pedagogy, which argues that it would be better if students took the test before student teaching and after some courses on pedagogy. However, some wonder what will happen to students if they do not later pass the test.

Currently, the state also requires students to be assessed on the TPEs and Teaching Performance Assessment (TPA). TPEs are infused throughout the preservice program and students must pass the TPA at the end of the program before being recommended for the credential. As a result, CSUN spent a great deal of time ensuring that its teacher education programs aligned with the TPEs and TPA. However, the role of the TPA is unclear at this point. Although the TPA is in pilot testing and the original time line called for all teacher education programs to develop an implementation plan by June 2003, funding for implementing the TPA has not yet been received. Therefore, a moratorium was placed on the submission of a TPA implementation plan.

New Induction Requirements. The state now requires that teachers either go through an induction program or complete a fifth-year program to obtain a professional clear credential. CSUN will need to position its TNE induction activities within this context and new teachers who are already overburdened may not feel they have time to participate in the new TNE induction on top of the district induction. Faculty also noted a few general concerns about the new requirements:

- The new standards are burdensome and overly detailed so that it is hard to fit content into the framework, especially for the joint master's programs.
- The district is now responsible for recommending teachers for the clear credential and there is some concern about its ability to document and judge whether teachers have met standards.
- Faculty raised questions regarding the quality of mentors and how they will be supported and trained.
- Districts offer free courses and workshops to meet the induction requirements while teachers must pay to take fifth-year courses at the university.
- Due to state budget constraints, state funding for the mandated induction is in doubt.

Limitations on Number of Credits for Teacher Education. The proposed new legislation SB81 seeks to limit the number of credits for teacher education; as a result, previously approved ITEP programs require too many credits and will have to be redesigned. The CSU faculty across the campuses are working on the length of the integrated program and making suggestions to the state.

Michigan State University: Profile at Baseline and Year 1 Implementation

Overview of the Teacher Education Program at Baseline

General Description of Programs

Michigan State University's teacher education program is delivered through the College of Education and the six other colleges that offer the disciplinary majors available for teacher certification. The primary program offered by the Department of Teacher Education is a five-year route to a bachelor's degree and a Michigan teaching certificate. The Department of Teacher Education also offers an 18-month certification program for postbaccalaureate applicants.

The Department of Teacher Education offers the elementary education major and also provides the five core undergraduate teacher education courses for students in other teacher education majors. MSU offers endorsements in two areas of special education: learning disabilities and deaf education. Candidates for elementary or special education credentials complete a planned program plus an integrated teaching major drawn from courses across colleges or two teaching minors or a major in an academic discipline. Candidates enrolled in the integrated teaching major concentrate in either language arts, general science, or social studies. Candidates for secondary education credentials complete a major and minor in academic disciplines. All teacher education candidates must complete their bachelor's degrees and pass the Michigan Test of Teacher Competency in their subject area(s) as a prerequisite for entrance to the year-long internship, upon successful completion of which they are recommended for state certification.

Just prior to TNE, MSU undertook a major restructuring of its elementary education program due to concerns that the preexisting requirements for a complementary studies block of courses plus two disciplinary minors (for those majoring in education) or one disciplinary major (for those majoring in that discipline) had not provided sufficient depth, as well as breadth, to serve the needs of elementary teachers. MSU believes the planned program for elementary education (effective 2002), provides a stronger and more common foundation in core subject-matter understanding. In addition, a set of integrated teaching majors (language arts, general science, social studies) have been developed and constitute the majors in which most elementary education candidates now enroll.

Formal admission to the teacher education program is necessary for all majors. To be admitted, applicants must reach junior status (56 credit hours of course work) by the end of the summer session. To be eligible for consideration, an MSU student must have a GPA of 2.5, have passed all three components of Michigan's Basic Skills Test for prospective teachers, and meet basic skills requirements in mathematics and writing. Applicants are also required to write an essay in a proctored setting as part of their application packet. Essays are weighted 40 percent and the applicant's overall GPA is weighted 60 percent. Total scores are ranked within each certificate area (i.e., elementary, secondary history, secondary English, secondary biology, etc.). Ranked lists are distributed to the colleges of the majors. Each college then selects the number of students within the quota assigned to the college by MSU's Teacher Education Council, which reviews decisions about how many students will be admitted to each of the majors. The College of Education retains 10 percent of the overall quota to add candidates who will help diversify the teaching population. Students from the Honors College who meet the minimum application criteria are guaranteed admission to the program.

Postbaccalaureate applicants may apply throughout the year. However, they must have overall scores (essays and GPA) that meet or exceed the mean score of the most recent pool of admitted undergraduates.

Clinical Component

MSU's teacher education program incorporates K–12 classroom experiences throughout the curriculum. Field experience begins in the preeducation courses on diversity and multiculturalism with a 25-hour service-learning project. For all students, the junior year education course includes 25 hours of observation and practical activities in K–12 schools. In their senior year, candidates spend about four hours each week working in schools, often in pairs or groups, building toward small-scale practice teaching of individual lessons and eventually small units. Students generally complete approximately 175 hours of field experiences before they begin their student teaching internship.

MSU students fulfill their student teaching requirements through a yearlong internship beginning with the K–12 placement school's academic year and ending with MSU's academic year early in May. During that time, candidates average about 24 hours per week in their schools, with alternating periods of extensive field involvement and lighter loads in their course work. This model brings the total hours spent in fieldwork to 900.

MSU's two major placement areas are the Lansing region and Southeast Michigan; smaller numbers of students are placed in Flint, Grand Rapids, and Jackson. In all these placement areas, MSU tries to accommodate all interns who request placements in urban schools and to recruit other interns to join them.

In an elementary school or a close pair of elementary schools, MSU typically places six interns together with their quarter-time field instructor (called "school liaison" in some teams). This concentration allows the interns and collaborating teachers to form a group of colleagues who share experiences and allows the field instructor to know and be known in the school. Because of the range of subjects and numbers of interns in them, secondary interns tend to be somewhat more dispersed.

Field experiences are coordinated by teacher preparation teams that combine partner schools, their teachers, a set of MSU course and field instructors, and a set of teacher candidates with whom they all work. Each team has a senior faculty leader and a coordinating staff that supports field instructors, visits schools and teachers, arranges early field experience and internship placements, arranges cooperation between mentor teachers and MSU course instructors, and monitors teacher candidates' progress. The coordinating staff work closely with school principals and with teachers who serve as liaisons between their schools and the campus. Feedback is systematically elicited from field instructors and shared regularly with interns. For both elementary and secondary candidates, there are regular conferences with the collaborating teacher and field instructor.

MSU did not have a formal induction program at the baseline.

Faculty

The regular faculty of the Department of Teacher Education and other selected faculty from the College of Education who participate in the education of the prospective teachers includes 44 tenure-track professors. Other participants in teacher education include 372 arts and sciences faculty, 101 adjunct faculty, and 94 graduate assistants. A considerable number of fixed-term teaching assignments are held by practicing teachers, former teachers, and graduate assistants. The two former categories are involved in the field experience components of the program, while most of the graduate assistants serve as instructors. MSU notes that this is consistent with the clinical model employed by Holmes Partnership programs and with the nature of a research-based program.

All the regular teacher education faculty hold doctorate degrees and work full-time; 91 percent are tenured, and 9 percent are in tenure-track positions. About 90 percent have previous experience as K–12 teachers.

Data on Students

In fall 2001, the College of Education received 548 applications for the elementary education program and 436 for the secondary education program. Sixty-one percent of applicants were admitted to the elementary education program, and 72 percent were admitted into the secondary education program. Approximately 95 percent of those admitted entered the program. The accepted class typically includes approximately 600 MSU juniors and transfer students and 50 postbaccalaureate candidates.

All categories of students entering the teacher education program had GPAs above 3.0 and ACT scores above 22. Students entering the secondary education program had slightly higher GPAs and ACT scores than their elementary education counterparts.

Less than 10 percent of students entering the teacher education program between 2000 and 2002 were minorities. The proportion of minorities in the teacher education program is somewhat lower than that of the entire university, which is 9 percent non-Hispanic black; 5 percent Asian; and 3 percent Hispanic.

Data on Graduates

MSU prepares approximately 550–600 teachers a year. In 2001, 591 students were recommended for certification, including 149 men, who accounted for 40 percent of program completers in secondary education and 14 percent of program completers in elementary education.

MSU's Teacher Education department faculty estimate that about half their graduates teach in Michigan and about half move out of state. Faculty members noted that their graduates are highly recruited by districts and because urban school districts tend to be slow in making hiring decisions, many MSU graduates tend to teach in other types of districts.

Evaluation Component

Evaluation of Students. MSU used Michigan's teacher standards as the basis for its own standards for its teacher education candidates. Currently, course instructors evaluate students using their own criteria. Teacher education faculty also formally evaluate seniors twice a year.

MSU uses a set of published criteria to determine eligibility for advancement to the fifth-year internship; elements include passage of external testing, academic requirements, and professional criteria. In fall 2001, 93 percent of MSU's elementary education candidates and 99 percent of MSU's secondary education candidates passed all required portions of the Michigan Tests for Teacher Certification and were able to begin their internships. During the internship, candidates meet regularly with their field instructors and collaborating teachers to receive formative and summative evaluations. Interns are evaluated on standards that cover candidates' knowledge of subject matter and how to teach subject matter; and ability to work with students, create learning communities, and work as a professional. Regular meetings of field instructors and workshops for field instructors and collaborating teachers aim to ensure that evaluation standards are applied consistently. Most interns also prepare professional portfolios that are presented in mock job interviews and at end-of-year convocations.

Evaluation of Graduates. In 1999 and 2000, MSU recommended 1,056 candidates to the state for teacher certification. All these graduates were surveyed by the College of Education and approximately 50 percent responded. Through this survey, the College of Education found that in the first year out of the program, 92 percent of responding graduates were employed full time as teachers and 5 percent were employed part time or as substitute teachers. About 76 percent were employed in the position they most wanted and three-quarters had only applied for jobs in Michigan.

Over 80 percent of both cohorts reported feeling well prepared for their teaching positions. Areas in which the graduates reported that they had been particularly well prepared by the program included: effective communication skills, respect for different points of view, ability to work effectively with peers as a member of a community of learners, and commitment to lifelong learning. Respondents were very positive about the internship experience.

Graduates reported feeling less well prepared to help students access and use information technology; to incorporate technology into classroom practice; to understand issues related to the legal and ethical dimensions of teaching; to use community and home resources to enhance school programs; and to teach in urban settings. Graduates also felt that advising by MSU faculty was a weakness of the program.

In a survey of superintendents from school districts throughout Michigan, as well as several out-of-state districts, the College of Education found that superintendents identified the reputation of the MSU program, past success with MSU alumni, MSU graduates' substantive content knowledge, and MSU's full-year internship as particularly attractive factors in hiring decisions. Eighty-five percent reported that first-year MSU graduates were performing more than adequately, while 69 percent felt that MSU graduates were outstanding or better than average in comparison to teachers prepared at other schools.

Program Evaluation. One of the parallel program evaluation efforts under way at MSU is the Delta Project. As mentioned earlier, the Delta Project is an initiative launched by the Carnegie Foundation for the Advancement of Teaching. The aim of this project is to bring together several universities to develop a set of assessment tools in various subjects, for both teacher education and arts and sciences, that will help teacher preparation programs assess the learning growth of their students and will provide a diagnostic toolkit that can serve to assess both programs and students.

MSU has a long history of conducting high-quality education research and using insights from that research to revise its teacher preparation program. Since 1976, MSU has conducted this research under a series of major grants through its Institute for Research on Teaching, the Center for the Teaching and Learning of Elementary Subjects, the National Center for Research on Teacher Education (NCRTE), National Center for Research on Teacher Learning (NCRTL), and the Center for Improvement in Early Reading Achievement.

Recently, work of the NCRTL—the successor of the NCRTE—influenced the redesign of teacher preparation at MSU. Specific work of the NCRTL includes study of

- preparation for teachers to work with diverse learners, particularly those historically underserved by schools
- interactions between prospective teachers' entering beliefs and opportunities to learn about ambitious teaching
- mentoring
- contribution of arts and sciences courses to the preparation of teachers
- the ways teacher educators understand their role, purposes, and practice.

The findings from these research efforts have led to changes in the course work of the teacher education program. For example, rather than teaching multicultural education in separate courses, the overall program tries to help students develop a clear sense of their own ethnic and cultural identities and examine their attitudes toward other groups throughout their course work.

Collaboration with Arts and Sciences Faculty: Selected Examples

- The Division of Science and Mathematics Education (DSME), jointly administered by the colleges of Natural Science and Education, seeks to "improve science and mathematics education, from kindergarten through the undergraduate years, through the professional development of preservice and in-service teachers and faculty members." DSME is supported by the university and the Towsley Foundation, with funding for projects from other federal and private sources. Faculty from the colleges of Education and Natural Science are active participants in the DSME, and the director has a joint appointment in the departments of Mathematics and Teacher Education. Joint searches for new faculty in mathematics and science education are conducted through the DSME.
- The Center for the Scholarship of Teaching, created by the College of Education, seeks to find ways to support a community of scholars who want to study teaching practice and student learning. Four purposes are central to its mission: providing insight into how to improve teaching in the broader MSU community, establishing rigorous and alternative means for faculty review and promotion, creating more cross-college communication, and contributing to the national discourse concerning the scholarship of teaching.
- Arts and sciences faculty participate on the Teacher Education Council, in which they discuss curriculum and policy changes.
- The Integrated Teaching Major in Social Studies, housed in the College of Social Science, is one of the largest majors in that college.
- The Department of Mathematics includes six faculty whose academic specializations are in mathematics education. This group has collaborated on teaching, research, and development projects with College of Education faculty for many years.

Collaboration of University Faculty with K–12 Schools

College of Education faculty are involved directly in K–12 schools. Some faculty members are given leave from the university to spend time in the schools as teachers and researchers. For example, both Deborah Ball and Daniel Chazan, former MSU faculty members, spent a year in K–12 schools and wrote books about the experience.

Arts and sciences faculty also have considerable interaction with the public schools. Below are listed a few examples of such collaborative efforts.

- Faculty in mathematics operate the Connected Mathematics Project, a nationwide reform of the middle school mathematics curriculum.
- The College of Arts and Letters works with teachers of foreign language across the nation through the Center for Language Education and Research.
- H-NET (Humanities and Social Sciences Online) provides access to national and international resources in the humanities and social sciences that can be utilized in school classes.
- Kids Learning in Computer Klubhouses (KLICK) is an innovative after-school program that works with students in rural and urban middle schools. MSU has already established clubhouses in nine schools, and plans to expand to 11 more. KLICK students learn to use technology and become important resources for their schools and communities.
- The Center for the Improvement of Early Reading Achievement (CIERA) is a collaborative center of MSU and the University of Michigan. Its mission is to present research-based solutions to persistent problems in the teaching and learning of early reading both to the teaching profession and to the public. To date the center has issued more than 30 reports. Partners in CIERA include teachers, reading specialists, teacher educators, parents, leaders in professional organizations, and educational publishers of reading materials and assessments.

Design Proposal

As mentioned in the introduction, each institution developed a design proposal for Carnegie that outlined their plans for how TNE would be implemented. This section outlines the major activities that MSU presented in its design proposal. Obviously, these were plans and, as such, will undergo revision during the implementation process. However, they do provide an idea and vision for how TNE will be implemented in the institution. We present the information in narrative form around major categories of activities—development and thematic groups, assessment, recruiting, program improvement, and induction—that MSU planned to undertake to produce high-quality graduates who produce better pupil outcomes. We also present this information organized under the design principles in Table C.1.

Development and Thematic Groups. MSU adopted the theme of "making content and context central" as the guiding force for a fundamental review and revision of teacher education under TNE. MSU proposed to form seven groups made up of faculty from the arts and sciences, education, and K–12 schools to conduct TNE activities. Faculty from arts and sciences and education would colead the teams. Four groups would concentrate on subject areas: mathematics, literacy and English, social studies, and science. The other groups would work on the themes of assessment, induction, and teachers for urban schools.

Table C.1
Major Proposed Activities, by Design Principle, Michigan State University

Design Principle A: Decisions driven by evidence	*Drawing on Research* • Develop TKS for what candidates should know and be able to do in the areas of subject matter, assessment, and pedagogy based on review of state and national standards, research, and current preparation in the MSU program. • Train faculty and K–12 partners to use existing and newly developed assessments to evaluate teacher education candidates as they progress through the different parts of the program, including content courses, education courses, and clinical and induction settings. • Make teacher education program improvements based on assessment of teacher candidates and on the relationship between candidates' knowledge and pupil achievement. • Train teacher candidates in the effective use of classroom and accountability assessments to guide instruction. *Role of Pupil Learning* • Explore value-added modeling and other methods to measure pupil learning gains and links to teacher and program characteristics. • Conduct a set of evaluation studies to examine the relationship between teacher knowledge and pupil learning.
Design Principle B: Engagement with the arts and sciences	*Subject-Matter Understanding* • Ensure that teacher preparation programs based on the TKS adequately address teacher candidates' knowledge of subject matter developed in academic majors, subject matter for teaching school subjects, and PCK. • Involve arts and sciences faculty in all areas of TNE work, including development of TKS and assessments aligned with the standards, design of clinical experiences and induction, and revisions of courses, curriculum, and programs. • Use cross-university seminars and a Council of Centers to involve all interested university faculty in learning about the process of reforming the teacher education program. *General and Liberal Education* • Evaluate the degree to which the current general education requirements in literacy, numeracy, and other areas of the liberal arts and sciences comport with the knowledge standards, especially for teachers who will serve in generalist positions in elementary schools, and work through academic governance to promote appropriate changes.
Design Principle C: Teaching as an academically taught clinical practice profession	*Pedagogy* • Examine pedagogy-related courses and experiences as part of program redesign. • Design curriculum components to help teachers learn about their students' communities. *Schools as Clinics* • Redesign the teacher education program to allow for the joint participation of K–12 faculty, arts and sciences faculty, and teacher education faculty in the planning and supervision of field experiences and courses in education and the arts and sciences. *Teachers on Faculty Appointment* • Establish formal roles for K–12 faculty in TNE activities. *Residency (Induction)* • Explore options for two-year induction programs, including new master's degree programs, joint programs with school districts, and technology-based induction activities. • Include mentoring that is subject-specific and assists new teachers in using appropriate assessments, analyzing their practice, and modifying teaching. *Preparation of Candidates for Professional Growth* • Connect students to professional networks and societies and technological resources, especially in subject-matter areas. • Develop curriculum and instruments to help candidates and graduates continually adjust their teaching practice in light of results from the assessment tools they use.
Additional issues to be addressed jointly by faculties in education and in arts and sciences	*Pedagogical Content Knowledge* • Ensure that teacher preparation programs based on the TKS adequately address teacher candidates' knowledge of subject matter developed in academic majors, subject matter for teaching school subjects, and closely related PCK. *Literacy and Numeracy Skills* • Address literacy and numeracy issues as part of the development of the TKS and the redesign of general education requirements and integrative studies courses.

Table C.1—Continued

Elementary and Middle School Education
- Prepare elementary and middle school teachers to be subject-matter specialists with integrative majors offered jointly by the appropriate disciplinary departments and the College of Education

Technology
- Develop new TKS that will address what teachers need to know about technology as a tool to support the learning of subject matter in reading and writing, mathematics, social studies, and science.
- Build on the extensive technology infrastructure already in place to ensure that teacher candidates are prepared to meet technology standards.

Cultural Considerations in Teaching and Learning
- Encourage faculty in K–12 schools and across colleges to draw on relevant literature and experiences to incorporate cultural considerations in teaching and learning into teacher preparation.

Recruitment of Underrepresented Groups in Teaching
- Increase efforts to recruit and support members of underrepresented groups as part of the related effort to prepare teachers for urban schools.
- Recruit urban community members (e.g. parents, substitute teachers, paraprofessionals) into an alternative certification program developed especially for these individuals.

Late Deciders in an Undergraduate Program
- Institute procedures to provide potential late deciders with advisors from both education and arts and sciences.
- Institute a pilot program for juniors with strong mathematics or science preparation.

The subject area groups would review the existing content preparation in education courses, arts and sciences courses, and in clinical experiences. They would also examine state and national standards for content knowledge for teachers and review research on content knowledge and assessments. Based on these resources, the groups would develop teacher knowledge standards (TKS) that would guide program improvements.

MSU proposed to hold cross-university seminars to help connect the TNE initiative to the broader range of activities at MSU and move teacher education to the center of the institutional agenda. The seminars would involve MSU faculty, administrators, staff, and K–12 personnel. MSU also would create a Council of Centers to connect the various MSU centers relevant to teacher education to the TNE initiative. The council would coordinate the activities of the centers with TNE for the benefit of TNE efforts and the work being done in the centers.

Assessment. MSU believes that the work of implementing TNE must be supported by the development and use of valid and reliable assessment tools. These tools would be part of a system that makes use of assessment data in three important ways. University and K–12 faculty would use assessment tools to measure teacher candidates' knowledge as they progress through the program and induction activities. Teacher candidates would learn to use a variety of assessment tools effectively. And finally, evaluation and revision of the teacher education program would be based on assessment of teachers' knowledge and the achievement of their K–12 pupils.

The Assessment team would gather and evaluate existing assessment tools, such as the Praxis assessments, Interstate New Teacher Assessment and Support Consortium (INTASC) tests, and portfolios that could measure teacher candidates' knowledge as they move through the program and induction. When needed, new assessment methods would be developed. These efforts would be coordinated with work already under way as part of the Carnegie Foundation Delta Project. MSU noted that relating teacher knowledge to pupil learning will be a major challenge for the Assessment team. The team planned to review current and emerging student achievement data systems in Michigan and explore value-added and other methodologies that might link programs, teacher knowledge, and pupil outcomes. A set of studies would be initiated to evaluate the relationship between teacher knowledge and pupil learning.

Recruiting Teacher Education Candidates. MSU intended to increase recruitment of candidates from underrepresented groups as a complement to a new program focus on urban teachers. Based on a review of current policies at MSU and other universities, recruitment programs would be improved. Supports for candidates from underrepresented groups and candidates interested in urban teaching would be increased and would include expanded internship programs and increased guidance and support from faculty. MSU also proposed to initiate efforts to recruit paraprofessionals and others already working in urban schools as a source of new students likely to teach in urban schools.

Currently, most students apply for admission to the teacher education program in their sophomore year. MSU proposed to institute procedures to make it easier for late deciders to enter the program. Faculty from education and arts and sciences would jointly advise these students and customize programs to meet individual needs and experiences. For example, a small pilot program would recruit strong science and mathematics students into customized teacher preparation programs.

Program Improvements. The new TKS developed by the subject area groups would be formalized and applied to all phases of teacher preparation. The array of tools provided by the Assessment team to measure candidate progress in meeting these standards would be integrated into education and arts and sciences courses. In addition, teacher candidates would receive increased training in how to effectively use assessment as a guide to instruction.

MSU would use the standards and evidence generated by the TNE work groups as the basis for creating new courses and revising existing courses in education and arts and sciences in terms of both substance and pedagogy. Field experiences, likewise, would be revised to align with evidence and standards.

The Urban Teachers team would coordinate with subject-matter teams, the Induction team, and K–12 schools to increase MSU's capacity to prepare teachers to work in urban schools. Partnerships with urban districts and schools would be strengthened, resources would be developed to support teaching in urban settings, and a specialization in urban teaching would be offered.

Induction Program and Support. MSU proposed to develop an induction program that would provide support for teacher education graduates through their first two years of teaching. First steps would include a review of best practices and research. MSU also planned to review data from recent MSU graduates about assistance and support they would find useful. The program would be expected to blend several components and resources. Mentors, who would play a key role, would be trained. Teachers would be linked through Web technology and would have access to such resources as a video library of exemplary lessons aligned with standards. Supports would focus on urban teaching and issues related to diverse learners. MSU also could link its induction activities to a master's program option.

Michigan State University combined progress in implementing its work plan in the first year with considerable success in raising matching funds for the TNE project.

First Year Implementation

Project Structure and Staffing

Leadership. The leadership team for MSU's TNE initiative consists of the Assistant Provost for Undergraduate Education and Academic Services, who serves as the project manager, and two coprincipal investigators: the Director of Research in the College of Education and the Associate Dean for Science and Mathematics Education in the College of Natural Science, who holds a joint appointment in mathematics and teacher education. MSU believed that the project required three experienced, senior project leaders because of its size and complexity.

In addition to the overall responsibility for the project, the project director manages all data requests from MSU's TNE teams; because of her long experience in the provost's office, she knows what data are available and can help refine questions and analyses. She also is working with the State Department of Education to secure access to a Michigan Department of Education (MDE) database that will track the locations of all Michigan public school teachers over time.

The coprincipal investigator from the College of Education has the primary responsibility for representing and ensuring effective involvement within the college. He also oversees all issues of budget, personnel, and evaluation. The other coprincipal investigator represents the colleges of Natural Science, Arts and Letters, and Social Science and is responsible for ensuring that arts and sciences faculty are involved with TNE and for ongoing communication with the different colleges.

Oversight of the TNE teams (described below) is divided among the three leads, and they meet weekly for a couple of hours to discuss progress. The leadership meetings now include the new chair of the Department of Teacher Education.

MSU formed a Coordinating Council that is headed by the provost and includes—in addition to the deans of the various colleges at MSU—the Michigan Superintendent of Public Instruction, the head of the school principals association, representatives from the teachers unions, the head of the middle schools initiative, representatives from business, the Dean of Wayne State University, and the superintendent of the Lansing school district. MSU hopes that the council will disseminate TNE information and provide members information about potential changes in state policy directions that would affect the TNE efforts. At the first meeting, a couple of the teams provided the council with a general overview and updates and members were invited to connect to teams in which they had a particular interest. The council decided it wanted to meet two to three times a year and asked to be provided read-aheads prior to the meeting. MSU pays travel and other expenses for the council members but no honorarium.

In addition to being a member of the Coordinating Council, the Dean of the College of Education meets with TNE leadership every couple of weeks and tracks TNE's progress and ensures that TNE is consistent with the College of Education's other activities. The dean meets with other deans formally at least once a month and more often informally, particularly with the College of Natural Sciences because it is so involved in mathematics and science education. The deans also are responsible for raising other money to support TNE, creating another link across the colleges.

Team Structure. As discussed earlier, the overarching theme of MSU's design proposal is "making content and context central." To do this, MSU established seven teams organized thematically rather than by design principle. There are four subject-matter development teams, K–12 Mathematics, K–12 Literacy and English, K–8 Social Studies, and 7–12 Science, and three cross-cutting teams, Assessment, Induction, and Urban Teachers. The subject-matter development teams are charged with benchmarking MSU's programs to state and national standards, developing a new teacher knowledge standards for what MSU-educated teachers should know and be able to do, collecting data on the program that could be used to redesign key elements, and initiating academic governance procedures to adopt and institutionalize the changes. The three other teams work with these subject-matter development teams to respectively: (a) assess the learning of MSU's teacher candidates and graduates and eventually the learning of pupils being taught by their graduates; (b) develop an induction program that recognizes the centrality of content and context, the overarching theme of MSU's design proposal; and (c) formulate TKS that are grounded in urban contexts and to develop a program that provides a specialization within the MSU teacher education program that prepares teachers for urban schools.

Each team comprises arts and sciences, education, and K–12 faculty, with faculty from the College of Education and from an arts and sciences college acting as coleaders.

Five of the seven teams were slated to begin work in Year 1. However, the Science and Social Studies development teams, which were not scheduled to begin work until much later, began some preliminary work without promise of funding.

Each of the three TNE project leaders meets with the teams for which they have oversight every couple of weeks to discuss progress, to keep apprised of any problems or barriers, and to facilitate cross-team communication of information.

Budget

The proposed budget included about $140,000 for overall project management and leadership. This included one-quarter time for each of the two coprincipal investigators, a half-time project manager, and two half-time secretaries, one working in the College of Education and one in the College of Natural Science. Funding for one half-time graduate assistant was also included, as are funds for central supplies, services, and consultants.

For each development team, the budget allocated release time or summer salary for the two coleaders of the team; graduate assistant support; and an allocation for purchase of materials, visits to other institutions, consultants, additional faculty or graduate student time, and pilot activities. The Literacy team had extra funds for additional coleaders (of which there are four instead of two) and graduate assistants. Other faculty who were invited to participate in the teams were expected to serve as part of their regular workload. In addition, each team received between $15,000 and $20,000 as a team budget to be used for miscellaneous expenses.

The budget included about $45,000 for supporting the participation of K–12 teachers. K–12 teachers received $100 per day plus travel expenses. MSU also paid for districts to provide a substitute when needed.

Although the budget did not include funds for the Social Studies or Science teams, which were not to begin work until Years 2 and 3, respectively, they did receive a small allocation for supplies, etc., when they decided to begin their work earlier than planned.

A faculty member from the MSU Office of Medical Education Research and Development is MSU's local site evaluator and about $20,000 was set aside for his salary offset and expenses.

The budget for equipment and supplies, approximately $40,000, included funds for computers, software, and video- and audiotaping equipment. The taping equipment was used by the teams to gather examples of teaching for discussion and in designing assessments. Another $40,000 was set aside for travel.

Overall, MSU spent about 41 percent of its proposed budget in Year 1. The Literacy and Mathematics teams spent 52 and 42 percent of their allocated budgets, respectively, while the other teams spent less than a third. Because K–12 teachers were involved so late in the process, none of the funds allocated for their participation were spent in the first year.

Matching Funds and University Contributions

The MSU provost contributed both the project director's time and also funds for an administrative assistant. In the first year, MSU already met the TNE matching funds requirement, having a total of $10,943,000 in confirmed matching gifts and grants. These matching funds include $1.25 million that was redirected from the Lappan-Phillips-Fitzgerald endowment royalties derived from the sale of the Connected Math curriculum. These funds have been used to help establish an endowed chair in mathematics education in the Mathematics department with one-quarter time allocated to TNE-related work.[1]

MSU is still trying to raise additional TNE funds. It has submitted applications for additional grants that include matching funds and is soliciting additional gifts for TNE work. MSU featured the TNE initiative at the Council of Michigan Foundations' annual meeting. Although its fundraising efforts have been successful, most of the funds received to date are for student support. In its progress report (Michigan State University, 2003), the university reports that it feels short of funds for actual TNE-related work.

Implementation Progress

Because the work of the teams MSU created covers key subject areas and themes rather than design principles, discussing the implementation under the design principle categories requires us to often reference work that is being done in other areas. Because of this, it may be helpful to remind the reader of the rationale behind the teams, as described in MSU's design proposal (MSU, 2002, p. 11):

> The main work of the Subject Matter Development Groups will be to agree on standards and expectations for what MSU teacher education students should know and be able to do in subject matter, assessment, and pedagogy. We will call these MSU TNE *Teacher Knowledge Standards*. To see whether students are meeting these standards, the Subject Matter Groups will work with the Assessment Group to identify, adapt, or develop tools for assessing teacher knowledge. (Throughout the proposal, we use "knowledge" broadly, to include skills as well as cognitive understanding.) The Knowledge Standards themselves will address teachers' knowledge about assessment and its connection to instruction. For overall program improvement, our assessment system will include ways to connect aspects of the program to the learning of K–12 pupils in the classrooms of program graduates.

Design Principle A: Decisions Driven by Evidence. The Assessment team is headed by three coleaders—a faculty member from the Department of Educational Psychology and Measurement; the Director of the Center for Integrative Studies in Science in the College of

---

[1] The current chair is held by Anna Sfard, who holds a joint appointment with the University of Haifa.

Natural Sciences; and a faculty member from the Department of Teacher Education, who is charged with evaluating the teacher education program. The center director became involved because he is interested in improving teaching across the university and has experience in assessing general education. The leaders meet once every two weeks.

The team itself consists of about 10 to 12 faculty members, with representatives from (among others) Mathematics Education; Teacher Education; Mathematics; Biology; Psychology; University Outreach and Engagement; and Counseling and Educational Psychology and Special Education. The coleaders divided the team into several subgroups (described in more detail below). The team typically did not meet as a full group; rather, subgroups met about once a week or every two weeks. Some team members participated more actively than others. Teacher education faculty who saw a potentially large payoff in terms of improvements to the program and some faculty from more "service-oriented" departments participated more actively than team members who viewed potential payoffs as uncertain or indirect.

The first subgroup is conducting a transcript analysis, studying characteristics of students prior to admission to the teacher program, including their ACT scores, in hopes of identifying characteristics that would help predict success in the classroom. This information could then help redesign the teacher education admissions process. In addition to the transcript analysis, the subgroup is attempting to obtain noncognitive interest inventory information collected as part of the ACT but that is not usually analyzed by ACT. The subgroup hopes to get data on the 2000–03 teacher education cohorts. It does not foresee problems with privacy issues as long as the data do not go outside MSU and are reported only in aggregated fashion.

The second subgroup is examining assessment in the disciplinary majors and in the general education courses. The latter is an extension of work conducted by the Center for Integrative Studies under a grant from the Hewlett Foundation. Under this grant, MSU has identified some broad learning goals and is attempting to measure through pre- and post-tests whether students are making progress toward these goals. Faculty explain their assessments and talk about how to use the feedback for change. In particular, the center is interested in comparing the effectiveness of different ways of delivering the same course.

Under the TNE work plan, the Assessment team was supposed to identify assessment instruments that could be used for assessing student outcomes in the disciplinary areas. However, the team decided that developing TKS in these areas was a necessary first step and so postponed this particular effort to the second year, when it could work with the disciplinary groups charged with this task. It is trying to make sure the subject-matter teams keep assessment in the forefront as they write the TKS. One of its team members is attending the Mathematics team meetings and believes that the group will be able to translate the standards into observable measures, in part because the Mathematics team understands the link between content and pedagogy and is enhanced by the presence of the mathematics education faculty.

The Induction team and the Literacy team undertook an overview study of the preinternship field experience components of the education program with a view to measuring the nature and consistency of the experience. The results of the study will be used to redesign the preinternship and internship components so that they produce the kinds of outcomes outlined in the TKS.

The Assessment team also wants to examine data on MSU's teacher graduates—where they locate, the kinds of jobs they get, and how long they stay in teaching. The team is looking at ways to improve current data collection efforts and response rates. The College of Education surveys practicing teachers and principals as part of its program evaluation and attempts to get some measures of their satisfaction with MSU graduates. The college also survey graduates as part of program assessment. The Career Services and Placement Office surveys seniors at the end of the 4th year, but this survey misses teacher education graduates because theirs is a five-year program.

The Assessment team has also been thinking about how to link learning gains of pupils to teacher characteristics and training, including using data from the Michigan Educational Assessment Program (MEAP), the state assessment. MSU noted that the MEAP is not a very good measure of student achievement but probably as good as some others. The fact that the MEAP is changing raises issues about using these data to measure longitudinal growth. Another problem is that the MEAP data system is not integrated, as the previous governor placed student-level MEAP data under the Department of the Treasury, while the Department of Education had data on schools. The Department of Education has regained control of all the data and is trying to develop an integrated database that will contain characteristics of schools and how they are functioning (they will receive letter grades), as well as characteristics of teachers and students. The TNE project manager is working with the Michigan Department of Education to see whether MSU can obtain data to track its graduates, although it is not clear whether the data will allow students to be linked to teachers.

One of the Assessment team coleaders is actively involved in the Delta Project. However, the Delta Project institutions have not made much progress toward their original goal of developing and using a set of common assessments to measure the learning of teacher candidates. MSU is interested in developing low-stakes, high-yield assessments rather than summative evaluation tools. They are also in touch with the University of Pennsylvania, which is developing instructionally embedded assessments that will cut across courses.

Design Principle B: Engagement with the Arts and Sciences. Altogether there are 80 faculty, including education and arts and sciences faculty and graduate assistants involved in TNE. The provost urged faculty to get involved and drew substantive participation from departments with strong links to teacher education, such as mathematics, the social sciences, English, and the natural sciences. Overall, the teams have good representation from across the arts and sciences and education colleges. The teams could not absorb all the faculty members who were interested, and the leaders went through a careful selection process and vetted candidates through the deans. They had a very good response from Arts and Letters. Only three faculty members across the university who were asked to participate refused. Leadership noted that making TNE a university project is important so arts and sciences faculty feel they have an equal voice.

Of the 310 faculty in the College of Natural Sciences, about 12 to 15 people are involved in TNE. The college has always had connections to the College of Education, so participation in TNE is a natural extension of existing work. The colleges made two new joint-appointment hires, one in fall 2003 and one in fall 2004. Also, a $35 million National Science Foundation project led by the College of Natural Sciences and DSME will help support TNE efforts.

Of the 290 faculty in the College of Arts and Letters, about 15 to 16 are participating in TNE, with about 4 to 5 forming the core. These individuals tend to be senior faculty with national reputations and some of their time was bought out for TNE. More faculty may be involved in later projects. The Writing Center also is involved in the Literacy and English teams. The dean is actively promoting the program and talked to faculty about TNE at the last retreat for chairs and directors. Work done in the Center for Language Research and Language Acquisition on second language and language acquisition is feeding into TNE.

Of the 225 faculty in the College of Social Sciences, eight are participating in TNE. While this represents the smallest involvement among the colleges, the Social Studies team is not yet fully operative and the Urban Teachers team continues to add faculty with relevant expertise. The college is interested in teacher education because the context of education is "the turf of Social Sciences." For senior faculty, the main incentive to get involved in TNE is to improve their own teaching. There is an overlap between those who are active in the college and those who are active in TNE. The college will be offering workshops in social sciences next summer for the teachers of an intermediate school district; this is an important area, given that scores on the MEAP for social studies throughout the state are low.

The directors of the integrative studies programs in social studies, arts and humanities, and general science held a crosscutting university seminar in spring 2003. They spoke about general education issues and, in particular, general education courses for teachers. The next seminar will focus on assessment, because these directors are in the second year of a Hewlett grant that requires them to assess student learning in these courses.

Teacher Knowledge Standards. TKS are a centerpiece of MSU's TNE work. The standards map what teachers should know and be able to do across a seven-year career. MSU has divided the seven-year-long career into three stages: emergent (four years of undergraduate work), novice (one year of internship), and target (two years of induction). The TKS are linked to these developmental stages. The standards were largely developed by the Literacy team, which wanted a general framework before developing subject-specific standards. They had strong input from the College of Arts and Letters.

The standards framework identifies six "knowledge sites" for learning to teach, in which *knowledge* includes knowledge, attitudes, and dispositions. The six knowledge sites are:

1. **Subject-Matter Knowledge.** This standard outlines for each subject area (literacy and English, mathematics, social studies, science) the habits of mind, specialized subject-matter knowledge, PCK, subject-matter knowledge for teaching, and the general knowledge that teachers need to have to teach.

2. **Student Knowledge.** This standard describes the knowledge about children's development and characteristics that teachers need to have and the actions they need to take based on that knowledge as informed decisionmakers, researchers, and caring professionals.

3. **Classroom Knowledge.** This standard delineates the knowledge that teachers must have to manage classrooms and to build communities of learners and the actions they should take to create a safe, caring, and productive classroom environment, to make the class an inclusive community, and to treat the classroom as a site of inquiry in terms of analyzing and improving the classroom environment.

4. **Professional and Institutional Knowledge.** Standard 4 discusses the knowledge that teachers need about the profession and institution of schooling and the actions they can be expected to take to adapt to, improve upon, and participate in the life and community of the school.

5. **Self-Knowledge.** This standard talks about the kinds of self-knowledge, such as personal philosophy of teaching and one's values and beliefs, that teachers should aim for and the kinds of actions that should be expected of teachers as they attempt to enhance and deepen their self-knowledge in these areas.
6. **Community Knowledge.** This standard outlines the knowledge that teachers should have about community and home environments, including local history, economics, politics, and the kinds of supports that are available, and the kinds of actions that would help the teacher develop and use this knowledge to support the learning of students.

These standards will inform the assessment work and will help target changes and improvements in the program by clarifying expectations; for example, at what point students should be expected to have mastered the knowledge and actions at a novice level.

In May, a workshop on TKS was held for all TNE participants, at which this framework was unveiled. Once the framework was approved, the Literacy and Mathematics teams began creating the disciplinary knowledge and teaching knowledge standards through the summer. A cross-team committee with members from the Literacy and Mathematics teams was charged with developing the other four standards. As of October 2003, the first draft of the standards was near completion and was to be reviewed by the full teams. In Year 2, there will be a meeting with undergraduate chairs and directors at which the TNE group will brief them on the standards and alert them to possible programmatic changes to get buy-in. Without the support of the chairs, such changes are unlikely to occur.

Already, there is some discussion about numeracy and literacy standards regarding what all teachers should learn—for example, what a high school mathematics teacher should know about literacy. One important limit to all changes to the teacher education program is that no more credits can be added, so only substitutions or changes are possible.

Literacy Team. The Literacy team has several coleaders and several associates from the following departments: Speech and Audiology, Linguistics, Teacher Education, English and Writing, Rhetoric, and American Cultures. While the coleaders met for weekly two-hour meetings, they decided only to include associates when necessary, to reduce the time burden on these members. The Literacy team also met three times with the associate members from other departments, whom they use as a review group. They have not yet identified K–12 teachers to work on the team, but they hope to engage them more in the clinical component.

The Literacy team took on development of the general framework and produced the original standards framework, as discussed above. The literacy coleaders wrote the standards together during their meetings. They often had substantive disagreements and there was considerable conversation around the standards attempting to find common ground.

They reviewed a number of sources to define these standards including National Council of Teacher Education (NCTE), the INTASC, the Michigan standards, and NCATE. The six knowledge "sites" they developed differ from those of the other organizations they studied, in the sense that they do not just offer a different level of detail but provide different categories of knowledge about actions and performance that correspond to each category. Their work integrates knowledge frameworks to accommodate changes over time, as a teacher moves through his/her career.

Mathematics Team. Like the Literacy team, the Mathematics team devoted its attention to the development of standards, and the process was quite similar. They examined multiple sets of existing standards to come up with a framework that might work for all the disciplinary teams. As mentioned above, the Literacy team developed the overall architecture for the standards and the Mathematics and Literacy teams are working on fleshing out Standards 1 and 2 to be content specific.

Unlike the Literacy team, the three coleaders of the Mathematic team chose to actively work with its three to four associates as a whole group. Also, unlike the Literacy team, the Mathematics team involved K–12 teachers early in the process, holding an early retreat to solicit input from them. The retreat focused on the variety of needs felt by the teachers and mathematics curriculum directors.

Science Team. As mentioned earlier, the Science team started work earlier than expected partly because of the changing state rules for elementary science certification. The state is establishing a new integrated science major for certification at the elementary level, replacing the general science major. There is concern about how best to do this while still meeting the definition of "highly qualified" teacher under the provisions of the No Child Left Behind Act.

The Science team is led by the Associate Dean of the College of Natural Science and a science educator who holds joint appointments with DSME and the Department of Teacher Education. The team has members who are scientists from biology (including one who has done work in curriculum development), chemistry, physics, science education, geology, and teacher education. There is a lot of communication among faculty from the two colleges and a real passion about wanting to develop this major and the science standards. They recognize that there are bound to be disagreements among the team members from the two colleges, but members are willing to work through these differences. Although they have yet to involve K–12 faculty, they want to get teachers involved sooner rather than later.

Because its work was not scheduled to start until Year 3, the Science team had limited resources this year—one-quarter time for a graduate assistant but no buy-out time for faculty. Team members expect that their new NSF grant can offer them resources for release time. The grant is to engage in research and faculty development in 70 school districts in Michigan and Ohio that will lead to the improvement of math and science teaching and pupil achievement in K–12 schools. This work will obviously intersect with TNE.

There are four faculty members who form the core group but there are several who are involved in short-term tasks. The core group met every two weeks for 3–4 hour meetings and will meet with the larger group twice a semester. The team's focus is developing science standards, and they hope to have a set of standards completed by the end of Year 2. This past year, they have focused on grades 7–12 and reviewed state standards and research on teaching science for motivation and understanding, which they plan to use as a resource for the development of standards. They are not starting with science content but rather with problems teachers encounter. This work is linked to one of their NSF grants, under which they are developing diagnostic questions for teachers.

Social Studies Team. The Social Studies team also started earlier than expected, looking at K–8 social studies. There was no money for the Social Studies team, and, like the Science team, they have been working all year with minimum funding. They have completed a literature review and begun developing standards for social studies. Unlike science and mathematics, it is difficult to find additional funding for work on social sciences, so lack of funding may be an issue.

Design Principle C: Teaching as an Academically Taught Clinical Practice Profession. Some of the work under this design principle is carried out by the subject-matter teams in terms of designing changes in the teacher education programs to help teachers meet the TKS for pedagogy and for involving K–12 faculty in the program. The largest segment of the work, however, is being carried out by the Induction team, which, with the help of the Literacy team, is looking at the entire range of clinical experiences in the program and attempting to design an induction program for MSU graduates.

The team includes experienced members who have worked with other induction programs. For example, one of the team leaders spent eight years at the University of Georgia, where she coordinated an induction program with other universities that was funded by a Title II teacher quality grant. Her work included creating a virtual online resource, working with the state certification program, and developing a mentoring program.

The team consists of two coleaders and 15–20 members, including representatives from social studies, mathematics, science, and English, as well as representatives from the teacher education faculty who specialize in each of the subject areas. The team also includes six K–12 teachers and three graduate students who are paid to work approximately 10 hours a week on the project. The Induction team has met as a whole group four times since the start of TNE and the two coleaders meet every week and talk even more frequently.

Believing that induction has to be more than just mentoring, the team is examining multiple formats and the feasibility of building multiple credentials (such as a master's degree, a certificate, etc.) into the program. The current state-mandated induction program requires that each new teacher have a mentor and receive a certain number of hours of professional development, though the program is not funded through the state. Schools and districts are intent on developing their own induction programs, so the Induction team is keenly aware that they need to work with the schools and districts to develop shared objectives. In the second year, they are planning to break the team into two subgroups to work on mentoring and online resources respectively.

The team contacted 80 MSU first-year teachers and found 16 willing to participate in a research study that will identify the needs of first year teachers with respect to induction and how prepared they were to teach literacy. These teachers are also working with the TNE initiative and will continue to consult with the project in the second year. Teachers were interviewed, observed, and completed a survey on national language arts standards. The findings suggest that elementary teachers are not well prepared to teach writing and secondary teachers are not well prepared to teach reading. The team provided feedback to the teachers at a daylong retreat at which the team also developed TNE induction goals.

The team wrote a one-page memo about what Michigan teachers need after the one-day retreat with the new teachers (from the research study) that will guide their induction work plan. The results help highlight how to improve teacher preparation and how induction can be used to fill gaps not covered in preparation.

In Year 2, the team will follow a new cohort of five graduates who are teaching in the same school, although they hope to get more teachers to participate, to study mentoring.

The Induction team has identified several tasks for the upcoming years:

- Review other programs and talk to experts. The team also feels that it would be helpful to share ideas with the other sites.
- Examine the current elementary program (which is currently delivered by three separate teams that are autonomous and operate differently) and the clinical experiences

that are a part of the program to determine how to connect them better. The team is finding that the clinical experiences differ across the three teams.

- Identify core mentoring practices. MSU cannot provide face-to-face mentoring to all its graduates, so it needs to build district and school capacity for mentoring. The team wants to work with the state to establish a knowledge base around mentoring practices and to develop effective programs to train teachers to be mentors.
- Determine how best to use induction to deepen graduates' subject-matter knowledge. The team needs to involve content-area expertise in the induction component. It has considered an "Ask Jeeves" format, in which teachers could submit questions to subject area faculty members. Faculty members could then be assigned on a rotating basis to answer questions. However, the team unsure how responsive this would be and how to make this a two-way learning process.
- Examine how to use technology to establish learning communities as a way of connecting new teachers and provide an electronic resource network so that various resources, such as writing and science materials or video cases of best practices, are readily accessible. One possibility is to have new teachers enter unit lesson plans and share their work. The team has hired a Web expert to think through possible Web programs, platforms, audiences, and links to support induction. The biggest challenge is to determine what will motivate teachers to use the program. They realize that they need to build in a large public relations component to sell their induction model to teachers and schools.
- Consider how best to make the induction program self-sustaining, perhaps by converting the induction program into a graduate program.

Progress on Other Issues Identified in the TNE Prospectus. The TNE prospectus asked the sites to recruit underrepresented groups into teaching. MSU has made preparing teachers for urban schools a central part of its design, and its efforts on this issue also address issues regarding engagement of arts and sciences faculty and schools as clinics. The goals of MSU's urban agenda focus on the recruitment and retention of teacher candidates committed to teaching in urban schools; development of a postbaccalaureate program to recruit people from urban areas; and "the infusion of theoretical knowledge and practices into the standards that will enable MSU-prepared teachers to implement enriched teaching practices in urban schools" (Michigan State University, 2003, p. 3).

The Urban Teachers team, which has been charged with this task, is currently headed by two coleaders, one from the College of Education and the other from the College of Social Science, who has a background in social work. In addition to the coleaders, six faculty members from teacher education, psychology, Chicano studies, and two graduate students were on the team, although there were no K–12 teachers. The team met twice during the first year.

The Urban Teachers team faced several challenges that made progress difficult in the first year. The University's urban programs configuration was undergoing change, compromising the ability to make helpful connections, and there is a dearth of faculty expertise in urban specialties that incorporate a focus on education. Second, the teacher education coleader found himself overcommitted by virtue of multiple grant activities and thus needed to change his status to associate member. Third, the recruitment of faculty from across the university brought together a set of people whose interests were not specifically urban focused. Fourth, the set of topics they were asked to examine did not form a coherent task and were only somewhat loosely related. As a result, the members were unsure as to their role and how they could contribute to the project.

The team noted that while the concept of urban education is easily identified, operationalizing it is much harder and it is not clear how this is or should be linked to the larger TNE project. The team needs a common language and common definitions for the language, which is challenging, given that team members are coming from different disciplines and departments. In a session designed to explore TNE work with the teacher education faculty, there was a lively discussion about what is meant by urban education and what an urban preparation program would imply for the regular program.

The Urban Teachers team expects to make better progress as it develops common understandings and a clearer sense of how to deal with its multilayered agenda under its new leadership. In addition, they will receive a lot of support from the new chair in teacher education, who has emphasized urban initiatives as one of her departmental goals. The work being done in the department will complement and further the work of the Urban Teachers team.

Will MSU expect its ability to obtain additional outside resources for pieces of the urban agenda help move the work forward in the coming years? For example, MSU was awarded a grant of over $6 million to recruit and retain students from the Detroit area who will return there to teach in exchange for full scholarship support during the program. Additionally, a Noyce grant of $1.4 million has been awarded to MSU by the National Science Foundation to recruit and educate mathematics and science teachers for urban schools.

Participants' Views on Year 1 Implementation

This section presents some early impressions reported by participants about progress and the effects of TNE on the institution and themselves.

Importance of Leadership. The three coleaders (now joined by the chair of teacher education) are viewed as very strong leaders with complementary skills and a lot of credibility across the various departments.

The fact that the project director is the assistant provost and has been in the office of the provost for a long time is seen as a strength and as a signal that the provost considers TNE important.

Problems with Time and Communication. The coleaders are provided TNE support in the form of release time or summer salary; some deans have provided additional support for faculty work on the project. However, the associates do this as committee work, so their work is voluntary. The project directors are worried about human capacity, given that so many who are involved as volunteers are already overloaded with teaching, outreach, and research activities. There have been several complaints about too many meetings.

Concerns were expressed by and for junior faculty who were taking time away from research and publishing. If there are defined tasks, this may be feasible; with more amorphous tasks that use up a lot of time, this is a serious concern. While the culture is changing and there is greater recognition of the TNE work as "service," more efforts to sell the project are needed.

Communication is also a big challenge. As one faculty member noted, "This is a big, unwieldy project with over 70 people involved. The question is how to get everybody connected, while still moving it along." One suggestion was to use Web sites to post progress or even a monthly newsletter.

Some participants pointed out the leaders do not have much release time to work on TNE and are overcommitted, so "it often feels like the central piece is missing."

Participants noted that funding is an issue, as "$5 million does not go very far with a project this size." MSU has been very successful in raising matching funds, so this may help pick up some of the burden for additional costs and involve more people. Participants also pointed out that it was harder to raise money for the work being done by some of the teams (such as Social Studies team) than for others (such as the Urban Teachers team).

Collaboration Among Arts and Sciences, Education, and K–12 Faculty. One of the biggest challenges is "making real the notion that teacher education is a cross-university endeavor." Mathematics and science faculty were always involved in teacher education, and this was one of the reasons that TNE was possible. Arts and Letters now has greater involvement with teacher education, and they are forging stronger relationships there with the establishment of the Social Studies team. Some participants expressed concern that teacher education faculty dominated the TNE work and the teams. On the whole, though, there has been real change over the past year, with faculty from different departments becoming more cooperative and participatory.

A larger question was raised about the TKS and the extent to which the core colleges will accept them and use them to redesign their courses.

Regular faculty sometimes are concerned about joint appointments. For example, when the issue of hiring a chemistry educator was raised, faculty wondered how they were going to judge him/her and how they would communicate or work together.

MSU found it more difficult than expected to involve K–12 faculty. The university needs to find methods to engage teachers in helpful ways. Some teams have been more successful than others in this regard; for example, the Mathematics team integrated K–12 faculty into their work, while the Literacy team had problems recruiting K–12 faculty. MSU would like to convene a group of teachers drawn nationally to come together for one day to focus on standards, etc.

Although MSU had hoped to hire someone from a K–12 school to work full time with induction, it found that even bringing someone half time requires a large investment because adjusted for cost of living, Michigan has the highest-paid teachers in the nation. They have not tried to recruit TIRs because of costs and because of concerns about how best to use them.

Some participants expressed concern that there was no representation from K–12 education when developing the TKS, which may raise issues of credibility in the community.

Problems with the Urban Teachers Team. The urban initiative is one of the most important pieces but difficult to implement because of both political and institutional considerations. There is an ownership issue: Many departments deal with urban issues, so there is no one logical department in which to house it and the particular interests of the faculty involved do not necessarily touch on urban education. As mentioned earlier, there were also issues of trying to develop a common language and a clearer focus for the team.

Looking Forward to Year 2

The challenge in Year 2 is to map standards to the program(s), to identify the curricular gaps, and to look at the changes that are needed to fill holes in the program. Over the next year,

MSU plans to finish the draft of the TKS and start a serious review process with multiple constituents. The university needs to build in ample time to get people engaged, to obtain feedback, and to revise based on the reviews. In addition, it will review course work taken by teacher education students to measure opportunities to learn and to target areas for revision, based on data. MSU needs a clearer vision of what is realistically possible.

A serious issue that is likely to arise in the second year is the willingness of the undergraduate chairs to consider program revisions based on the TKS. Programmatic changes cannot be undertaken lightly because they affect the core courses that all students are expected to take. A real effort will be made to involve the undergraduate chairs to bring them into the loop and to sell the standards.

MSU is looking to make progress with its urban work. The team's tasks will include an online review of what other colleges and universities are doing in urban education and conducting focus groups with teachers in small, urban areas to ask them about their teacher preparation programs.

MSU also plans to improve and increase communication both within and across the TNE teams, as well as with broader audiences outside of TNE. Among other efforts, this would include developing Web sites for the teams, holding small localized meetings and cross-university seminars, and cosponsoring events with different university leaders. As part of this effort, MSU will be keeping a close eye on political issues that might affect its current TNE plans.

Effect of State Policy Context

Budget

In 2003–04, state funding to MSU was reduced by 10 percent, bringing state support per student to the 1995–96 level of state funding. The budget cuts have hurt MSU somewhat: It is not filling open positions (for example, the College of Natural Sciences is down 10 FTEs), is eliminating some departments or combining them, and is closing some centers. Further cuts seem likely in the next two years. However, the $1.2 billion capital campaign started in 1999 and expected to continue until 2007 is progressing better than expected. In terms of TNE, as mentioned earlier, the university has been very successful in raising over $10 million in matching funds.

Policy

By and large, TNE participants did not raise any major concerns with respect to state policy on teacher education. They had jump started the Science team because of the changing certification requirements for science teachers while the Induction team seemed sensitive to and willing to work in conjunction with the Michigan state-mandated induction program.

University of Virginia: Profile at Baseline and Year 1 Implementation

Overview of the Teacher Education Program at Baseline

General Description of Programs

The Curry School of Education and the College of Arts and Sciences offer a five-year integrated teacher education program, which culminates in both the baccalaureate (BA) and the Master of Teaching (MT) degrees. In addition, the Curry School of Education offers a two-year postbaccalaureate program in which students with a completed BA degree in a noneducational field earn a Master of Teaching degree. These two programs are designated as the BA/MT and the PG/MT programs, respectively. Both programs prepare students for licensure and endorsement in elementary education (PK–6), secondary education (6–12 in English, mathematics, science, and social studies), or PK–12 programs (health and physical education, foreign languages, and special education). Curry started a new early childhood and developmental risk program in 2002.

Students in the five-year program have advisors in both the College of Arts and Sciences and the Curry School of Education. Students begin professional studies in their second year and take courses that fulfill both university requirements and education school requirements interfaced throughout the four-year sequence. Students move to graduate status at the start of the spring semester of the fourth year. Students entering the PG/MT program are essentially interfaced with the last two years of the five-year program. All students in the Curry programs take at least 30 hours of graduate education course work. There were 124 students in the graduating class of 2002, including both the BA/MT and PG/MT programs. The Curry School teacher education programs have been growing in recent years, and officials project that there will be 150 graduates in 2004.

Undergraduates apply to Curry in the spring of their first or second year. Students who apply in their second year must complete some summer school To make up missed courses. Students interested in mathematics, science, foreign language, and special education may apply as late as their third year in the college. Others who miss the deadline may apply to the PG/MT program as early as the spring of their fourth year in the college.

To apply to the Curry School, BA/MT and PG/MT candidates must have SAT or GRE scores of 1000, an overall GPA of 2.7, and a major GPA of 3.0. To advance to graduate status, students must pass the Praxis I, which tests pedagogy, attain GRE scores of approximately 1000 or better, have an overall GPA of 2.7, and an academic major GPA of 3.0. Students must also demonstrate satisfactory performance in education courses and in field experiences.

Clinical Component

Students in the teacher education program have varied experiences working in classrooms. The field placement activities, which begin in the second year for BA/MT students, gradually increase in complexity and responsibility as students go through the program. Each field experience is guided by a clear set of objectives and an associated field manual. These experiences include

- conducting structured observations of children, schools, and communities in the second year
- tutoring an individual student and developing a case study in the third year
- planning and teaching a multilesson sequence and developing and implementing conflict resolution strategies within schools during the fourth year
- completing full-time student teaching in the fall semester of the fifth year.

Cooperating teachers serve as clinical instructors and are considered adjunct members of the Curry School of Education faculty. Clinical instructors are selected for their ability to provide instructional models and to serve as supervisors of entry-level professionals. During the third and fourth years of the program, Curry faculty who teach field-related courses provide necessary supervision of the students. A university supervisor is assigned to supervise a candidate's student teaching experience during the final year in the program. University supervisors are either faculty or doctoral students with experience in public school teaching within the content area.

UVa had no formal induction program at baseline.

Faculty

In 2002–03, the Curry School employed 128 faculty members, 28 of whom worked in the teacher education program. Three-fourths of the teacher education faculty were tenure-track professors; 21 percent were general, non–tenure-track faculty; and 4 percent were adjunct faculty. Teacher education faculty were somewhat more likely to hold non–tenure-track positions than Curry faculty in the other departments (Human Services and Leadership, Foundations, and Policy). Ninety percent of the teacher education faculty members have had public school teaching experience. All teacher education faculty members hold doctorate degrees.

Data on Students

UVa compiles data on students' entry qualifications, such as GPA and SAT or GRE scores. The average GPAs and SAT or GRE scores of Curry candidates exceed the minimum requirements. For example, for the classes of 2001–04, the average student SAT scores exceeded 1200. Candidates in both the BA/MT and PG/MT programs on average had a combined verbal and quantitative GRE score of over 1100 for all graduating classes. Further, the average fourth year GPAs for all graduating classes ranged from 3.1 to 3.4.

The vast majority of students in the BA/MT program were female (85 to 90 percent) while the PG/MT program attracted a comparatively larger proportion of males (20 to 34 percent). The percentage of minority students varied across programs and years (from 4 to 20 percent) but small numbers make it difficult to compare trends over time.

Data on Graduates

In addition to these entry-level quality indicators, UVa also keeps data on the performance of its graduates on the teacher licensing examinations. Praxis II exams, which measure subject area proficiency, are required in Virginia. Almost all UVa students passed the Praxis II exams in all years and certification areas.

While UVa does not systematically track the placement and careers of its graduates, faculty estimated that about 40 percent of graduates teach out of state, some graduates teach overseas, and that most Curry School students teach in suburban schools, although a few teach in challenging urban schools for shorter periods of time. Faculty also noted that Curry students tend to be leaders in their schools—some become mentoring teachers by their third year and many move into administration or other leadership roles in the education fields. Some return for further graduate work and then teach in teacher preparation programs.

Evaluation Component

Evaluation of Students. UVa considers assessment of student competence an ongoing process that relies on multiple measures. Student subject-matter knowledge is assessed by course grades and the completion of required course work for the academic major. Typically, the grading of students in individual courses is determined by the instructor of record and is based on class participation, course assignments, and curriculum-based assessments.

Permission to advance through the teacher education program depends on multiple factors including: standardized test scores, GPA, field evaluations, and faculty review. Faculty review involves either a written statement or a discussion among faculty members of a student's performance in class and in the field, the student's overall attitude and sense of professionalism, and the perceived development and potential of the student as a teacher. Faculty discuss the performance of all students one semester prior to their student teaching and faculty approval is required to advance BA students to graduate status within the MT program. At this same time, PG/MT students are also reviewed.

Peer teaching experiences and field-related courses in pre–student teaching semesters include opportunities to observe and assess students' developing teaching skills. Students receive feedback on these experiences from the course instructor and peers. Each year's field placement has a corresponding evaluation component that reflects increasing expectations for professional and pedagogical skills. Students' teaching skills are judged by assessment of a student's progress across the two field-experience courses' evaluations and a midplacement assessment used during student teaching. These assessments are based on INTASC standards. Field placement and student teaching evaluations focus on professional responsibility and commitment, reflection, professional relationships, instructional strategies, and diversity. Further, at the end of each field placement, an evaluation form is completed by the clinical instructor and the university supervisor.

The Curry School has a Curry Teacher Education Warranty that guarantees that the Curry School will provide assistance to its graduates during the professional induction year if a school or district expresses a problem or difficulties with a graduate.

Evaluation of Graduates. UVa did not follow its graduates at baseline.

Program Evaluation. According to the Curry School (UVa, unpublished document, 2001), emphasis is placed on student performance outcomes, not course syllabi. UVa evaluates the program's achievement in creating high candidate performance using student grades, field-based evaluations, national and professional tests, feedback from clinical instructors and graduates, recruitment by employers, and ultimately the satisfaction and performance of the students.

The Curry School reports that courses and program requirements are discussed regularly and revised as needed to incorporate new ideas and empirically supported procedures. UVa's teacher education programs align with the INTASC guidelines and adhere to Virginia's regulations for the licensure of teachers (Virginia Department of Education, 1998), which specifies competencies for all teachers.

The Curry School tracks its program's quality through licensure of graduates; Praxis I and II scores, which, respectively, measure pedagogy and content; and its warranty program. It also tracks program recognition through education school rankings, teacher education program rankings, and faculty and student recognition.

The Curry School analyzed data from 1999 to 2001 provided by supervising teachers and including evaluations of field experiences from two cohorts of students, as well as their midplacement evaluations for student teaching placements. Data were divided into five areas of competence: professional responsibility and commitment; reflection on their teaching; relationships with students, teachers, clinical instructors, and other teaching professionals; instructional activities, such as planning and carrying out lessons, managing the classroom, and assessment; and diversity, involving attention to differences among children's backgrounds and learning abilities.

The Curry School found that preservice teachers' GPAs were not correlated with their performance in any of their teaching competencies. UVa anticipated this finding, believing that teaching competency is not necessarily related to academic success as traditionally measured. The Curry School also found that ratings of preservice teachers' five competencies correlated with each other. The Curry School also looked for differences among the three graduating classes on the five teaching competencies. It found only one statistically significant difference. The ratings of relationships with children and other teaching professionals were higher for the class of 2000 than for the other two classes.

The Curry School continuously cycles through self-reviews as part of its development process and is currently involved in a strategic planning process. One of the five strategic directions for the entire school is the assessment of all Curry programs to demonstrate the effectiveness of the programs on the graduates and the K–12 students whom the graduates teach. Near-term goals include focusing on the multiple needs of all young children, including vulnerable children; strengthening existing leadership in advancing and applying educational technology; becoming a national resource for knowledge and practice based upon evidence of the effectiveness of programs; and creating organizational structures to unlock Curry's potential, both on and off campus.

Collaboration with Arts and Sciences Faculty: Selected Examples

- Teacher education policy and curriculum are determined by the Curry School's Teacher Education Advisory Committee, consisting of faculty from the various departments and chaired by the director of teacher education. The Curry School of Education's Academic Affairs Committee provides the final approval of teacher education policies. A committee made up of faculty from the Curry School and the College of Arts and Sciences provides advice on policy and curriculum matters that affect the five-year programs.

- The Dean for Arts and Sciences, Ed Ayers, has collaborated with Curry faculty to develop curriculum materials around the Civil War for use in middle schools and high schools. His project, "Valley of the Shadow: Two Communities in the American Civil War," provides K–12 teachers and students online access to primary documents from two communities during the Civil War and is part of the Center for Digital History. Curry School social studies educators use this Web site when working with K–12 teachers during professional development training.
- The Center for Technology and Teacher Education is a cross-disciplinary group of faculty and students working to develop appropriate uses of technology in teacher education. The center's goal is to prepare the next generation of technology leaders and to influence educational technology policy.

Collaboration of University Faculty with K–12 Schools: Selected Examples
- The Virginia School–University Partnership is a consortium of 21 central-Virginia school districts and the Curry School of Education that serves the leadership and professional development needs of its students, administrators, and faculty members. Housed at the Curry School for the past 16 years, the organization has sponsored numerous conferences, workshops, seminars, and meetings and has provided technical assistance directly to its members to accomplish its goal of mutually improving K–12 and higher education.
- The Teacher Education Office has created a Clinical Instructor Advisory Board consisting of outstanding practicing teachers who represent all program areas and extend across grade levels and school districts. The purpose of the board is to help develop procedures for all field-related activities including assessment procedures, clinical instructor training, supervision policies, and recommendations for new clinical instructors.
- The Center for the Liberal Arts provides K–12 teachers around the state with professional development experiences, typically in two- and three-week summer institutes and weekend workshops. These institutes and workshops are taught by arts and sciences faculty members and sometimes cotaught with Curry faculty. They focus on increasing teachers' knowledge of subject matter. Faculty are also sent to conduct courses at particular schools, if the school district so desires; for example, English professors have gone to the Virginia Beach school district for many years.
- The Curry School is involved in many projects and programs in the local schools, including a program using the Internet to support mentoring of new teachers and Teaching Early Decoding Effectively, a project developing a set of ten CDs on early reading instruction that is disseminated to every reading coordinator in the state of Virginia.

Design Proposal

This section outlines the major activities that UVa included in its design proposal. Obviously, these were plans and, as such, will undergo revision during the implementation process. However, they do provide an idea and vision for how TNE will be implemented in the institution. We present the information in narrative form around major categories of activities—assessment, recruitment, program improvement, and induction—that UVa planned to undertake to produce high-quality graduates who produce better pupil outcomes. We also present this information organized by design principles in Table D.1.

Assessment

UVa listed four major categories of variables that will be included in its integrated assessment model—teacher characteristics; teaching performance; pupil learning; and context, to include the school, classroom, and community. These variables would guide the assessment of teacher preparation at UVa. Questions it planned to answer through its model included the following: How do teachers perform? How does context influence teaching? What and how well do pupils learn? To answer these questions, the Teaching Assessment Initiative members would develop a body of data that would support an evaluation of the effectiveness of graduates in terms of pupil learning, including an integrated database system that tracks teacher candidates from preservice education through their first two years of teaching. Faculty, staff, and students would construct new measures of PCK and use a variety of measures to build online profiles (electronic portfolios) of teacher education students. UVa proposed to draw on its work with the Delta Project during this development. The data would allow the university to conduct cross-sectional and longitudinal studies of graduates' performance in achieving pupil-learning gains, and it would like to compare these gains to those of other institutions and other TNE sites. Further, UVa noted its commitment to ensuring that its teacher graduates know how to use a variety of assessment tools, including curriculum-based measurement, teacher-made assessments, and standardized state and national tests, to improve their own teaching. UVa planned to use electronic portfolios to assess its teacher candidates.

Recruiting Teacher Education Candidates

UVa proposed a few initiatives to recruit more and different students into its teacher education program. First, UVa proposed to create an alternative option for late deciders. While UVa currently has a fifth-year graduate program that can be considered a late-decider option to its five-year BA/MT program, it planned to develop another alternative, so that students could enter the five-year BA/MT program as late as the beginning of their senior year. Second, UVa planned to attract students into the BA/MT program through a series of new courses:

- **Teachers for a New Era Seminars** would be a group of 100-level seminars on teaching to generate interest and encourage critical examination of teaching. All freshmen would be encouraged to take these courses.
- **Common Courses** would be 200-level interdisciplinary courses that incorporate a lab section focusing on the PCK aspect of the course. Students in the BA/MT program would have priority access to the teacher education sections; however, other arts and sciences students would be able to sign up for these as well. UVa hoped that the general emphasis on pedagogy and its integration into the content of the courses would raise awareness among students about the challenges and rewards of teaching, and perhaps inspire some to become teachers.

Table D.1
Major Proposed Activities, by Design Principle, University of Virginia

Design Principle A: Decisions driven by evidence	*Drawing on Research* • Revise the teacher education program based on the research base and federal and state initiatives. • Conduct evaluation studies linking teacher candidates' characteristics, teaching performance, and pupil learning in different contexts. Results will lead to changes in the program. • Develop mechanisms and processes to ensure that all teacher education programs can be evaluated and strengthened over time, based on ongoing analysis of teacher effectiveness in schools. *The Role of Pupil Learning* • Develop a body of data that enables evaluation of effectiveness of graduates in terms of pupil learning. • Develop an integrated database system that tracks teacher candidates from preservice education through the first two years of teaching. • Conduct cross-sectional and longitudinal studies of graduates' performance in achieving pupil-learning gains and compare these to other institutions and other Carnegie sites. • Ensure that teacher candidates know how to use data from curriculum-based measurements, teacher-made assessments, and standardized state and national tests to assess students and improve their own teaching. • Provide fifth-year teacher education candidates the option of full-time student teaching in their last semester and have these candidates measure their pupils' progress and take responsibility for getting the lowest 20 percent of the class to achieve at grade level by the end of the term.
Design Principle B: Engagement with the arts and sciences	*Subject-Matter Understanding* • Foster an interdisciplinary approach to content knowledge learning through Common Courses, Counterpoint Seminars, summer institutes, and weekend workshops. *General and Liberal Education* • Foster an interdisciplinary approach to content knowledge learning through Common Courses, a new advising structure, and the Center for Liberal Arts' summer institutes and weekend workshops for in-service teachers.
Design Principle C: Teaching as an academically taught clinical practice profession	*Pedagogy* • Develop a series of new courses, jointly taught by arts and sciences and education faculty, that explicitly link how one teaches to what one teaches. • Use the Teaching Resource Center to engage faculty universitywide in conversations about effective pedagogy. *Schools as Clinics* • Offer fifth-year students the option of full-time student teaching during their last semester. • Create an Expert Educators Group of teachers and principals to represent the school district in decisionmaking regarding the TNE program. • Develop a collaborative relationship with school districts to provide induction services. *Teachers on Faculty Appointment* • Fund one K–12 teacher as a teacher-in-residence (TIR) to team-teach methods courses, work with the Teacher Education Advisory Committee, and engage in joint research with university faculty. • Potentially add additional TIRs and draw them from a pool of nationwide applicants in later years. *Residency (Induction)* • Create summer and weekend workshops focused on PCK that bring graduates back to the university. • Provide induction services for all new teachers in one or more local school districts, regardless of where they graduated. • Attempt to engage other Research I institutions in developing such an induction model. *Preparation of Candidates for Professional Growth* • Create a system in which teacher candidates develop program goals that are revisited throughout their education and prepare a professional development plan for their induction years. • Ensure that graduates maintain a meaningful connection with the academic community and participate in their disciplines beyond graduation.

Table D.1—Continued

Additional issues to be addressed jointly by faculties in education and in arts and sciences	*Pedagogical Content Knowledge* • Develop new courses, such as Common Courses, that integrate pedagogical knowledge more fully with study in the disciplines. • Redesign the culminating course to focus on PCK. • Bring together education, arts and sciences, and K–12 faculty in the mentoring program to foster PCK. • Create mathematics and science positions dedicated to teaching courses for elementary education and special education students. *Literacy and Numeracy Skills* • Assess teacher candidates' literacy and numeracy skills through course work and Praxis, SAT, and GRE scores. *Elementary and Middle School Education* • Assess required course work in the program review. • Develop courses in physics, biology, and mathematics that will be offered to elementary and special education majors. • Provide elementary education students with multiple arts and sciences mentors. *Technology* • Use technology and model the way teachers might use technology to support assessment of their own students. *Cultural Considerations in Teaching and Learning* • Provide fifth-year teacher education candidates the option of full-time student teaching in their last semester and have these candidates measure their pupils' progress and take responsibility for getting the lowest 20 percent of the class to achieve at grade level by the end of the term. • Redesign the program to include a focus on teaching at-risk student populations. *Recruitment of Underrepresented Groups in Teaching* • Create an Emerging Teachers Program to recruit underrepresented minorities into the BA/MT program. *Late Deciders in an Undergraduate Program* • Create a program option for students to enter the program at the start of their fourth year.

- **Counterpoint Seminars** would be 300-level courses linked to popular survey courses and would focus on the pedagogy associated with the course content. These courses would be for teacher education students who have already taken the survey course, as well as graduate students in arts and sciences.

In its efforts to increase the diversity of its teacher candidate population, UVa also planned to institute a competitive Emerging Teachers Program that would encourage students from underrepresented groups to enter the BA/MT program or inspire students to enter the teaching profession through other pathways. The program would include a seminar, internships and independent studies at one of the research institutes in the program, and a one-week summer conference covering a range of professional concerns for minority students and addressing key topics of interest for the teaching profession.

Program Improvements

To improve the quality of its graduates, UVa proposed a number of program improvements, many of which would eventually be informed by assessment data. The first goal was to align teacher education courses and field experiences with existing evidence on teacher preparation. Using evidence would become an ongoing process at UVa, and knowledge that is continuously generated about the program would be used to continuously improve the program.

UVa also proposed to create a greater programmatic focus on at-risk populations. In addition to creating course work focused on at-risk populations, UVa proposed to offer the option for teacher education candidates to engage in full-time student teaching during their last semester. Fifth-year students who choose the option of full-time student teaching would measure student progress using assessment tools and would take responsibility for bringing the lowest 20 percent of the class up to grade level by the end of the term.

UVa sees its teacher education program as a joint product of the College of Arts and Sciences and the Curry School of Education. Teacher education students at UVa are advised first by an arts and sciences faculty member and then by a faculty member from teacher education. UVa proposed to strengthen the advising process by creating faculty mentor teams in each of the disciplines, consisting of an arts and sciences faculty member, an education faculty member, and a cooperating K–12 teacher. UVa noted that the close relationships that students will establish with their mentor team members may extend throughout the induction period and help foster a lifelong identification with a community dedicated to teaching.

UVa would also adopt an interdisciplinary approach and team teaching in many classes, particularly the common courses, TNE seminars, and counterpoint seminars, which will be used to recruit students for teacher education. This interdisciplinary approach would help improve students' PCK.

To support improvements in PCK, UVa would establish new mathematics and science positions dedicated to teaching courses for elementary education and special education students and refocus its capstone course to focus on PCK.

UVa also proposed to improve the program through involvement with K–12 schools by including K–12 schools and teachers in decisions about teacher preparation and by increasing the involvement of faculty, particularly arts and sciences faculty, in K–12 schools. UVa planned to hire K–12 teachers as TIRs who would team-teach methods courses, work with the Committee on Teacher Education, and engage in joint research with university faculty. The university would begin by hiring one TIR and seek additional funding for more in later years. As part of this later effort, UVa would even contemplate drawing TIRs from a national pool of applicants.

UVa would also form an Expert Educators Group (EEG) that would include ten teachers and principals from local schools to represent the local school districts in decision-making and to ensure their participation in all TNE programs. The EEG also would help provide hands-on K–12 experiences for arts and sciences faculty.

To create teachers who think of themselves as continuous learners and to help bridge the progression from preservice to induction, UVa proposed to have teacher candidates develop program goals that would be revisited throughout their teacher education program. In addition, teacher candidates would prepare a professional development plan for their induction years.

Induction Program and Support

UVa proposed to offer induction support to two groups of new students. First, UVa planned to work with local school districts to provide induction services for all new teachers in the divisions, regardless of where they received their training. UVa noted that one benefit to this model is that it provides a control group to compare the pupil-learning gains of UVa graduates against. Second, UVa would also provide induction support to all its own graduates. Since many UVa graduates leave the area, UVa planned to develop online induction support. In addition, UVa would create opportunities to draw its graduates back onto the campus and into the university community through summer and weekend workshops focused on PCK. UVa noted it wants to ensure that its graduates maintain a meaningful connection with the academic community and participate in their disciplines beyond graduation. In addition to its own efforts, UVa proposed to engage other Research I institutions in developing such an induction model.

State Policy

UVa explicitly mentioned state policy as a factor that influences the quality of its program and graduates. Because UVa's program is influenced and must abide by state policy, UVa proposed to take an active role in helping to shape state policy so that the state is supportive of its TNE efforts.

First Year Implementation

This section documents the progress UVa has made over the first year in implementing the TNE initiative.

In our conversations with the TNE leadership at UVa, a consistent theme that emerged was the challenge of raising the stature of participation in teacher education within a Research I University setting. The leadership at UVa has worked to draw individuals into the TNE efforts rather than trying to force the issue or create demands. In doing so, it has focused on a set of first-year activities that draw upon the research interests and strengths of its faculty, seeking to encourage participation by emphasizing scholarship. When engaging K–12 institutions, UVa is attempting to forge a partnership that meets the needs of the K–12 partners, as well as those of UVa.

Project Structure and Staffing

Leadership. The University of Virginia's Director of Teachers for a New Era reports to the provost. UVa recruited its TNE director from the arts and sciences but looked for a faculty member who would have credibility with the Education department as well. The current project director previously directed the Center for Liberal Arts, which provides professional development to teachers. The TNE directorship was originally billed as a full-time vice-provost position; however, budget constraints did not permit the creation of such a position. Instead, the director is covered half-time by the provost's office and TNE funds and half time by his department. In Year 1, the project director received some help from an administrative assistant in the provost's office (one-quarter time).

The director is assisted by an implementation team, consisting of deans and faculty members from the Curry School of Education, deans and faculty from the College of Arts and Sciences, the head of the Faculty Senate, the associate director of the Teaching Resource Center, the holder of the Goldsmith Distinguished Teaching Professorship, the Director of University Outreach and Executive Assistant to the Provost, and representatives from local school districts.

Selected members of the implementation team form a core leadership group: the director of TNE; the Director of Teacher Education; the Associate Dean for Academic Affairs of Curry School; the Chair of Curriculum, Instruction, and Special Education of the Curry School; and a faculty member from the Department of Leadership, Foundations, and Policy Studies. This core group is primarily responsible for the day-to-day implementation and planning of TNE. Although the group does not have an official name, in this report, we will refer to them as "TNE leadership." In addition, the executive assistant to the provost, who played a key role in developing the proposal, works closely with the director of TNE and updates the provost on TNE progress.

The EEG comprises representatives from the two major local school districts. This group was established in the spring 2003 semester and functions as an advisory group, particularly in the area of induction.

TNE leadership updates faculty through teacher Education Advisory Board meetings and department faculty meetings. Also, in Year 1, UVa started to develop a TNE Web site that can be accessed both internally and externally.

In its proposal, UVa wrote that it would form a Coordinating Council to help work with state agencies, the legislature, and accreditation groups to promote fundamental changes required for the success of the program. The council was to include top officials from the Virginia Department of Education, the Virginia State Board of Education, the U.S. Department of Education, and various professional community and business organizations. However, UVa chose not to form the council during the first year, because the leadership believed that it was premature to form such a group during the planning and initial implementation phase.

The TNE leadership reported meeting formally on a weekly basis, while the full implementation team met approximately twice a semester. The EEG met three times.

While the director is assigned half time to TNE, he reported spending well over half time on TNE activities. The rest of the leadership team reported spending a substantial amount of time working on TNE activities; however, none of them holds an official TNE title or is compensated for his/her time (except for one faculty member, who received a summer stipend). The TNE work is simply added on top of their other responsibilities. In particular, the Director of Teacher Education, who has taken the lead from the Curry side for TNE activities, reported feeling particularly overextended.

New Faculty. During the first year of TNE, UVa filled a number of new TNE positions:

- a director of the Teaching Assessment Initiative
- a postdoctoral fellow to lead the performance-based evidence work
- a head of recruitment to focus on recruiting minorities into teaching.

UVa had a failed search for a person to work on the late-deciders program. When reviewing the applicants for the posted position, they realized that none of the applicants had the experience necessary for this position. As a result, UVa will reopen the search for this position in Year 2, with a clearer job description. In the interim, UVa hired a new Curry Ph.D. graduate to work part time on the late-deciders issue.

Budget

UVa's total budget for TNE amounted to a little over $460,000 for Year 1. The university chose to ramp up in Year 3, so its proposed budget for that year was about $1.6 million. The largest items in the budget were for the start-up of the Teaching Assessment Initiative or more generally to support assessment: approximately $137,000 for faculty time, including one-half of a faculty member's time to act as senior advisor for the Teaching Assessment Initiative, six months of a new faculty member to serve as the Director of the Teaching Assessment Initiative, and a senior programmer to work half time on designing technology to support assessment activities. It also included $40,000 for summer salary for faculty and funds for graduate students to conduct research on assessment and $20,000 for consultants (videographer, measurement expert, programmer, etc.). Another $30,000 was included for one postdoctoral fellow to work on the curriculum outcome measurement program and to help faculty incorporate systematic assessment procedures into their courses. The fellow worked closely with the Teaching Assessment Initiative faculty. Another $32,000 was allocated for summer salaries for faculty selected to develop the new Common Courses and $6,500 for teaching assistants to work with these faculty in course development. The budget included $30,000 for a half-time coordinator of induction to work with the director of teacher education on induction mentoring, undergraduate advising, etc. Two full-time administrative assistants (one for the Curry school and one to work with arts and sciences faculty) were budgeted at $30,000 apiece. In addition, $14,000 was allocated for the EEG. Other items include $17,500 for external evaluators and $11,000 for a six-week training workshop for Common Course teaching assistants. In Year 1, UVa spent approximately one-fourth of its proposed budget.

Matching Funds and University Contributions

In Year 1, UVa is provided matching funds totaling a little more than $135,000. This included $25,000 for faculty summer grants to develop new courses; close to $40,000 to help pay for the project director's time; half-time support for an administrative assistant to work with the project director ($12,500); $50,000 to pay for half the senior programmer's time; and $5,000 for a grant writer.

Implementation Progress

We focus our discussion around the major areas in which UVa has been working in its first year: assessment, the creation of new courses, strengthening of advising teams, and induction. As with the other chapters, we organize the sections around the design principles, but the reader should note that many of the activities are designed to address more than one design principle.

Design Principle A: Decisions Driven by Evidence. Under the leadership of a veteran faculty member and the new director of the Teaching Assessment Initiative, the Assessment Center has begun the process of gathering data to help inform the teacher education program. UVa has been in active communication with the state to obtain student test data linked to teachers. However, UVa faculty noted that if they are not able to obtain state assessment data, they will pursue obtaining assessment data from local districts. UVa is looking into qualitative measures, such as motivation, in addition to state assessment scores. The school wants to determine what teacher characteristics lead to positive pupil outcomes.

The Assessment Center issued a request for proposal (RFP) in spring 2003 for research on the connections between and among teacher characteristics, teaching processes, and pupil learning in a variety of educational contexts. University faculty, local K–12 school personnel, and students with faculty support were invited to submit proposals. They funded 15 research studies at approximately $3,000 to $5,000 apiece. Four studies will examine the value added to public education by UVa teacher education as defined at the program level; five studies will focus on specific teacher education courses or discrete features within the teacher education programs; and four studies will investigate attitudes and practices of in-service teachers. One additional study will assess the development of preservice teachers' beliefs and abilities as they progress through the five-year teacher education program.

Many of these studies will require the participation of students enrolled in the Curry School of Education and the College of Arts and Sciences. Initially, these will be drawn from a pool of volunteer student participants. However, faculty in the Assessment Center would like to require Curry students to participate as subjects in research projects for five hours per year. This ongoing participation would allow the Assessment Center to track students over time and encourage further research studies. They are currently working through their Internal Review Board to work out human subject protection issues around this plan.

One of the most prominent pieces of UVa's first-year work in assessment is a series of assessment seminars that are hosted by the provost. The purposes of this seminar series include raising awareness of assessment techniques, developing a culture of research and practice, and engaging teacher education and arts and sciences faculty with one another.[1] In Year 1, the provost hosted three assessment seminars that focused on issues around urban schools and rural schools. Approximately 15 individuals participated in the series at the invitation of the deans, the provost, and the director of TNE. The fact that the provost hosted these seminars sent a signal to all faculty members that this was an important activity and underscored his personal support.

UVa had begun working on an electronic portfolio system prior to TNE, and it was piloted in Year 1.[2] The Open Portfolio contains data on all field placements, student evaluations, and student artifacts. In addition, student teachers submit their lesson plans for faculty comment 48 hours before they plan to teach the lesson. Faculty members are expected to respond quickly. After teaching the lesson, the student teacher enters reflections from the teaching experience. This system allows Curry to look at data across programs. For instance, the data showed that teacher education candidates in special education were the strongest in classroom management and candidates in secondary science were the strongest in technology. UVa hopes to use this system during induction as well. The goal is for UVa students to use the portfolio and update it continuously.

As mentioned earlier in the staffing section, in Year 1 UVa hired a staff member to work on developing performance-based evidence. She started working with faculty to collect evaluation data on candidates that can be fed into the teacher education system. She will also eventually work with teachers in the field.

Also, as part of the work done for the Delta Project, the Department of Teacher Education has surveyed its existing assessment instruments. Two faculty members are creating a manual for field experience courses containing a set of chapters with curriculum-based assessments and assessments for motivational outcomes.[3]

Design Principle B: Engagement with the Arts and Sciences.

New Courses and Seminars. As part of its attempt to engage arts and sciences faculty in TNE and to interest more students in teaching, UVa wanted to develop and offer TNE Common Courses. These courses are expected to be large survey courses (300–500 students), often team taught, with discussion sections led by graduate teaching assistants. One discussion section is to be devoted specifically to pedagogical issues and will be led by a Curry instructor and is intended for students enrolled in the BA/MT program or interested in the

---

[1] As such, these seminars are also designed to address Design Principle B: Engagement with arts and sciences faculty.

[2] Note that this also addresses Design Principle C: Teaching as an academically taught clinical practice profession.

[3] This too will feed into Design Principle C activities.

teaching profession. UVa piloted two Common Courses in the arts and sciences—the Ethics of War and Environmental Decision Making—to develop a model for the TNE common courses. In spring 2003, UVa solicited proposals from faculty to develop common courses but received few applications. While the reviewers liked one proposal, it was proposed for SY2004–05. The reviewers felt that none of the other proposals they received were appropriate for the Common Course series. The two associate deans from the arts and sciences who are working closely with TNE are now targeting certain professors and soliciting applications from them, including a chemistry professor who they hope will lead a science-based Common Course.

During Year 1, UVa developed two Counterpoint Seminars that will be offered in Year 2. As discussed earlier, Counterpoint Seminars are targeted to BA/MT students and are designed to increase PCK. The seminars are linked to a survey course that the students have taken and focus on how that course's content can best be taught in a middle school or high school setting. The seminars will be highly interactive and focused on practical teaching challenges. The seminar that is linked to a literature course is being offered in fall 2003 and will be co-taught by two graduate students, one from the Curry School of Education's teacher education program, and one from the English department in the College of Arts and Sciences. The second Counterpoint Seminar will be offered in spring 2004 in association with a survey course in American history.

Advising Teams. The work of reconfiguring the advising teams will begin in Year 2, but in Year 1 the structure for doing this work was put into place. As discussed earlier, UVa planned to create improved advising teams in seven major subject areas (English, mathematics, history, etc.) to create better links among the departments and stronger ties with arts and sciences faculty. These teams would consist of an arts and sciences faculty member, a teacher education member, and a K–12 member.[4] There was initial uncertainty regarding whether the teams should begin by convening as a large group or should start their discussions autonomously. Also, there was uncertainty regarding how much input K–12 schools should have into the advising teams. A school district representative on the implementation team felt that K–12 teachers should be involved in the advising as well to emphasize the realities of the classroom; however, some felt that Curry faculty could speak authoritatively about schools and districts. As a result, each of the seven teams will have one K–12 teacher who will consult with the teams.

Design Principle C: Teaching as an Academically Taught Clinical Practice Profession. Under this design principle, UVa has been focusing on induction. As discussed in the description of UVa's theory of change, UVa planned to have a two-part induction system—one focused on its graduates, and the other focused on all new teachers in the local area. In Year 1, UVa began developing a program for all new teachers in the local area.

As a first step, UVa formed its EEG to assist in this planning. To get buy-in at the higher levels, invitations to form the EEG went from the provost to the superintendents of the local school districts. The school districts selected people who would work well with the rest of the EEG. UVa did not hire a Director of Induction in Year 1; instead, the TNE Director did most of the work coordinating with the EEG.

The EEG is playing a major role in the planning for a UVa community induction program. While UVa had originally planned to engage new teachers in content from the

---

[4] Note that this also addresses Design Principle C: Teaching as an academically taught clinical practice profession.

beginning, the opinion of the EEG was that first-year teachers are generally so overwhelmed that they are unlikely to benefit from or realize that they need help with content. In addition, the feelings of isolation among new, single teachers often led them to leave the area and teaching, so this is something that the university could help address. The EEG noted that positive initial experiences at the university would make teachers more likely to take advantage of its educational resources. UVa also realized that local school districts are proud of their induction work, so it would be inappropriate for UVa to "take over" induction. The university wants to work with the districts and to consider what its optimal role should be within the district model.

As a result, UVa revamped its plan and now intends to focus first on activities to help connect new teachers with their community. Given that UVa's new single faculty members also have a difficult time getting settled in the Charlottesville community, the university is developing a network of "new educators" that brings together new K–12 teachers and UVa faculty. UVa hopes that this will encourage a two-way relationship in which K–12 teachers will feel comfortable at UVa and with UVa faculty, and UVa faculty will develop an interest in K–12 schools.

The original TIR model was not met with enthusiasm: It was unclear what the TIR's role would be and what the benefits would be to students. As a result, no TIRs were hired during Year 1. Their role will be reconceptualized in Year 2.

Progress on Other Issues Identified in the TNE Prospectus. UVa's proposal made recruiting students into teaching, particularly from underrepresented groups, a priority. The proposal suggested establishing an Emerging Teachers program based on UVa's Emerging Scholars program. However, the implementation team was skeptical about whether it would work in the teacher education context; further, no one at UVa was assigned responsibility for this effort. As a result, the leadership team revised its plan and, as discussed earlier, hired a faculty member specifically to work on this issue. The new hire has K–12 experience and arts and sciences admissions experience, so she has the respect of all the players in the TNE project. The provost has agreed to contribute funding to this position after Year 1. The new hire is expected to build minority support on campus; work with arts and sciences faculty to make them aware of the BA/MT option, so they can provide this information to students during initial advising; and work in the local K–12 schools to help recruit and retain minority teachers.

Participants' Views on Year 1 Implementation

As mentioned in the earlier chapters, this section reflects participants' views.

Importance of Leadership. Faculty from the Curry School and the College of Arts and Sciences noted that the Director of TNE has been key to the program's progress. He is credible to the arts and sciences faculty, has the trust of the Curry School, and is familiar with the local schools. He is attuned to how each group views decisionmaking and process, and is adept at making each group feel valued. Further, he attempts to use everyone's time efficiently; as a result, when he asks people for time, they are "pleased to do it."

Faculty repeatedly mentioned that having the provost host the assessment seminars sent a clear signal of the importance and significance of TNE.

Problems with Structure, Coordination, Scheduling, and Timing. UVa has a limited formal TNE structure and members of its core leadership team, other than the TNE director, did not receive formal TNE titles or release time for their activities. This structure was selected so that the work of TNE would be incorporated and institutionalized into the general work of teacher education and to increase the chances of replicability in other Research I institutions, as it is unlikely that another university would be able to have a full-time implementation team. However, the lack of structure has meant that the TNE work has been added on top of the already heavy workload of these faculty members. The lack of formal recognition makes it difficult to include these activities on curricula vitae. It has also led to some confusion regarding the respective roles of the various leaders.

TNE leadership reported that coordinating the timetables of the different players, particularly the school districts and the university, was a challenge. For example, K–12 representatives often can meet only after 4:30 p.m. and K–12 school and university spring breaks and semester breaks are at different times. Also, due to limited space and the cost of parking at the university, it is an administrative challenge even to have K–12 representatives park at the university.

One individual noted that there seem to be more practical and personal sensitivities among the various constituencies than there are philosophical differences. This has led to problems in doing business and suspicion among the groups. Also, there are cultural differences that lead to practical challenges. For example, one respondent noted that arts and sciences faculty respond promptly to email, Curry faculty respond promptly when telephoned, and that work with the school districts was executed most promptly in person.

When hiring for TNE positions, TNE leadership had problems coordinating among the provost's office, the College of Arts and Sciences, and the Curry School. Each has different administrative procedures and unfamiliarity with the procedures and the people led to delays and problems in posting job descriptions and processing salaries for new hires.

Because the TNE funding was not received until January, first-year implementation was slower than expected and delayed. Further, response to the RFP for Common Courses was low, as most faculty already had courses planned for the subsequent academic year.

Collaboration Among Arts and Sciences, Education, and K–12 Faculty. The dean of the College of Arts and Sciences and the two associate arts and sciences deans who worked on the first year TNE implementation are very committed, which sends a strong message to other arts and sciences faculty and will help them recruit the key arts and sciences faculty needed to work on TNE.

Although K–12 faculty are not widely involved, UVa has been responsive to advice from the EEG, revising its initial induction plan to reflect their concerns and suggestions.

Looking Forward to Year 2

UVa plans to make two key hires during Year 2—one to serve as a coordinator of induction to lead the induction work for both the school districts and the UVa graduates and the other to work on the late-deciders issue. Based on its experiences with the first round of hires, UVa feels that hiring in Year 2 will go much more smoothly and efficiently. Once individuals have been hired to fill these positions, UVa believes its progress in these areas will greatly increase.

To involve more arts and sciences faculty in TNE activities, the TNE leadership has invited two associate deans from the College of Arts and Sciences to join them twice monthly at meetings. In addition, UVa seeks to actively recruit faculty who may be predisposed to participate in TNE. As a result, the university has hired a graduate student to help identify arts and sciences faculty who have a scholarly or personal interest in K–12 schools.

The assessment seminars will continue to be hosted by the provost in Year 2, and the number of arts and sciences faculty who are invited to attend will expand. The Year 2 seminars will focus on the research studies funded by TNE through the assessment center.

To increase communication between the school districts and the university, UVa plans to have school district representatives speak to groups of faculty in Year 2.

Effect of State Policy Context

Budget

In 2002–03, UVa's state funding was cut by $24.5 million in the academic areas. UVa instituted a mid-year tuition surcharge in spring 2003 and raised tuition in the fall. UVa has been dedicated to retaining staff because layoffs lower morale and hurt the school's ability to move forward. The university has taken a tiered approach to cuts, first asking all departments to bear the burden equally and then taking a more strategic approach, with a greater influence on auxiliary units. It has cut faculty travel, money for copiers, telephones, etc. This is not a sustainable situation, but the objective was to preserve faculty lines. Funding for teacher education was preserved, but it was noted that the program has grown by almost 50 percent over four years (100 graduates in 2000 to an expected 151 graduates in 2004) and has not received any increases in funding.

The state cutbacks in university funding have had an effect on the TNE work in that university faculty are more stretched and TNE is asking them to do additional work. There is simply no extra time in faculty members' workloads due to the budget cuts on the arts and sciences side. The proposed TNE seminars were derailed by budget cuts, but UVa is planning to offer a university seminar about minorities in education in 2003–04.

Policy

UVa Curry School faculty expressed concern about some of the state initiatives and proposed changes in state policy.

New Majors for Elementary Education. Virginia has been considering requiring one of five majors for elementary education—English, history, mathematics, science, or an interdisciplinary degree consisting of all four majors. Regardless of state policy, such an interdisciplinary degree is not likely to happen at UVa, as there would be too little content in any one of the disciplines to suit any of the departments. There is some concern that the elementary education might lose some students because psychology would no longer be considered an acceptable major; however, these students might be attracted to special education, which would still retain psychology as an acceptable major.

UVa has been exploring the possibility of creating a mathematics and science major for students seeking to become elementary school teachers. These new certification regulations would make such a major unlikely. Faculty members are planning on presenting their ideas to the state legislature in the hope of getting it approved.

Alternative Licensure. Alternative licensure is a big issue in Virginia. Any expanded alternative licensure provisions would have a decided effect on the five-year program and on late deciders. As it is, even now, more than 100 UVa graduates who are not graduates of the Curry School seek teaching positions after graduation.

State Policy Contexts

As mentioned in Chapter One, this appendix describes the state policy contexts that provide the backdrop for the TNE reform in the four states. For each state, we provide a brief overview of the state education system and the fiscal condition of the state. Then we describe state policies dealing with teacher certification, teacher education programs, additional routes to teaching, new teacher induction, continued professional development, and teacher recruitment and retention.

California

California educates more than 6.14 million K–12 students: 44 percent of students are Hispanic/Latino; 35 percent are non-Hispanic white; 8 percent are Asian; 8 percent are non-Hispanic black; 2 percent are Filipino; and 1 percent are Native American (California Department of Education, 2003). One quarter of California students are English language learners. Currently, California employs 306,940 teachers and certifies approximately 20,000 new teachers each year. Seventy-eight California institutions of higher education have approved teacher education programs, as do eight of its school districts. Approved district programs are district intern programs, which provide an alternate route into teaching. About 2 percent of newly credentialed teachers are district prepared. Approximately 19 percent of newly certified teachers were prepared out of state. CSUN is California's third largest producer of new teachers.

Like many states, California is facing lagging state revenues due to a downturn in the economy. General Fund revenues from major tax sources were expected to fall by $65.8 billion in 2003–04. This decline marked the most dramatic revenue loss California has experienced since World War II. Declining revenues meant reductions in expenditures in many areas, including higher education. Under the 2003–04 budget, the CSU system received $3.5 billion. However, this represented a 7 percent reduction (about $409 million) in funding from the 2002 Budget Act.[1] Due to these budget constraints, it is uncertain whether cuts will be made to funding for mandated teacher programs, such as induction programs and teacher performance assessments in future years.

As described below, California has recently instituted policy changes for teacher certification and preparation. Thus, teacher preparation programs are under pressure to revamp

---

[1] To offset these budget losses, in 2002–03, for the first time in eight years, the CSU Board of Trustees increased student fees. Further increases in student fees are expected in coming years.

their curriculum, demonstrate to the state that they meet new requirements, and position themselves in a changing environment.

Certification Requirements

California has two stages of certification—preliminary credential, a five-year, nonrenewable initial certification, and a professional clear credential, a five-year, renewable certificate. To receive a preliminary credential, candidates must possess a bachelor's degree from a regionally accredited college or university in a subject-matter major (not education); have completed course work in subject matter and pedagogy; complete a course on the U.S. and California constitutions; pass basic skills tests in reading, mathematics, and writing; and take a subject-matter exam *or* approved course of subject-matter study, though as of summer 2003 all teachers will be required to pass subject-matter exams. At the end of five years, teachers must apply for a professional clear credential. The professional clear credential needs to be renewed every five years. To be eligible for renewal, teachers must have completed 150 clock hours of professional development and have been employed one-half year.

Over the past decade, the education requirements for initial certification in California have changed from having to hold a bachelor's degree in a subject-matter major to needing a master's degree in education back to holding a bachelor's degree in a subject-matter major. Requirements for teacher testing also have changed. Previously, candidates who completed an approved teacher education program were exempt from most pedagogy and content tests. However, due to the requirements set under the federal No Child Left Behind Act for highly qualified teachers, the testing requirements have increased.

To receive a preliminary credential, candidates must hold a bachelor's degree in a subject-matter major and pass several tests. Currently, California requires teacher candidates to take the CBEST before admission to a teacher preparation program, but passage of the test is not required for entry into the program. Students who have not passed the exam before admittance to a teacher preparation program must pass it before advancing to the supervised classroom-teaching portion of the program. There is no limit to the number of times a candidate may take any or all sections of the CBEST before passing it. The purpose of the CBEST is to verify acceptable proficiency in reading, writing, and mathematics skills in English. The exams are designed to measure basic reading, writing, and mathematics skills that are needed and used by professional staff members in schools that offer academic programs in kindergarten, grades 1–12, and adult education (see http://www.cbest.nesinc.com/ CBESTUpdatedTestSpecs.pdf for test specifications). The score for each section ranges from 20 to 80. The passing score on each section of the test is a scaled score of 41. A total scaled score (the sum of reading, mathematics, and writing scaled scores) of 123 is required to pass. However, it is possible to pass the CBEST with a scaled score as low as 37, on one or two sections, provided that the total score is 123 or higher. Passing rates are high, ranging from 93 to 100 percent for traditional teacher programs and 91 to 100 percent for alternative preparation programs.

Potential teachers are also tested for their subject-matter knowledge. All candidates for multiple-subject-area teaching credentials (positions with self-contained classrooms) must now pass the (CSET) Multiple Subjects Exam. Candidates for secondary school positions (generally departmentalized classrooms) must either pass the CSET Single Subject Exam or complete an approved subject-matter program in the relevant subject.[2] The purpose of the assessment is to help ensure that credential candidates have demonstrated the level of subject-matter knowledge and skills required to teach satisfactorily in the classroom.

In addition, elementary and special education teachers are required to take the RICA, a measure of PCK in reading. The intent of the RICA is to ensure that California-trained elementary and special education teachers have the knowledge, skills, and abilities to provide effective reading instruction. This is the only exam that is designed specifically for testing professional knowledge and pedagogy acquired through a program of professional preparation. The test is available as *either* the four-hour, paper-and-pencil RICA Written Examination (which contains both multiple-choice and constructed response items) or the self-paced RICA Video Performance Assessment. The scale for the written exam is from 0 to 120, with a passing score of 81. The scale for the video assessment is from 6 to 24 with a cut score of 17. Pass rates for traditional preparation programs range from 94 to 100 percent. Pass rates for the RICA for alternative routes range from 87 to 100 percent.

In addition to these changes, California is instituting new regulations, as of 2004, which require newly credentialed teachers to complete an approved induction program or a fifth year of study to receive a professional clear credential. While induction programs will be offered by the districts and will be free to participants, teachers seeking to engage in a fifth year of study at an institution of higher education will have to pay the costs themselves. Specific components of the teacher induction programs are discussed later.

Teacher Education Program Requirements

All teacher education programs must align with the CSTP, a set of standards for the teaching profession, which align with the K–12 content standards. California also developed TPE that detail standards teacher candidates must meet before receiving their preliminary credential. All teacher education programs must demonstrate to the state that they prepare their candidates to meet the CSTP and the TPE. To do so, teacher preparation institutions submit a crosswalk of how the competencies taught in each of their courses maps to these standards.

In California, teacher preparation course work must cover a number of pedagogy topics, including child and adolescent development; theories of learning; social, cultural, and historical foundations of education; teaching English language learners; and teaching special populations (i.e., students with disabilities and gifted and talented students). However, pedagogy courses must not exceed a year of full-time study; and no more than nine pedagogy courses may be taken prior to student teaching.

The state also requires that teacher education candidates complete at least one semester of student teaching as well as fieldwork (e.g., classroom observation, tutoring small groups of students, etc.) prior to student teaching. Student teachers are required to be in the field for a minimum of one K–12 grading period, including full-day teaching for at least two weeks. Student teachers are evaluated on explicit standards by their university supervisor and

[2] Middle schools have increasingly hired teachers with multiple-subjects credentials. California law prohibits schools from assigning a multiple-subjects credential holder to a full day of classes in one subject (for these assignments, middle schools still hire single-subject credential holders). However, schools can and do assign multiple-subjects credential holders to daily teaching schedules in which one teacher is responsible for three consecutive "core classes" that encompass two subjects (e.g., science and math, or English and history). As a result of this growing pattern, increasing numbers of students in grades 6–8 are taught core academic subjects for entire school years by teachers whose subject-matter competence was traditionally assessed in relation to the typical curriculum in grades K–6.

cooperating teacher. Overall, during all their fieldwork experience, teacher education candidates must observe or participate in at least two K–12 classrooms, including an experience in a hard-to-staff or underperforming school; have at least one experience in a public school setting; teach English language learners; and should have the opportunity to experience all the phases of the K–12 school year. Multiple-subject candidates should experience two or more grade spans, and single-subject candidates should gain experience with two or more content areas.

Teacher education candidates also must pass a TPA before being recommended for a preliminary credential. The TPA measures performance on a range of TPEs and requires the completion of four tasks. Three of these tasks require candidates to document how they respond to the needs of students they are teaching while the fourth task includes observation of candidates' teaching. The results of the TPA inform the development of an individual induction plan. While the TPA has been developed, it is not yet funded or implemented.

Additional Routes to a Teaching Career

California has instituted a number of routes to teaching in addition to completing a traditional teacher preparation program. Internship programs, offered by districts or universities, allow candidates with a bachelor's degree who demonstrate subject-matter competence (either through a subject area major or passing a test) to complete professional development (at least 120 clock hours) or course work (approximately 32 semester units) while teaching in the classroom. Like candidates going through a traditional teacher preparation program, interns are required to pass the TPA before being recommended for preliminary credential.

Districts also offer a preintern program that provides additional training to candidates who cannot yet demonstrate subject-matter competence. Candidates who successfully complete a preintern program earn a one-year preintern certificate, during which time they are expected to participate in an intern or postbaccalaureate preparation program.

The California Commission on Teaching Credentialing (CCTC) also operates an Intern Early Completion Option that allows candidates with a bachelor's degree and demonstrated subject matter, teaching, and subject-matter pedagogy knowledge to bypass course work and professional development and use passing performance on the TPA to obtain the preliminary credential.

New Teacher Induction

In 1988, SB148 (The Bergson Act) established the California New Teacher Project (CNTP) to examine models of induction and assessment. CNTP was funded at $8.8 million, served 37 local pilot programs, more than 3,000 new teachers, and 1,500 experienced teachers. In 1992, an evaluation of CNTP, Success for Beginning Teachers: The California New Teacher Project, showed that participating teachers used better instructional practices than other new teachers and motivated and set high expectations for all students. In addition, the retention of minority teachers and teachers in hard to staff schools was high.

In 1992, SB1422 was passed, largely based on recommendations from the CNTP evaluation. The act established the BTSA program and commissioned a comprehensive evaluation of the teacher credentialing system. The goals of BTSA were to provide effective transition and feedback for new teachers to enable success and retention of promising teachers and improve student performance; improve teacher performance assessments; and establish a coherent assessment system to ensure acceptable competence of teachers remaining in the profession. BTSA induction programs were offered by school districts, county offices of education, and/or institutions of higher education. The program was voluntary for districts and teachers. Over the years, BTSA moved from a small program to a large part of California's strategy to improve the quality of teaching and reduce attrition.

From 1992 to 1997, BTSA grew from $4.9 million to $7.5 million in statewide funding (matched by local funds in 2:3 ratio from state funded Mentor Teacher Program), served 33 local programs, and between 1,700 and 2,480 teachers per year. The key features of BTSA were sign-off by the local teacher bargaining agency on the program; support provider training for mentors, site administrator training, diversity training for teachers, and performance-based formative assessment that was distinct from the formal employment evaluation. Many of the programs used the California Teaching Portfolio from WestEd or Pathwise Observation System from the Educational Testing Service.

California is now implementing provisions under SB2042 that require teachers to complete an induction program or an extra year of study to receive a professional clear credential. Candidates who complete a teacher preparation program will first receive a five-year preliminary credential. To earn a professional clear credential, candidates must complete either an approved induction program or a fifth year of study. Teacher induction programs will require participants to complete the following requirements:

- documentation of TPA outcomes from the professional teacher education program, when available
- an annual Individual Induction Plan, documenting planned professional growth activities based on formative assessment information and individual needs
- demonstrated application of the California Standards of Teaching Profession and state-adopted frameworks and adopted curriculum materials in one content area in the context of his/her instructional practice, showing response to individual diverse student needs, beyond what was demonstrated for the preliminary credential
- evidence of participation in professional development activities, including
  - attendance at planned events
  - consistent communication with a support provider
- demonstrated knowledge of the following
  - using technology to support student learning
  - equity, diversity, and access to the core curriculum
  - creating a supportive and healthy environment for student learning
  - teaching English learners
  - teaching special populations.

While BTSA programs may convert to SB2042 induction programs, the nature and scope of the BTSA program will shift under the new requirements. First, all induction programs will need to meet certain standards, although they are given flexibility in how those standards are met. Second, they will be mandatory, requiring the participation of all newly certified teachers. One should note that some newly certified teachers may already have years of classroom experience if they were working on an emergency permit. Third, by making successful participation a requirement to gaining a clear credential, the nature of the program becomes dual purpose: to provide support for new teachers and to serve a gatekeeper function. All current induction programs must meet the standards under SB2042 by 2004.

Professional Development

Teachers are required to complete 150 hours of professional development for renewal of their professional clear certificate every five years. Teachers develop goals and a plan for professional development in consultation with their school-approved professional growth advisor, and submit a Professional Growth Plan and Record to the CCTC. Activities may include university courses; conferences, workshops, institutes, academies, symposia, teacher center programs or staff development programs; a systematic program of peer observation and teaching analysis; service in a leadership role; and educational research. Teachers must include at least two different types of activities for every renewal cycle. The California Professional Development Consortia and the California Department of Education produced guiding principles for high-quality professional development in *Designs for Learning* (California Department of Education, 2002).

California has a number of statewide professional development programs available to schools and teachers. For example, the Peer Assistance and Review program allows veteran teachers to earn professional growth credit by assisting less experienced colleagues in developing their subject matter or pedagogical knowledge. The California Professional Development Institutes are university-based summer sessions for school teams of teachers with follow-up sessions during the school year and stipends for participants. The Subject Matter Projects program, run by the University of California with state support, offers opportunities for intensive subject-matter learning in various teaching fields. California also offers a one-time award of $10,000 to teachers who complete their National Board certification, with an additional $20,000 available to teachers who teach in low-performing schools.

Recruitment and Retention

California faces teacher shortages in a number of areas. Statewide, approximately 16 percent of teachers were not fully certified in 2001–02. The percentage of uncertified teachers was particularly high in special education (36 percent) and in high-poverty districts (23 percent). The state issues emergency permits and waivers to uncertified teachers in cases where a district is unable to hire a fully qualified teacher. In 2001–02, the state issued more emergency permits than full certifications in foreign language, mathematics, science, and special education. The Center for the Future of Teaching and Learning has projected that California will need more than 300,000 new teachers over the next decade.

To help meet this demand and remedy shortages, the state has a number of recruitment and retention initiatives in place: The California Teaching Fellowship program offers $20,000 awards to teacher candidates who earn credentials and teach for at least four years in low-performing schools. The Teacher Scholars program is a 15-month credential and master's degree program at the University of California that offers full scholarships for teachers who go on to work in hard to staff schools. Teachers may accelerate their preparation program by attending state-supported Summer Session Teacher Preparation programs at various CSU campuses. California offers teachers tax credits of up to $1,500 after four years of service in public schools. The Assumption Program of Loans for Education offers loan awards to teachers who teach for at least four years in subjects with teacher shortages. Below-market mortgages are available to teachers who work for at least five years in low-performing schools, and the state also offers one-time cash awards to staff in low-performing schools that significantly improve student performance. Low-performing schools may receive grants from the state for discretionary teacher recruitment and retention incentives through the Teaching as a

Priority program. Finally, the Loaned Teacher Tax Credit offers a 50 percent tax credit to employers who loan their employees to teach math and science in California public schools.

Michigan

Michigan educates nearly 2 million K–12 public school students. Of these, approximately 75 percent are non-Hispanic white, 19 percent are non-Hispanic black, 3 percent are Hispanic, 2 percent are Asian, and 1 percent are Native American. Thirteen percent of the state's students receive special education services, and 3 percent are classified as English language learners. The state employs almost 100,000 public school teachers, and issues more than 8,500 initial certificates each year. Eleven percent of these are granted to teachers trained out of state. The remaining 89 percent of newly certified teachers are trained by teacher education programs at Michigan's 32 approved institutions. In 2003, approximately 8 percent of Michigan's teacher education program completers were Michigan State University graduates, making MSU the 4th largest producer in the state.

Michigan's state revenue has declined by nearly 20 percent over the past three years. The state constitution requires a balanced budget, so the state has been forced to make cuts in a number of areas. However, education funding has been a top priority for both the current governor and her predecessor, so K–12 school aid has fared relatively well in recent budgets. For FY2004, the original school aid budget maintained full funding for the per-pupil allowance and for at-risk and school readiness preschool programs; however, a midyear Executive Order issued in December 2003 mandated additional budget cuts to remedy a $900 million deficit, including a 2.3 percent reduction of per-pupil school aid. Higher education funding has fared less well. Support for public universities and community colleges was trimmed by 10 percent from FY2003 to FY2004, and an additional $73.2 million was cut by the December 2003 Executive Order. Adult education was cut by 75 percent in the FY2004 budget. The administrative budget for the MDE has been cut by 55 percent since FY2001; as a result, MDE employees have been taking furlough days and pay cuts.

The Michigan State Board of Education formed task force groups to study five important educational issues: teacher quality, educational leadership, community involvement, early literacy, and educational technology. The Ensuring Excellent Educators Task Force delivered its report to the board in April 2002. Key policy recommendations of the task force include development of a new institutional accountability system for teacher preparation programs; implementation of a standards-based induction period for new teachers; development of standards for alternative teacher preparation pathways; adoption of performance standards for professional development; support for collaborative partnerships for teacher development; and the development of a marketing campaign in support of teaching as a profession.

Certification Requirements

Michigan offers two teaching certificates, the Provisional Certificate, and the Professional Education Certificate. Teachers may be certified in elementary education, which qualifies them to teach all subjects in self-contained classes for grades K–8 or subject areas in which they hold a major or minor in grades 6–8, or secondary education, which qualifies them to teach subject areas in which they have a major or minor in grades 7–12.[3] Additional endorsements are available in early childhood education, bilingual education, general elementary education, and middle school education, and require completion of an 18 semester hour planned program of study. Certification is required for all Michigan teachers, including nonpublic school teachers except in cases where sincerely held religious belief contradicts teacher certification.

The Provisional Certificate is Michigan's entry-level teaching certificate. Applicants are required to pass the state teaching assessment and complete an approved teacher education program, including 40 semester hours of general education, demonstrated depth in a substantive teaching field, and 20 semester hours of professional education. For secondary teachers, demonstrated depth requires a subject area major and minor, while elementary teachers may complete a subject area major and minor or three subject area minors. Professional education for all teachers includes course work on human development, foundations of education, methods and materials for instruction, and at least six semester hours (180 clock hours) of directed teaching. Teachers must also complete course work in reading instruction—six semester hours for elementary teachers and three semester hours for secondary teachers.

The Provisional Certificate is valid for six years, and may be renewed twice for three years each time. The first renewal requires that the teacher has completed at least 10 semester hours of study in a planned program since receiving initial certification; the second renewal requires at least 18 semester hours.

The Professional Education Certificate is awarded to teachers who have completed the requirements for the Provisional Certificate, have three years of successful teaching experience, and have completed an 18-semester-hour planned program of study since initial certification or hold a master's degree. The Professional Education Certificate is valid for five years, with unlimited renewals available. Renewal requires six semester hours of postsecondary credit, or completion of 18 State Education Continuing Education Units, or a combination of the two.

Michigan uses the Michigan Test for Teaching Certification (MTTC) for basic skills and subject area testing. Scores range from 100 to 300, and the passing score on all tests is 220. All teacher candidates must pass both the basic skills test and the subject area test to complete their teacher education program and be recommended for certification. The basic skills test includes reading, math, and writing subtests, and must be passed before admission into a teacher education program. The subject area tests are offered in elementary education, special education, and a variety of subject areas, and must be passed before progression to a teaching internship.

Teacher Education Program Requirements

The Michigan State Board of Education is responsible for evaluating and approving teacher education programs, with help from MDE. Teacher education programs must maintain an 80 percent minimum collective pass rate on specialty area MTTC tests. Programs should utilize a variety of assessment instruments, and should use assessment data for continuous program improvement. All teacher education programs are expected to address the require-

---

[3] A major consists of at least 30 semester hours in a single discipline, or 36 semester hours for interdisciplinary programs; a minor consists of at least 20 semester hours in a single discipline, or 24 semester hours for interdisciplinary programs.

ments for Michigan teacher certification, including required course work content in general, subject area, and professional studies. In addition, the state has instituted several sets of standards that teacher education programs must meet.

Standards address the design of the program, characteristics of the teacher education candidates, characteristics of the program faculty, and the governance and support of the teacher education unit. For example, the school's teacher education programs should be based on a conceptual framework that is knowledge-based, coherent, consistent, and continuously evaluated. Teaching in the programs should be high quality and research based, and the program should use multiple indicators to assess and monitor teacher candidates. Candidates should have a variety of field experiences, including full-time student teaching or internships of at least ten weeks. The programs should also help candidates learn how to integrate general, content, and professional and pedagogical knowledge. The programs should have clear and rigorous academic entrance standards, including a required minimum 2.5 GPA. Programs should have active diversity and recruiting programs, male and female students, and faculty members from at least two ethnic or racial groups.

Higher education faculty should hold terminal degrees and should not carry a load that exceeds 12 semester hours per quarter of undergraduate teaching or nine semester hours per quarter of graduate teaching. Faculty who supervise student teaching or direct graduate projects should receive adequate adjustments to their teaching load. Supervising faculty should have specific preparation for their role as well as K–12 teaching experience, and their assignments should not exceed 18 students per faculty member. Associated K–12 classroom teachers should have at least three years of teaching experience. Faculty in the teacher education program should collaborate with both arts and sciences faculty and K–12 teachers.

Teacher education programs must also respond to the Entry-Level Standards for Michigan Teachers, which are aligned with the state's K–12 standards and curriculum and with INTASC. The standards include an understanding and appreciation of the liberal arts, a commitment to student learning and achievement, knowledge of subject matter and pedagogy, the ability to manage and monitor student learning, the ability to systematically organize teaching practices and learn from experiences, commitment and willingness to participate in learning communities, and an ability to use information-age learning and technology operations and concepts to enhance learning and professional productivity. The standards were revised in October 2002, and IHEs have two years to respond to the changes. Programs also are required to develop and implement an instrument for assessment of student teaching based on the Criteria for Assessment of Pedagogy, which is aligned with the entry-level standards.

Individual endorsement programs must meet specific state standards for the teaching field, which have been recently revised. The state also outlines standards for reading instruction that all teacher education programs must address in candidates' required reading instruction courses. The standards relate to professionalism, content, knowledge about students, knowledge about assessment, knowledge about reading instruction, knowledge about inquiry, and knowledge about communication with the community.

Finally, once fully approved, programs must continue to meet quality indicator standards for seven critical accountability factors in the periodic review and program evaluation process. The factors relate to teacher candidate performance in content, pedagogy, and dispositions; field placements, which should ensure that candidates are placed in schools or classes that meet the state's academic performance standards; diversity and multicultural experiences; faculty knowledge; parent and community interaction and involvement; educational technology; and statutory, regulatory, and policy requirements.

Specific program requirements may be waived on a temporary basis for innovative experimental teacher education programs. Institutions may apply for an initial three-year waiver, which may be reapproved for an additional three years if the experimental program shows promise.

The Ensuring Excellent Educators Task Force has recommended the development of a new state data–based institutional accountability system that uses publicly shared information on teacher candidates' performance and graduate and employer satisfaction.

Additional Routes to a Teaching Career

Michigan offers two alternative routes to licensure: the Michigan Alternative Route to Teacher Certification (MARTC) and the Limited License to Instruct (LLI). The MARTC is a collaborative effort of the MDE, participating IHEs, and local school districts and teachers unions.[4] The program includes 20 semester hours of professional education covering human development, exceptional children, methods and materials of instruction, and reading instruction. Program participants complete course work while holding fully paid, full-time teaching positions under the guidance of an assigned mentor. Entry into the program requires a bachelor's degree with at least a 2.5 GPA, a major and at least two years of occupational experience in the intended area of specialization, and passing scores on the MTTC basic skills and subject area tests. The program is only offered in grade levels, locations, and endorsement areas where a critical need has been verified by the district, union, participating IHE, and MDE. Participants are expected to complete at least one year of employment in the state after finishing the program.

The LLI is a newer program intended for substitute teachers, paraprofessionals, career changers, and recent college graduates. Candidates are required to hold a bachelor's degree in a noneducation field and to have occupational experience in their intended teaching field or experience as a substitute teacher. LLI participants are admitted to existing approved teacher education programs, with adjustments made to fast-track the curriculum to meet their particular needs. Participants complete a mentored teaching assignment while they complete their certification requirements. The program has been piloted by Wayne State University with a cohort of substitute teachers from Detroit Public Schools and is intended to be expanded throughout the state.

The Ensuring Excellent Educators Task Force has recommended that the state formalize content and performance standards for these alternative routes to certification.

New Teacher Induction

Michigan's New Teacher Induction and Teacher Mentoring Program has been in place since 1996. The program requires all new teachers in their first three years of classroom teaching to be assigned a master teacher as a mentor and to receive at least 15 days of specialized, intensive professional development. Mentors should have the same teaching area as the new teacher and, if possible, should teach in the same building. Mentoring is explicitly separated from teacher evaluation. Professional development activities for new teachers should address a number of core experiences, including knowledge of the community, classroom manage-

---

[4] Only three institutions were offering MARTC programs in 2003; Michigan State was not one of them.

ment, parent and guardian interaction, alignment of curriculum, diversity in the classroom, networking, knowledge of teacher evaluation, use of volunteers, time management, use of resources, and knowledge of legal issues. The state does not provide financial assistance to schools and districts for mentoring and induction programs.

MDE currently is developing new standards for mentoring and induction. One of the five policy action recommendations of the Ensuring Excellent Educators Task Force calls for linking standards-based induction to the teacher licensure requirements, including pay and quality incentives for induction and mentoring.

Professional Development

Michigan school districts are required to provide at least five days of professional development for teachers each year, in addition to the 15 days over three years for new teachers required by the mentoring and induction program. Teachers are required to complete 18 State Board Continuing Education Units (SB-CEUs) for renewal of the professional certificate. One SB-CEU is equivalent to 10 contact hours, while one semester hour of academic study is equivalent to three SB-CEUs. Activities for SB-CEUs must be approved by the state, and may include attendance at seminars, workshops, and conferences; service as a mentor, supervising teacher, member of a state-approved advisory committee, member of an accreditation review board, or member of a school improvement team; or completion of National Board certification or a portfolio for the National Board application. Michigan offers subsidy grants for teachers applying for National Board certification. The state is also implementing new approval standards for IHEs that wish to offer professional development courses without a full teacher preparation program.

The Ensuring Excellent Educators Task Force recommended that the state develop standards for professional development based on instructional improvement, and implement practice-based professional development as a condition for certificate renewal.

Recruitment and Retention

Michigan has faced teacher shortages in a number of areas. In 2002–03, approximately 2percent of all classroom teachers were teaching on waivers because they were not fully certified to teach in their assigned area. Areas with particularly high concentrations of uncertified teachers include bilingual education (12 percent), environmental studies and computer science (7 percent), foreign language (4 percent), and special education (3 percent). In 2003–04, the state identified as critical shortage disciplines elementary grades, English and language arts, mathematics, music, reading, science, social studies, foreign language, bilingual education, and special education.

The state has addressed these shortages in several ways. First, several types of temporary teaching permits are available for teachers employed by districts that can demonstrate that open positions could not be filled with fully certified teachers. The state board also recently ruled that noncertified, nonendorsed teachers who hold a bachelor's degree in the teaching field and have at least two years of occupational experience may be hired to teach high school mathematics, science, and foreign language. For candidates preparing to teach in the identified critical shortage areas, deferment or reduction of loans under the Federal Stafford, Paul Douglas Scholarship, and Federal Perkins Loans programs are available. Retired teachers may reenter the workplace in the critical shortage areas and receive an exemption from the postretirement earnings limitations under Michigan law. The state has a

Troops to Teachers program for retiring active duty and reserve military personnel, which offers either a $5,000 bonus for teaching preparation expenses or a $10,000 stipend for teaching at least three years in a Michigan high-needs school. Finally, the marketing campaign recommended by the Ensuring Excellent Educators Task Force is intended to enhance the image of teachers in the state.

New York

New York State educates nearly 3 million K–12 public school students. Of these, approximately 55 percent are white, 20 percent are non-Hispanic black, and 18 percent are Hispanic. Eight percent are classified as English language learners. New York City has more than 1 million K–12 public school students, of whom 38 percent are Hispanic, 35 percent are black, and 15 percent are white. Eighteen percent are classified as English language learners. New York State employs more than 225,000 public school teachers, and issues more than 25,000 certificates each year. New York City has more than 74,000 teachers; 39 percent of the city's teachers are minorities. New York State has 110 teacher preparation programs. Regular teacher preparation programs produced 19,182 graduates in 2003, while alternative route programs produced 10,539 program completers. Bank Street College produced 1 percent of the state's regular teacher preparation program completers, which ranked it as the 30th largest producer in the state.

Like many other states, New York has faced lower than expected revenues in recent years, which has resulted in significant budget shortfalls. The state faced an $11.5 billion gap in January 2003, which amounted to approximately 12 percent of the state's total $95 billion budget. The governor proposed closing the shortfall in part through $6.3 billion in budget cuts, including a $1.4 billion reduction in school aid. The state legislature rejected many of the cuts and restored school aid in most areas to 2002–03 levels, but the enacted budget still cut school aid by $199 million, or 1.36 percent, the first year-to-year decrease in school aid in 12 years. State economists have estimated that local districts will need to increase property taxes by an average of 8 percent to maintain all services and programs. In addition to school aid cuts, the state also reduced funding for teacher recruiting and teacher mentoring programs by 20 percent each, and reduced general fund higher education spending by 25 percent while raising tuition at SUNY and CUNY campuses by 33 percent for residents and 50 percent for nonresidents. Estimated budget gaps of $3.9 billion and $4.8 billion still loom in the next two fiscal years.

New York City's public school system has also faced stagnating revenues, resulting in an inflation-adjusted decrease in expenditures in FY2002. Although revenues recovered somewhat in FY2003, the district still ran a $14.1 million budget shortfall. At the beginning of FY2004, district officials were preparing to implement a $28 million budget reduction program, which amounts to approximately 2 percent of all FY2003 spending.

Certification Requirements

The State Professional Standards and Practices Board for Teaching advises New York's Board of Regents on issues related to teaching, including certification, preparation, induction, evaluation, and professional development. The board includes K–12 teachers and administrators, representatives from higher education, representatives from the public, and one teacher education student.

The Initial Certificate is New York's entry-level teaching certificate. Applicants may earn the Initial Certificate by completing a teacher education program at an approved New York State institution, or by applying directly to the State Education Department for individual evaluation of their credentials. Candidates for the Initial Certificate must complete a bachelor's degree with a minimum cumulative GPA of 2.5. Course work requirements include 30 semester hours in the general education core, 30 semester hours in a content area, and 21 semester hours in the pedagogy core, which includes study of human development, students with disabilities, literacy skills, curriculum and instruction, and foundations of education. Six semester hours must be related to student development. Candidates must also complete 40 days of supervised teaching, and must pass the state teacher examination. The Initial Certificate is valid for three years, with a one-year extension possible for those who have completed at least 24 semester hours of study.

The Professional Education Certificate is New York's new permanent teaching certificate; previously, this certificate was known as the Permanent Certificate. Earning the Professional Education Certificate requires holding an Initial Certificate, teaching for three years with mentoring during the first year, and completing a subject area master's degree in the teaching field or completing a graduate-level teacher education program. The Professional Education Certificate is continuously valid with the completion of required professional development hours every five years.

New York's current teacher certification structure is new as of February 2004. The Initial and Professional Education certificates replace the old Provisional and Permanent certificates. The changes created new middle school and early childhood certificate titles, and revised the requirements for the certificates in a variety of ways, such as mandating a minimum GPA, eliminating the old requirement for foreign language study, adding a general education core requirement, mandating content area testing for all applicants, requiring course work on reading instruction, and changing the content area requirements for the initial certification. For the full certificate, the major changes include the addition of a third year of required teaching experience and mandated mentoring during the first year of teaching, the elimination of the video TPA, the revision of the master's degree requirements to specify a degree in the teaching field or graduate-level study in teacher education, and the addition of a continuing professional development requirement to maintain the certificate's validity. Although the Provisional Certificate has been discontinued, the Permanent Certificate will continue to be issued to teachers who earned Provisional Certificates.

Teachers may add an additional certificate in another teaching field by completing at least 30 semester hours in the content core of the subject area and passing the content examination.

New York uses several assessments in the New York State Teacher Certification Examination for teacher testing.

- The Liberal Arts and Sciences Test covers general knowledge in history, social sciences, science, mathematics, art, and the humanities, and is required for the Initial Certificate in most teaching fields.
- The Assessment of Teaching Skills–Written tests pedagogical knowledge. The exam is offered in elementary and secondary versions, and is required for the Initial Certificate in most fields.

- The Content Specialty Test covers subject area content in various teaching fields, and is required for secondary academic subject certification and elementary certification.
- The Bilingual Education Assessment is required for bilingual education certification, and tests listening, speaking, and reading skills in English and target languages.
- The Assessment of Teaching Skills–Performance consists of videotaped samples of teachers instructing in their classrooms and is required for provisional certification in some teaching fields, though not for the Professional Education Certificate.

Teacher Education Program Requirements

New York adopted new standards for teacher education programs in 1999. Teacher education programs must be registered with the New York State Education Department and accredited by either the state's board of regents or a professional education accrediting association.

To meet the requirements for registration, programs must have a written statement of philosophy and should maintain formal relationships with local schools. Programs leading to initial certification must require students to meet the state certification requirements for general education, the content core for their teaching area, and pedagogical knowledge, including study of human development, learning processes, students with disabilities, language acquisition and literacy, curriculum development, educational technology, student assessment, foundations of education, professional development skills, and child abuse identification and intervention. Programs should use various types of assessments to evaluate students. Programs should include at least 100 hours of field experiences, which provide candidates with experiences working with a variety of different students and settings. Programs leading to the Professional Education Certificate must lead to a master's or higher degree and should require students to meet the requirements for the Initial Certificate. Additional requirements for specific endorsement programs also must be met.

Faculty in both education and arts and sciences must cooperate to ensure the high-quality academic preparation of students. The majority of credit-bearing courses should be taught by full-time faculty. Faculty loads should not exceed 12 semester hours of undergraduate teaching or nine hours of graduate teaching. Supervision of student teachers should be considered in determining faculty load, and faculty members should not supervise more than 18 student teachers per semester. Faculty should have knowledge of and experience in high-need schools, and faculty involvement in K–12 schools should be promoted and valued as a component of teacher education faculty responsibilities. The program should make an effort to recruit and retain faculty and students from historically underrepresented groups.

Institutions are required to maintain a minimum 80 percent passing rate for all candidates on the state's teacher certification exams or be subject to corrective action and denial or reregistration. All programs must be accredited by the Board of Regents or a professional education accrediting organization within seven years of initial registration. The Regents Accreditation of Teacher Education requires rigorous on-site visits every seven years. The standards deal with commitment and vision; philosophy, purpose, and objectives; program registration; teaching effectiveness of graduates; assessment of candidate achievement; financial resources; support services; advertising; candidate complaints; public disclosure of accreditation status; and annual reports.

Additional Routes to a Teaching Career

New York's Alternative Teacher Certification (ATC) program allows teacher education institutions and local districts to cooperatively offer programs for career-changers and others to earn their certification by working as full-time teachers in hard-to-staff schools under the guidance of a mentor teacher while they complete their master's degree to earn their Professional Education Certificate. New York offers competitive federal grants of up to $3.5 million to expand capacity in ATC programs. The New York City Teaching Fellows program is a partnership between several ATC programs and the New York City Department of Education that places teacher candidates in New York City public schools while they pursue graduate degrees at various New York City universities.[5]

New York City also participates in the national Teach for America Program and operates a Peace Corps Fellows program in collaboration with Teachers College at Columbia University that helps returning Peace Corps volunteers complete course work to earn their teacher certification.

New Teacher Induction

New York's new teacher certification regulations require a mentored experience in the first year of classroom teaching to qualify for the Professional Education Certificate. The district is responsible for providing a mentoring program as part of the district professional development plan. Programs should have publicized mentor selection criteria, mentor preparation, defined mentoring activities, and time allocated for mentoring. The New York State Mentor Teacher Internship Program offers grants to support school mentoring programs; 58 districts received awards in 2003–04.

Professional Development

As of 2004, teachers holding the Professional Education Certificate are required to complete 175 hours of professional development every five years to maintain the validity of their licenses. Districts are responsible for determining the content, delivery, and providers of professional development, in accordance with the district professional development plan. New York also offers fee subsidies for teachers applying for National Board certification.

Recruitment and Retention

New York State (NYS) and New York City (NYC) face severe teacher shortages in a number of areas. The state defines teacher need as the difference between new certificates issued and the number of teachers on temporary licenses or of retirement age. By this definition, NYS faced a statewide shortage of 8,643 teachers, or 4 percent of the state's teaching positions, in 2000. For NYC, teacher need was 14,937, or 20 percent of the city's teaching positions. Areas of particularly acute need include mathematics (30 percent for NYS, 67 percent for NYC), sciences (22 percent for NYS, 70 percent for NYC), English (16 percent for NYS, 37 percent for NYC), foreign languages (24 percent for NYS, 34 percent for NYC), social studies (13 percent for NYS, 38 percent for NYC), and ESOL and bilingual education (17 percent for NYS, 23 percent for NYC).

New York State offers grants for teacher recruitment to both local school districts and colleges and universities through the Teachers of Tomorrow program and the Teacher

---

[5] Bank Street participates in the New York City Teaching Fellows program.

Opportunity Corps. Since 2000, more than $75 million has been distributed through these programs. New York also has received federal funding for a number of additional teacher recruitment programs under the Higher Education Act and the Elementary and Secondary Education Act, such as Troops to Teachers, Transition to Teaching, and the Teacher Recruitment Project. In addition, seven of New York's community colleges have partnered with senior colleges to offer joint teacher education programs. Finally, New York offers a Teacher of the Year program and the Better Beginnings Award to recognize outstanding teachers.

New York City also has a number of initiatives aimed at remedying teacher shortages by recruiting and retaining teachers:

- The Summer in the City program places college students in summer school classrooms with cooperating teachers to experience teaching and build their commitment to a teaching career. Participants are expected to develop and present two instructional lessons, attend weekly intern meetings, complete professional reading assignments, and participate in school-based professional development. Housing and transportation are provided by the program, and interns receive a $2,000 stipend for the six-week session.
- The Senior Year Initiative offers $3,400 in tuition reimbursement and a $1,500 stipend for preservice professional development to college students who major in Special Education and commit to completing three years of teaching in New York City public schools.
- The Loan Forgiveness Program provides student loan reimbursement of as much as $4,000 per year of public school teaching for up to six years.
- The Graduate and Undergraduate Scholarship programs offer full payment of tuition for completion of a master's degree or for the junior and senior year of a bachelor's degree for students preparing to teach in certain special education areas.
- The Teaching Opportunity Program Scholarship provides a fully paid master's degree at the City University of New York to highly qualified college graduates who have majors in Spanish, mathematics, or science or who wish to become literacy teachers.
- The Teacher Recruitment Program uses certified New York City public schools to attract new teachers by visiting college campuses and sharing their first-hand experiences.
- Newly hired certified teachers in Schools Under Registration Review or in designated high-needs schools may be eligible for annual grants of $3,400 for up to four years.

Virginia

In 2002–03, Virginia public schools educated nearly 1.2 million K–12 students. Of these, approximately 27 percent were non-Hispanic black, 6 percent Hispanic, and 5 percent Asian. Four percent were English-language learners, and 14 percent were enrolled in special education programs. Virginia had 88,609 full-time contracted classroom teachers. The state's 37 institutions of higher education with approved teacher education programs produced 2,646 new teachers in 2002–03. Approximately 5 percent were graduates of the University of Virginia, making UVa the eighth largest producer in the state.

Virginia has faced a significant budget crunch in recent years, as state revenues have consistently fallen short of projections. FY2002 saw a 3.8 percent falloff in revenues, the biggest decline since 1960. As a result, the state faced a cumulative $6 billion shortfall as of the beginning of FY2003. Large budget cuts of $797.7 million in 2002–03 and $764.5 for 2003–04 have been necessary, including an across-the-board reduction of 3 percent for nearly all agencies, exempting direct aid to public schools. Although K–12 education has generally been spared in the cuts, the state has reduced aid for several targeted programs for at-risk students. Higher education has faced substantial budget reductions of $290.8 million, or 21 percent, for the 2002–04 biennium. To help institutions remedy shortfalls, the state has granted its public colleges and universities the discretion to increase revenue from tuition and fees, ending a six-year freeze.

Virginia received a $13.5 million three-year Title II Teacher Quality Enhancement Grant in 2002. The state has developed a number of goals for the grant, including developing a comprehensive database on teacher quality, expanding teacher recruitment initiatives, supporting high-quality teacher preparation programs, retaining high-quality teachers, and evaluating teacher quality initiatives.

Certification Requirements

Virginia's Advisory Board on Teacher Education and Licensure, which is composed of teachers, administrators, teacher education faculty members, and other stakeholders, advises the State Board of Education on policies related to teacher licensure.

Virginia offers two full, five-year renewable teaching licenses: the Collegiate Professional License and the Postgraduate Professional License. To receive the Collegiate Professional License, individuals must possess a bachelor's degree with a major in an arts and sciences field, complete required professional studies course work and fieldwork, complete content area course work requirements in the desired teaching area, and pass the state teaching assessments. The Postgraduate Professional License requires an appropriate master's degree from an accredited institution in addition to the requirements for the Collegiate Professional License.

Required professional studies course work includes three hours on human growth and development, six hours on curriculum and instruction, three hours on the foundations of education, and three to six hours on reading and language acquisition. Additional topics to be covered include attention-deficit disorder, gifted and talented education, parent communication, the Virginia K–12 Standards of Learning (SOL), child-abuse recognition and intervention, and educational technology. Candidates must also complete at least 300 hours of fieldwork, including at least 150 hours of supervised direct teaching.

Content area requirements range from 24 to 60 hours of course work, depending on the teaching area. Early and elementary education candidates must fulfill requirements in seven subjects, while middle school candidates must complete requirements for two concentration areas as well as general education course work in nonconcentration areas.

Virginia uses the Praxis I for basic skills testing and the Praxis II for subject-matter testing. The state claims to have some of the toughest cut scores in the nation. Institutional pass rates on the Praxis I ranged from 83 to 100 percent in 2001–02, and statewide pass rates on the various Praxis II tests ranged from 82 to 100 percent. In May 2003, the State Board of Education approved a plan to implement a new assessment of knowledge of reading instruction for special and elementary education teachers and reading specialists. National

Evaluation Systems, Inc., is currently developing the test, which will be ready for the first administration in fall 2004. Cut scores will be set in 2005, and it is expected that teachers will be required to pass the test for licensure as of July 2006.

The licensure requirements are likely to undergo substantial revision in the next several years. The State Board of Education accepted a number of revisions to the licensure regulations on first review in June 2003 and authorized them for public comment. These revisions would align the competencies in the licensure regulations with recent revisions to the SOL, increase the required number of fieldwork hours, formalize the reading assessment requirement, respond to the highly qualified teacher provisions of the No Child Left Behind Act, require content areas course work for all teachers for license renewal, and make various other changes to the requirements for specific endorsements. However, as of the January 7, 2004, meeting of the State Board of Education, the revisions had not returned to the board for final review. Additional changes to the licensure regulations may result from Virginia's Title II grant, as part of the state plan for retaining high-quality teachers calls for the development of a multitiered, performance-based licensure system.

Teacher Education Program Requirements

Recent revisions to the state's accreditation standards for teacher education programs took effect in July 2002. The revisions aligned the regulations with the SOL and the regulations for school personnel (Virginia Department of Education, 1998). The accreditation process runs on a five-year review cycle, though institutions must submit annual reports in addition to institutional reports and on-site reviews in accreditation years.

Institutions must demonstrate that their teacher education program reflects the SOL, the teacher education research base, and a coherent program philosophy. Programs must collaborate with K–12 schools on program design and delivery, and must have in place processes for regular, systematic formative evaluation of the program.

The standards have no required courses that programs must offer; rather, they set out 20 competencies for beginning teachers that the program must address. Competencies include knowledge and skills related to English language communication; mathematical, scientific, and historical thinking; human development; language acquisition and reading; foundations of education; teaching methods and classroom management; and educational technology. Programs are limited to 18 semester hours of professional studies for all endorsement areas except elementary and special education, which are capped at 24 semester hours. Fieldwork must be integrated with course work.

Programs must require that students pass Praxis I and II for program completion. All approved endorsements must maintain a 70 percent pass rate on Praxis II.

Plans for the state's Title II grant related to teacher preparation programs include the development and dissemination of model teacher education programs and an incentive-based funding system to reward programs that are responsive to the needs of school districts and can demonstrate their graduates' effectiveness in raising student achievement.

Additional Routes to a Teaching Career

Virginia's primary alternative pathway to a teaching license is the Career Switcher Alternative Route to Teaching Program. Started in 2000 as a pilot for military personnel only, the program was expanded to include all career switchers in 2002. Currently, six state-approved providers participate in the program: four colleges and universities, one school district, and one consortium.[6] Candidates for the program must possess a bachelor's degree, complete content requirements for their endorsement area, pass Praxis, and have five years of full-time work experience. In their first year, candidates complete 180 clock hours of instruction and fieldwork. Participants spend the second year teaching full-time while collaborating with an assigned mentor and completing 20 hours of instructional seminars. After the second year, candidates receive a five-year renewable Professional License.

Outside of the Career Switcher program, nonlicensed teachers who are hired by school districts, hold a bachelors degree, and satisfy content requirements for an endorsement area may be given a three-year, nonrenewable Provisional License, and must pass Praxis and complete the state professional studies requirements to receive their Professional License. School districts and colleges and universities may—with state approval—offer alternative programs of professional study for these candidates.

New Teacher Induction

Since 1999, Virginia has required that all beginning teachers in the state work with a mentor during their first year in the classroom. Between 2000 and 2002, $2.75 million was allocated for the Mentor Teacher Program for Beginning and Experienced Teachers. Local school boards administer the program with the assistance of a statewide advisory committee of teachers, administrators, and representatives from partner IHEs. Mentors should work in the same building as beginning teachers; receive release time for mentoring; and receive training on the *Uniform Performance Standards and Evaluation Criteria for Teachers* (Virginia Department of Education, 2000), formative assessment for beginning teacher performance, development and use of individualized plans, and provision of individualized assistance.

Professional Development

License renewal in Virginia requires teachers to complete at least 180 professional development points given for various activities including conferences, peer observation, curriculum development, mentorship, and more. For teachers who do not hold master's degrees, half the required professional development points must be earned by completing a three semester hour course at the graduate or undergraduate level in content for their endorsement area.

The Clinical Faculty Program offers the opportunity for experienced teachers to serve as leaders in their schools by supervising, grading, and evaluating student teachers. Partner IHEs provide special training for clinical faculty members, who are designated as adjunct faculty at the university or college.

Virginia offers financial support and incentives for teachers who pursue certification from the NBPTS. The state provides grants of $1,000 to $2,000 for at least 75 teachers each year to help pay the NBPTS application fee. For teachers who complete the certification process, the state offers an initial $5,000 bonus and annual $2,500 awards for the ten-year life of the certificate. In addition, the state provides a number of supports, including symposia, information sessions, technical assistance, workshops, list servers, and retreats to help teachers learn about the certification and complete their application portfolio.

---

[6] The University of Virginia does not participate in the Career Switcher program.

Recruitment and Retention

Virginia has had shortages of teachers in a number of areas in recent years. In 2001–02, approximately 4 percent of contractual teaching positions in the state were unfilled or filled by unendorsed personnel. Twenty school districts had more than 10 percent of positions unfilled or unendorsed. The state has defined a critical shortage area as one where there are regularly fewer than three qualified applicants per position, and listed the top ten critical shortage areas for 2003–04 as mathematics, special education, science, career and technical education, foreign language, English as a second language, middle grades education, library media, art, and reading specialists.

To deal with these shortages, Virginia has implemented several initiatives on teacher recruitment and retention:

- The Virginia Teaching Scholarship Loan Program provides scholarship loans of up to $3,720 to students preparing to teach in one of the state's critical shortage fields. Recipients repay the loan by teaching in Virginia public schools for at least four semesters.
- The Virginia Community College System recently signed an articulation agreement with ten colleges and universities to facilitate transfers for teacher preparation candidates.
- Recent legislation allows retired teachers in the Virginia Retirement System to be hired to teach in critical shortage areas with no interruption to their retirement benefits.

Additional Teacher Quality Initiatives

As part of the state's work under its Title II grant, Virginia is in the process of developing a comprehensive database on teacher quality. In Phase I, the pilot Teacher Education and Licensure System was implemented in July 2003, featuring online Praxis scores, teacher education tracking, an interface with the National Association of State Directors of Teacher Education and Certification database, and other functions. The next phases of development include intensive data collection and the development of a Web access portal. Eventually, the database is expected to hold information on teacher qualifications and effectiveness, retention, teacher supply and demand, and shortage areas. The database should support research to link teacher effectiveness and student achievement.

Bibliography

American Association of State Colleges and Universities, *A Call for Teacher Education Reform*, Washington, D.C., 1999.

American Council on Education, *To Touch the Future: Transforming the Way Teachers Are Taught*, Washington, D.C., 1999.

Ball, Deborah, *Mathematics in the 21st Century: What Mathematical Knowledge Is Needed for Teaching Mathematics?* Secretary's Summit on Mathematics, Washington, D.C.: U.S. Department of Education, February 6, 2003. Online at http://www.ed.gov/rschstat/research/progs/mathscience/ball.html (as of June 1, 2004).

Bank Street College of Education, *Institutional Report*, New York, 2001.

_____, *Graduate School of Education Course Catalogue 2002–2003*, New York, 2002a.

_____, design proposal submitted to the Carnegie Corporation of New York, unpublished, 2002b.

Bardach, E., *The Implementation Game: What Happens After a Bill Becomes a Law*, Cambridge, Mass.: The MIT Press, 1977.

Barney, H., E. Eide, and S. N. Kirby, "Reforming Teacher Education Programs: A Review of Field-Initiated Programs," unpublished research, RAND Corporation, 2001.

Berends, M., S. J. Bodilly, and S. N. Kirby, *Facing the Challenges of Whole-School Reform: New American Schools After a Decade*, Santa Monica, Calif.: RAND Corporation, MR-1498-EDU, 2002.

Bodilly, S. J., *Lessons from New American Schools' Scale-Up Phase: Prospects for Bringing Designs to Multiple Schools*, Santa Monica, Calif.: RAND Corporation, MR-1777-NAS, 1998.

Bodilly, S. J., and M. Berends, M., "New American Schools' Designs: Evolving Maturation and Accommodation in the Design Concept," unpublished RAND research, 1999.

California Department of Education, *Designs for Learning*, Sacramento, 2002. Online at http://www.cde.ca.gov/pd/ps/te/designs4lrng.asp (as of June 2, 2004).

_____, Fact Book, 2003. Online at http://www.cde.ca.gov/re/pn/fb/documents/factbook03.pdf (as of June 2, 2004).

California State University, Northridge, Design Principle A Team, *Decisions Driven by Evidence: Year One Progress Summary*, September 13, 2003.

Carnegie Corporation of New York, *Teachers for a New Era Prospectus*, New York: Carnegie Corporation of New York, 2001. Online at http://carnegie.org/sub/program/teachers_prospectus.html (as of June 2, 2004).

Darling-Hammond, L., R. Chung, F. Frelow, and H. Fisher, "Variation in Teacher Preparation: How Well Do Different Pathways Prepare Teachers to Teach?" *Journal of Teacher Education*, No.53, 2002, p. 4.

Darling-Hammond, L., and M. B. Macdonald, "Where There Is Learning There Is Hope: The Preparation of Preservice Teachers at Bank Street College of Education," in L. Darling-Hammond, ed., *Studies of Excellence in Teacher Education: Preparation at the Graduate Level*, Washington, D.C.: National Commission on Teaching and America's Future, 2000.

Ehrenberg, R., and D. Brewer, "Did Teachers' Verbal Ability and Race Matter in the 1960s? Coleman Revisited," *Economics of Education Review*, Vol. 14, No. 1, 1995, pp. 1–21.

Elmore, R., *Building a New Structure for School Leadership*, Washington, D.C.: The Albert Shanker Foundation, 2000.

Ferguson, R., "Paying for Public Education: New Evidence on How and Why Money Matters," *Harvard Journal on Legislation*, No. 28, 1991, pp. 465–498.

Ferguson, R., and H. Ladd, "How and Why Money Matters: An Analysis of Alabama Schools," in H. Ladd, ed., *Holding Schools Accountable: Performance-Based Reform in Education*, Washington, D.C.: The Brookings Institution, 1996, pp. 265–298.

Fullan, M. G., *The New Meaning of Educational Change*, New York: Teachers College Press, 1991.

Fullan, M., G. Galluzzo, P. Morris, and N. Watson, *The Rise and Stall of Teacher Education Reform*, Washington, D.C.: American Association of Colleges for Teacher Education, 1998.

Gideonse, H. D., "Holmes Group III: Responsible in Goals; Remiss in Practicalities," *Journal of Teacher Education*, Vol. 47, No. 2, 1996, pp. 147–152.

Greenwald, R., L. Hedges, and R. Laine, "Interpreting Research on School Resources and Student Achievement: A Rejoinder of Hanushek," *Review of Educational Research*, Vol. 66, No. 3, 1996, pp. 361–396.

Hanushek, E. A., and R. R. Pace, "Understanding Entry into the Teaching Profession," in R. G. Ehrenberg, ed., *Choices and Consequences: Contemporary Policy Issues in Education*, Ithaca, N.Y.: ILR Press, 1994.

The Holmes Group, *Tomorrow's Schools*, East Lansing, Mich., 1990.

———, *Tomorrow's Schools of Education*, East Lansing, Mich., 1995.

Kain, J. F., "The Impact of Individual Teachers and Peers on Individual Student Achievement," paper presented at the Association for Public Policy Analysis and Management, 20th Annual Research Conference, New York, 1998.

Kain, J., and K. Singleton, "Equality of Educational Revisited," *New England Economic Review*, 1996, pp. 87–111.

Kirby, S. N., M. Berends, and S. Naftel, *Implementation in a Longitudinal Sample of New American Schools: Four Years into Scale-up*, Santa Monica, Calif.: RAND Corporation, MR-1413-EDU, 2001.

Kupermintz, H., "Teacher Effects and Teacher Effectiveness: A Validity Investigation of the Tennessee Value-Added Assessment System (TVAAS)," *Educational Evaluation and Policy Analysis*, Vol. 25, No. 3, 2003, pp. 287–298.

Mazmanian, D. A., and P. A. Sabatier, *Implementation and Public Policy*, Lanham, Md.: University Press of America, 1989.

McCaffrey, D. F., J. R. Lockwood, D. Koretz, and L. S. Hamilton, *Evaluating Value-Added Models for Teacher Accountability*, Santa Monica, Calif.: RAND Corporation, MG-158-EDU, 2004.

McCombs, J. S., S. N. Kirby, H. Barney, and S. Naftel, "Teachers for a New Era: Baseline Profiles of FY02 Grantees," unpublished RAND Corporation research, 2003.

Mendro, R., H. Jordan, E. Gomez, M. Anderson, and K. Bembry, "An Application of Multiple Linear Regression in Determining Longitudinal Teacher Effectiveness," paper presented at the 1998 Annual Meeting of the AERA, San Diego, Calif., 1998.

Michigan State University, design proposal submitted to the Carnegie Corporation of New York, unpublished, 2002.

____, interim progress report submitted to the Carnegie Corporation of New York, unpublished, October 2003.

National Network for Educational Renewal, Agenda for Education in a Democracy, undated. Online at http://depts.washington.edu/cedren/AED.htm (as of June 1, 2004).

National Research Council, Committee on Assessment and Teacher Quality, Board on Testing and Assessment, Mitchell, K. S., D. Z. Robinson, B. S. Plake, and K. T. Knowles, eds., *Testing Teacher Candidates: The Role of Licensure Tests in Improving Teacher Quality*, Washington, D.C.: National Academy Press, 2001.

Prestine, N. A., "Political System Theory as an Explanatory Paradigm for Teacher Education Reform," *American Educational Research Journal*, No. 28, 1991, pp. 237–274.

Rivers, J. C., *The Impact of Teacher Effect on Student Math Competency Achievement*, 1999 dissertation for the University of Tennessee, Knoxville, Ann Arbor, Mich.: University Microfilms International, 9959317, 2000.

Rivkin, S. G., E. A. Hanushek, and J. F. Kain, "Teachers, Schools, and Academic Achievement," Cambridge, Mass.: National Bureau of Economic Research, NBER Working Paper W6691, 2000.

Rowan, B., R. Correnti, and R. J. Miller, "What Large-Scale Research Tells Us About Teacher Effects on Student Achievement: Insights from the Prospects Study of Elementary Schools," *Teachers College Record*, 2002.

Sabatier, P., and D. Mazmanian, "The Conditions of Effective Implementation: A Guide to Accomplishing Policy Objectives," *Policy Analysis*, Vol. 5, No. 4, 1979, pp. 481–504.

Sanders, W. L., and J. C. Rivers, *Cumulative and Residual Effects of Teachers on Future Student Academic Achievement*, Knoxville, Tenn.: University of Tennessee Value-Added Research and Assessment Center, 1996.

Santrock, J., *Educational Psychology*, 2nd ed., McGraw-Hill Companies, 2004.

Scannell, D. P., *Models of Teacher Education*, Washington, D.C.: American Council on Education, 1999.

Scheirer, M. A., "Designing and Using Process Evaluation," in J. S. Wholey, H. P. Hatry, and K. E. Newcomer, eds., *Handbook of Practical Program Evaluation*, San Francisco: Jossey-Bass Publishers, 1994, pp. 40–60.

Schulman, L., "Knowledge and Teaching: Foundation of the New Reform," *Harvard Educational Review*, Vol. 57, No. 1, 1987, pp. 1–22.

University of Virginia, unpublished document with pre–site visit information submitted to Carnegie and the RAND Corporation, 2001.

Virginia Department of Education, *Guidelines for Uniform Performance Standards and Evaluation Criteria for Teachers, Administrators, and Superintendents*, 2000. Online at http://www.pen.k12.va.us/VDOE/newvdoe/evaluation.pdf (as of June 2, 2004).

____, *Licensure Regulations for School Personnel*, 8 VAC: 20-21-10 et seq., 1998. Online at http://www.pen.k12.va.us/VDOE/Compliance/TeacherED/nulicvr.pdf (as of June 2, 2004).

Walsh, K., *Teacher Certification Reconsidered: Stumbling for Quality*, Baltimore, Md.: The Abell Foundation, 2001.

Weatherly, R., and M. Lipsky, "Street-Level Bureaucrats and Institutional Innovation: Implementing Special Education Reform," *Harvard Education Review*, Vol. 47, No. 2, 1977, pp. 171–197.

Wisniewski, R., *Recreating Colleges of Teacher Education*, Atlanta, Ga.: BellSouth Foundation, undated.

Wright, S. P., S. P. Horn, and W. L. Sanders, "Teacher and Classroom Context Effects on Student Achievement: Implications for Teacher Evaluation," *Journal of Personnel Evaluation in Education*, No. 11, 1997, pp. 57–67.